RODALE'S
BASIC
ORGANIC
GARDENING

RODALE'S

BASIC

ORGANIC

GARDENING

A BEGINNER'S GUIDE
TO STARTING A HEALTHY GARDEN

DEBORAH L. MARTIN

ILLUSTRATIONS BY
MARGARET MAGRIKIE BERG

RODALE

Rodale books may be purchased for business or promotional use or for special sales. For information, please write to: Special Markets Department, Rodale Inc., 733 Third Avenue, New York, NY 10017.

Printed in the United States of America

Rodale Inc. makes every effort to use acid-free ∞ recycled paper ♻.

Book design by Carol Angstadt

Illustrations by Margaret Magrikie Berg
Illustrations on page 106 taken from originals by Signe Sundberg-Hall

Research by Anne Halpin White

Library of Congress Cataloging-in-Publication Data is on file with the publisher.

ISBN-13: 978–1–60961–983–1   trade paperback

Distributed to the trade by Macmillan

2   4   6   8   10   9   7   5   3   1   paperback

We inspire and enable people to improve their lives and the world around them.
rodalebooks.com

Gardening,
perhaps, offers more
opportunities to put
meaning and
productivity into our
lives than any other
leisure activity.

—ROBERT RODALE

CONTENTS

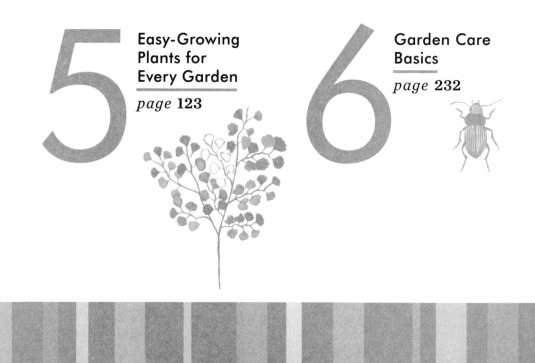

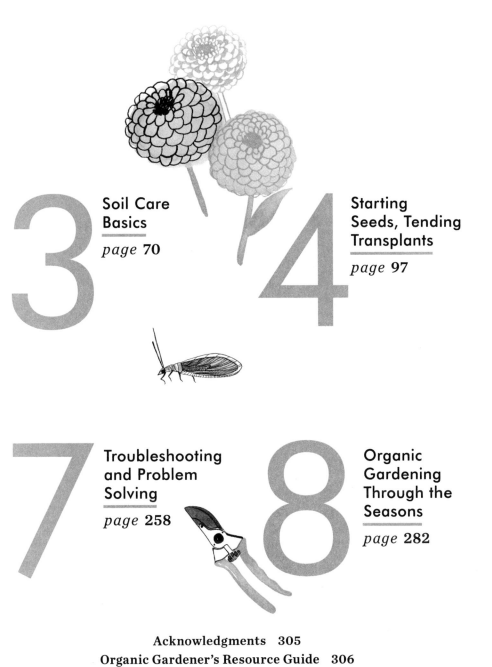

GO ORGANIC!

Welcome to *Rodale's Basic Organic Gardening!* Whether you are new to gardening or an experienced gardener who has been "hooked" on chemicals, this book will guide you through the process of planning, planting, tending, and harvesting a beautiful, successful, productive garden using organic methods.

In the pages that follow, you'll find time-tested techniques and the latest practical gardening know-how, gathered from more than 70 years of *Organic Gardening* magazine and Rodale gardening books. Chapter 1, Get to Know Organic Gardening, focuses on the origins of organic gardening and describes related trends such as community gardening and local food movements. If you want to know why organic gardening is vital to your health and well-being *and* to the health of the environment and all living things, check out Chapter 1. If you're already convinced that organic methods are the only way to grow and you want to know how to put them to work in your garden, skip ahead to Chapter 2, Getting Started, to learn how to choose and prepare a garden site, how to take climate into account in planning your garden, and what tools and equipment you'll need to get going. You'll also find some simple garden plans to help you arrange your plants to make the most of your garden space.

Healthy soil truly is the foundation of an organic garden. In Chapter 3, Soil Care Basics, you'll learn the ins and outs of organic soil stewardship, including compost-making techniques. Chapter 4, Starting Seeds, Tending Transplants is the place to turn for guidance on what to grow and how to grow it. Find out which seeds to start indoors and which ones to sow directly into the garden, as well as why you might want to grow your own transplants (and how to do it) rather than buying them from a store. Profiles of the most popular vegetables and herbs deliver planting-to-harvesting guidance in Chapter 5, along with complete care information for more than 40 surefire annuals and perennials for the flower garden.

Need to know what to do once the garden's planted? Turn to Chapter 6, Garden Care Basics, to find the fundamentals of watering, feeding, and ongoing care during the growing season and straight through the harvest. Should trouble arise in the form of pests, diseases, or other problems, look to Chapter 7, Troubleshooting and Problem Solving, for organic solutions to common garden woes and ways to prevent them from ever getting a foothold in your garden.

Chapter 8, Organic Gardening Through the Seasons, details what to do when in the major climate regions of North America. Learn how to increase garden productivity with simple season-stretching techniques, how to get started saving seeds, and helpful hints for good garden record keeping. Finally, the Organic Gardener's Resource Guide includes sources of seeds, plants, tools, soil amendments, and everything else you might need to make your garden a success from start to finish.

Enjoy fresh, wholesome vegetables and herbs, chemical-free flowers and fruits, and the satisfaction of knowing you've done what's best for your health and for the environment. Organic gardening is right for you and right for the Earth, and getting started is as easy as turning the page and putting the collected experiences of seven decades of gardening experts to work in your garden.

GET TO KNOW
ORGANIC GARDENING

I believe a whole new era of agricultural research is in the making—
one that will help to create a healthy society and keep it in close touch
with the land from which it gets its strength and sweetness.

—J. I. RODALE, *PAY DIRT*, 1945

Where did organic gardening come from? Where is it going? Why does anyone garden organically? Why doesn't everyone? This chapter explores what it means to garden organically and how the term *organic* is used and misused, as well as how it relates to widely applied labels like *green, natural, eco-friendly,* and *sustainable.* Trends and movements in gardening and in food also are described.

While news coverage of dying honeybees and disappearing monarch butterflies may make it seem as if we are just beginning to recognize the costs of chemical-dependent agriculture, concerned farmers, naturalists, and citizen scientists have been sounding the alarm for more than 70 years. The Rodale name has been linked with organic farming and gardening methods in the United States since the 1940s.

Here's a brief history of organic gardening, from the origins of *Organic Gardening* magazine to the present, in the words of third-generation organic visionary and current chairman and chief operating officer of Rodale Inc., Maria Rodale:

Maria Rodale

Most people do a double take when I explain that *Organic Gardening* was launched in 1942. Then they want to know who had the foresight—and the courage—to launch a magazine about a little-known subject that would become the mainstream movement we know today. Well, who else but some gardeners?

The first pioneers of the modern organic movement were minor members of the British nobility who were obsessed with gardening, farming, and soil, long the traditional reserve of the Empire's landed gentry. Chief among them was British diplomat Sir Albert Howard, whose 1943 book, *An Agricultural Testament*, records his observations and research into traditional methods of composting while he was serving in India. Also in 1943, amateur soil scientist Lady Eve Balfour wrote *The Living Soil*, and agronomist Lord Northbourne coined the term *organic farming and gardening* in his 1940 book *Look to the Land* (revised second edition published in 2003). They believed that what was being done to the land, the soil, and the farms and gardens of the time—all in the name of progress and the advance of industrialization—would eventually destroy our health and the environment.

My grandfather, J. I. Rodale, was anything but an aristocrat. But he was living the American dream—rising up from the tenements of the Lower East Side of Manhattan to start a profitable electrical engineering business with his brother. He had everything except his health, and so became obsessed with finding solutions to this problem. Moving his family to a Pennsylvania farm, J.I. found the answer in the soil, realizing that if it was healthy, alive, and chemical free, it would produce healthier food and thus healthier people.

In 1942, J. I. Rodale started *Organic Farming and Gardening* magazine as a hobby—a place to publish his experiments with growing and eating organic food and to share his thoughts about the natural world. Sir Albert Howard became his contributing editor and, eventually, fellow crusader. Together they braved ridicule and scorn from many, including other gardeners, as well as the government. But they had a firm faith in both the rigors of science and the healing power of nature.

Fast-forward to the 1980s when my father, Robert Rodale, began the Farming Systems Trials: the first scientific study comparing organic agriculture to chemical agriculture.

For more than 60 years, the Rodale Institute has been researching the best practices for organic agriculture and sharing findings with farmers and scientists around the world.

Little more than 2 decades ago, global warming and climate change were confusing concepts, there were no USDA organic standards, and Whole Foods Market employed 19 people. My father and friends like Wendell Berry also harvested their share of ridicule—especially from other farmers, who believed you had to spray [chemicals] to grow anything. Today, that study remains the foundation of the Rodale Institute's work, and the results continue to impress with their unequivocal support of organic practices in agriculture and horticulture.

First, the study has demonstrated that organic crops are more productive over time than chemically grown crops because organic soil is more biologically active and much more absorbent. Organic crops can produce more extensive root systems and benefit from the presence of beneficial fungi, which enhance moisture and nutrient uptake. So organic crop production is more resilient during wetter and drier years—weather events that are a farmer's greatest threat and are increasing globally. Second, those healthy root systems are another reason that organic farming is so powerful. Living among the roots are mycorrhizal fungi—tiny fungal threads that capture and store, or sequester, carbon at an astoundingly high rate. This makes organic agriculture the number-one solution in our quest for ways to cut the excess carbon in the atmosphere that is the leading cause of climate change. Chemical agriculture's toxic residues not only cause a variety of health problems but also destroy the soil's ability to do what it does naturally—pull carbon out of the atmosphere and keep it underground.

And so a radical idea from decades ago has become the solution to a problem that few had recognized. That is, in essence, what being a pioneer is all about, isn't it? Braving the risks, taking chances, and following your inner voice, hoping that you will create or find a better place for future generations. Like my grandfather and my father, you have the power to be an organic pioneer, too. Whether you have a pot on a windowsill, a suburban yard, or a farm, by tending your soil and plants organically, you are protecting and preserving our future on this planet.

America's Organic Founding Fathers

More than half a century ago, Maria's grandfather J. I. Rodale, patriarch of the Rodale family and founder of Rodale Press, made the following observation about the growing acceptance of organic farming and gardening methods as more people became convinced of the benefits:

J. I. Rodale

The Organic Revolution

The time was when the organic movement was not in good repute, and we were called all kinds of names, mostly vituperative and insulting. All of a sudden . . . or shall I say, gradually over a short period of a year or two we have become respectable. No longer are we considered crackpots. The reason for this is simple. There are too many people in our camp, including millions of young people. They refuse to be shoved around.

In his introduction to J. I. Rodale's book *Pay Dirt*, published in 1945, organic advocate and contributing editor Sir Albert Howard wrote of the connections between the health of the soil and human health:

PAY DIRT
Farming & Gardening with Composts
by J. I. RODALE
THE DEVIN-ADAIR COMPANY, NEW YORK

A Fertile Foundation

A revolution in farming and in gardening is in progress all over the world. If I were asked to sum up in a few words the basis of this movement and the general results that are being obtained, I should reply that a fertile soil is the foundation of healthy crops, healthy live stock, and last but not least healthy human beings. By a fertile soil is meant one to which Nature's law of return has been faithfully applied, so that it contains an adequate amount of freshly prepared humus made in the form of compost from both vegetable and animal wastes.

The remedy is to look at the whole field covered by crop production, animal husbandry, food, nutrition, and health as one related subject and then to realize the great principle that the birthright of every crop, every animal, and every human being is health.

Introducing *The Basic Book of Organic Gardening* in 1971, J. I. Rodale's son, Robert Rodale, wrote these encouraging words to a new generation of gardeners. Over the years, understanding of the advantages of organic practices continued to grow. While a few forward-thinking farmers began to adopt organic techniques, home gardeners remained the most receptive audience for the organic message:

How to Be an Organic Gardener

It's easy to be an organic gardener! In fact, it's so easy that we sometimes wonder why *all* gardeners aren't organic gardeners. Our prediction is that once everyone has a chance to see organic methods demonstrated, there will be few *artificial* gardeners left.

Robert Rodale

The main reason why organic gardening is easy and produces good results is because it forces people to pay attention to their soil and build its fertility. Organic gardening is basically organic soil building. We all know that probably 90 percent of all garden failures are caused by poor soil. By improving the fertility of the soil, the organic gardener prevents the major cause of poor gardening results.

The first step in becoming an organic gardener is to think about the step you are taking. Consider that you are embarking on a new adventure—a voyage of discovery into the world of nature's wonders. You are going to create in your own garden an environment for plant life that is supremely fertile and natural in conception. You are going to grow plants that are superior in size and in nutritional quality to the average produce available in the market—and immeasurably superior in taste.

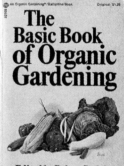

The Basic Book of Organic Gardening

Edited by Robert Rodale

Most important, think about the fact that your organic garden will be a demonstration of the cleanliness and spirituality of nature's design for life on this planet. Your organic garden will prove to you that our lives and the way we grow our food still are conducted best along the patterns set down by nature.

In 2010, Maria Rodale published her book *Organic Manifesto* to continue the fight started by her grandfather more than 60 years earlier. Her explanation of what motivated her to write the book appeared in *Organic Gardening* magazine:

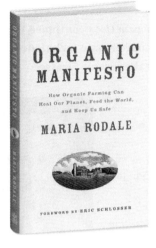

Why I Wrote *Organic Manifesto*

A few years ago, I began to worry.

When my oldest daughter was a teenager (she is now 27), the chatter was about how organic wasn't "good enough," that the government regulations were too lax and didn't take into account things like the humane treatment of animals, social justice, and health concerns. Some farmers began to think of themselves as "beyond organic" (an imprecise term that is generally considered a melding of the concepts of organic, local, and sustainable), and somewhere a marketer was probably dreaming up organic Twinkies. But at last, I thought, healthy discussions were taking place, conversations and debates that could lead to better regulations and broadened definitions of organic. All of this, I thought, would support the expanding market for organic food.

When my middle child was a grade-schooler (she is now 11), the local-food movement hit like a giant faddist food craze. The good news was that farmers' markets popped up all over the place, revitalizing local farm food communities. The bad news was that consumers soon became confused, as the movement became an either-or proposition: One was either "Local" or "Organic," 100 percent locavore or random grazer. Most of the local-vs-organic debate revolved around the use of fossil fuels to transport food. But this was a distraction from the more substantial and controversial aspect of the issue: using fossil fuels to create artificial chemicals that sustain nonorganic methods of food production.

I work in two worlds—the world of environmentalists and the world of health experts—and I realized that these two worlds were not communicating with each other. In the health world, where I sit on the advisory board of the Children's Environmental Health Center at Mount Sinai, headed by Philip Landrigan, MD, there is mounting concern over the impact of chemicals, especially agricultural chemicals, on our health and especially that of our children. Yet this did not feature in any of the discussions about our food choices or the expanding environmental crisis.

Is it any wonder that many Americans gave up trying to figure it all out? Our focus on what really matters most—the health and safety of our children, our families, and the future viability of life on this planet—was lost completely.

talk the talk
Organic Advocacy

BIODIVERSITY: The diverse variety of plant and animal species in an environment, the variability of species on Earth. Greater biodiversity is considered beneficial and is best preserved by conserving natural habitats.

BIODYNAMIC: A method of organic gardening or farming in which the garden/farm is viewed as a whole, incorporating soil, plants, and animals in an interdependent, unified ecosystem.

BIOTECHNOLOGY: Using or modifying living organisms to make products. Biotechnology is used to enhance disease resistance or improve yields of particular crops, for example.

GENETIC ENGINEERING: The process of introducing new traits into plants or animals by manipulating genetic material through biotechnology.

GMO (GENETICALLY MODIFIED ORGANISM): An organism whose genes have been altered using genetic engineering. The genes of food crops and animals are being manipulated in various ways, including across plant genera and families and even from animals to plants. Whether the resulting products must be labeled as such when they are sold to the public is an ongoing discussion.

MONOCULTURE: The cultivation of a single, genetically uniform crop, especially on a farm.

ORGANIC: Materials that are derived directly from plants or animals. Organic gardening uses plant and animal by-products to maintain soil and plant health and doesn't rely on synthetically made fertilizers or pesticides. In chemistry, "organic" describes compounds that contain carbon; this definition is sometimes used to characterize petroleum-based products as environmentally benign.

That's when I started to get really worried, and angry, too, and decided that I needed to write my recently published book.

My youngest child was an infant (she is now 3) when the economy tanked, and sure enough, the press began to chatter about the expensive elitism of organic food, saying people were struggling to afford food, period. But [I believe and hope you do, too] that organic is the sane lifestyle option, and that our survival may well depend on it. And, like me, [I believe] you're ready to turn this conviction into action. My kids are glad I did, and yours will be, too. That's my Organic Manifesto.

WHAT ORGANIC GARDENING MEANS TODAY

Its rich history notwithstanding, gardening organically remains a vibrant and viable practice, as relevant to today's gardens and gardeners as it was to J. I. Rodale and his colleagues in the 1940s. A popular catchphrase of the organic movement goes something like this: "What we call 'organic gardening' today is what my grandparents (or previous generations) simply called 'gardening.' " It suggests that before the development of agricultural chemicals—synthetic fertilizers, pesticides, and herbicides—gardening (and farming) was inherently organic, just because there was no other option. While it's true that the soil-turners of yore did not douse their genetically modified crops with glyphosate herbicides to wipe out competing weeds or seek to eradicate insect pests with carbaryl insecticides, the mere absence of manufactured chemical products does not define a farm or garden as organic.

Arsenic, copper, and sulfur are just a few of the products that farmers and gardeners have used for centuries to defend their crops against pests and diseases. Pesticides such as rotenone, nicotine, and pyrethrum underscore the reality that even botanically derived—and, in some cases, organically acceptable (see "The Arbiter of Organic," below)—products can be highly toxic and contrary to the nature of organic gardening.

At its heart, organic gardening is a system of working with nature to create conditions that benefit plants, people, and the environment. Instead of "See a bug? Spray a bug!" or "Spindly plants? Fertilize 'em!," organic gardeners replace reaction with prevention. A successful organic garden requires fewer inputs— like fertilizers and fungicides—but takes more involvement from the gardener. Initially, gardening organically may seem like more work than gardening with chemical products. Instead of spraying for weeds, you may have to hoe or pull them. Instead of pouring on the SuperGro, you have to build the fertility of the soil. Over time, however, an organic garden can achieve balance. Healthy soil yields healthy plants that are less susceptible to attacks from pests and diseases. Populations of beneficial organisms thrive in the absence of pesticides and provide further checks against problems.

Gardening is not natural—it is our effort to direct nature to serve our interests. But gardening in cooperation with nature is a much more likely path to success than constantly battling against the natural order.

Make Good Choices

There's much more to "going organic" than simply swapping organic products for chemical ones. In fact, it's safe to say that people who follow only that approach are in danger of falling back into garden-chemical dependency. Without a system of beneficial organisms cooperating to create a healthy growing environment, organic substitutes may seem like pale replacements for things like potent pesticides.

Still, using safer, more environmentally friendly organic products in place of harsh chemicals is a step in the right direction. Breaking your garden's chemical habit begins with good choices.

ORGANIC OPTIONS

Here are a few examples of good choices to make on the way to creating a healthy organic garden. Instead of concentrated chemical fertilizers that wind up washing into waterways when the nutrients exceed what plants are able to use, choose organic products that provide moderate amounts of nutrition in forms that are readily available to plants *and* beneficial to soil microbiology. Instead of chemical pesticides that kill a wide array of insects, including honeybees and other beneficials, choose the least toxic organics and learn to apply them selectively and only when absolutely necessary.

USE THIS	NOT THAT
Fish and seaweed fertilizer	Miracle-Gro
Insecticidal soap	Sevin (carbaryl)
Clove oil herbicide	Roundup (glyphosate)
Compost	Bagged synthetic fertilizer

THE ARBITER OF ORGANIC

When choosing products to use in your garden, how do you know what's okay— i.e., organic—and what isn't? One way is to look for a seal that says "OMRI" or "OMRI Listed" to identify products that have been evaluated and deemed acceptable for use in organic production.

OMRI, the Organic Materials Review Institute, is a nonprofit organization that focuses on agricultural inputs, such as nonsynthetic fertilizers, soil amendments, and naturally derived pest-control products. Farmers and food processors seeking organic certification under the USDA's National Organic Program (and the certifiers who inspect their lands and production processes) rely on the OMRI Products List and OMRI Generic Materials List, databases of products and substances that are approved for use on certified-organic land.

Foods that bear the "USDA Organic" label have rightfully earned a reputation for being carefully monitored and reliable. Organic certifiers annually inspect each producer, auditing operating procedures and record keeping and ensuring that all standards set by the USDA's National Organic Program have been met. Producers of organic foods must retain detailed records showing that only approved fertilizers, soil amendments, and other inputs have been used on the land. While home gardeners have only themselves to answer to regarding the use of approved products, looking for the OMRI seal is a reliable way to know that the inputs they're using in their gardens are truly organic.

Without OMRI, shopping for garden products can be complicated. Product labels can be confusing and misleading. Claims such as "organic" and "natural" on gardening products are, for the most part, not regulated. When a fertilizer package includes these words, it can simply mean that it contains carbon-based

Food Movements

CSA (COMMUNITY-SUPPORTED AGRICULTURE): A system in which individuals purchase shares in a farm's harvest at the beginning of the growing season to support the farmer's planting and raising of the crop, in return for which the contributors receive shares of the harvested crops.

FOOD MILES: The distance food travels from where it is produced to where it is sold and consumed. Measuring food miles is one way to gauge the environmental impact of commercial food production and distribution systems.

FOODSHED: A geographic area that supplies a population center with food.

LOCAVORE: Someone who eats locally grown or produced food as much as possible. Food from within a 100-mile radius is generally recognized as local.

matter or that some of its ingredients are natural. It does not necessarily show that the product is free from toxic and persistent chemicals or that it is appropriate for an organic garden.

Verified products for organic use will usually carry some sort of seal to support label claims. Be wary of misleading labels—if you want to be sure a product meets recognized organic standards (and your own personal ones), look for the OMRI seal. Before heading to the garden store, search the products and generic materials lists at omri.org, or download the products list, to help you find the right inputs for your organic garden.

AT THE INTERSECTION OF THE ORGANIC AND FOOD MOVEMENTS

One incentive for gardening organically is to ensure the food you eat is free of pesticides and other potentially harmful chemical residues. This same goal, along with concern for the environment and interest in sustainability, may be shared by the advocates of various food movements. Although they are not synonymous, the organic movement and many food-related trends share similar interests and objectives. Folks who start out trying to eat more locally grown food may take up gardening to enjoy the most local food they can get, and organic gardeners often consider sustainability to be a necessary element of their gardening practices, even if they are not food gardeners.

When these similar groups work together to pursue common goals, benefits like greater availability of organic produce and reduced use of toxic chemicals can extend throughout entire communities. The trick is for all involved to avoid developing a "greener than thou" mentality in which organic gardeners, for example, look down on the folks who prize locally grown food because not everything the so-called locavores eat is produced organically. And the locavores, in turn, may disparage those who eat only organic food because some of it is shipped over great distances, while whole-foods aficionados decry eating processed foods even if they're organic and/or local.

The reality is that local food, organic food, sustainable gardening and farming, community-supported agriculture, community gardens, farmers' markets, pick-your-own operations, and many other factions all are on the same path, working to bring fresh, healthy food to their families, their neighbors, and their communities.

Different Perspectives, Similar Goals

Is one food movement more valid, healthier, or more environmentally responsible than another? Just as vegans may claim superiority over mere vegetarians, so may locavores value their food choices over those of dedicated organic-only consumers. Here are a few views on the effects and benefits of eating locally and/or organically, from the pages of *Organic Gardening* magazine:

Menus Matter More Than Miles (2009)

Put down 2008 as the year the word *locavore* entered the popular lexicon. More and more consumers are actively seeking out locally grown foods in an effort to reduce their impact on the environment. But a study conducted at Carnegie Mellon University in Pittsburgh, Pennsylvania, suggests that what we eat may impact our ecological footprint more than where our food comes from.

The typical American family's consumption of roughly 10 pounds of food each day contributes about 8.1 metric tons of greenhouse gases to the atmosphere every year. Researchers Christopher Weber and Scott Matthews examined the total life cycle associated with producing and shipping food, and found out that moving food from farm to table generated only about 11 percent of the total greenhouse-gas emissions, while food production accounted for 83 percent. Focusing on individual food categories such as red meat, dairy products, and produce, the researchers discovered that the production of red meat and dairy products generated the highest greenhouse gas emissions. They found that far more energy is used to transport grain to cattle on feedlots than to ship food to the grocery store. The authors concluded that eating just 13 to 15 percent less red meat and dairy products would reduce an individual's output of greenhouse gases as much as eating a diet comprised entirely of locally produced foods.

So does organic gardening reduce global warming? "The conditions are extremely variable, and a lot depends upon the local chemistry and soil conditions," says Weber. "However, it's fair to say that growing your own organic food using compost and cover crops is the most sustainable way to feed yourself."

Banish the anonymity of food: That's the banner stretched across Main Street today. People are asking: Who made this bread? Who grew these vegetables? Are they fresh and local, or have they come from 2,000 miles away, picked too early, ripening in the cavern of a refrigerated tractor-trailer, their carbon footprint getting bigger by the mile? Consumers want to know just where the cheese and fruit and fish or meat their families will eat this evening come from.

The answer to many of these questions lies within the foodshed. Like a watershed, which is the geographic area drained by a body of water, a foodshed (as defined by Cornell University) is a geographic area that supplies a population with food. You can learn more about foodsheds and access a foodshed mapping tool on Cornell's Department of Crop and Soil Sciences Web site (http://css.cals.cornell.edu//extension/foodshed-mapping.cfm).

In many ways, mapping where our food comes from is an old-fashioned idea made modern. We started losing sight of food sources just after WWII, when agribusiness began ramping up. In fact, the term *foodshed* was coined by one W. P. Hedden in his book *How Great Cities Are Fed*, published in 1929. We are only now getting back to an idea that generations of people before us took for granted: The best food is locally grown. The words *sustainable, organic, locavore, carbon footprint* all in fact point back to a much simpler time, before the big rigs and interstate highways, before global food corporations. The foodshed map of your area provides the route to find healthy, delicious food to put on your table tonight.

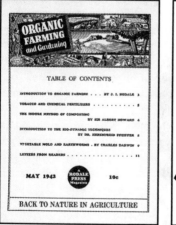

Left: *Organic Farming and Gardening,* 1942

Right: *Organic Gardening,* 2013

THE RODALE FAMILY
LEGACY CONTINUES

The Rodale family, including the grandchildren and great-grandchildren of J. I. Rodale, continue their work sharing the benefits of growing organically and their passion for healthy living. Maria Rodale's *Organic Manifesto*, excerpted here, "arms us all with the most powerful tool of change, information." By setting out "a lifetime of thinking," Maria tackles head-on the deluge of disinformation about the state of the global food supply and clears the way for us all to understand how important it is for us to demand organic.

We can feed the world with organic foods and farming. Despite the propaganda churned out by biotech and chemical companies, organic farming is the only way to feed the world. Transferring our toxic agricultural system to other countries is sure to bring about a global environmental collapse. The energy required, the toxicity of the chemicals, and the degradation of the soil will be fatal. Instead, we need to export the knowledge we have gained about successful modern organic farming and then help others adapt these practices to their climates, regions, and cultures.

Organic is more important than local, but local is also important. Numerous studies have shown that organic is much more critical when it comes to carbon than local. In one study commissioned by PepsiCo, an independent researcher determined that the most significant component of the carbon footprint for Tropicana orange juice (a PepsiCo product) wasn't transportation or manufacturing, but "the production and application of fertilizer" required to grow oranges.

The local food movement has been very important in revitalizing small farms and communities and bringing fresh, seasonal foods to many more people. However, as a means of saving the planet and improving our health, it only goes so far. Local chemical farming contaminates local communities and actually increases residents' carbon footprints and energy use. Local organic farming cleans up communities and decreases their carbon footprint and energy use. . . .

Organic farming increases and protects the planet's biodiversity. If you are an animal lover of any kind, organic is for you. A report by the International Union for Conservation of Nature documents that "life on earth is under serious threat." The report found that one-third of amphibians, at least one in eight birds, and a quarter of mammals are on the verge of extinction. Half of all plant groups are threatened. Development and logging are responsible, but agriculture is as much, if not more, to blame. . . . [T]he toxic effects of chemicals have reduced all species' abilities to survive and reproduce.

Growing organic is not going backward. When I proposed to chemical farmers that they switch to organic methods, they frequently replied, "Do you mean going back to the old way?" No! I believe in applying the best of modern science, technology, and resources to constantly improve our understanding of nature and our ways of growing and producing food. I also believe we cannot let corporations profit from killing us.

CAUSE FOR OPTIMISM

The launch, in 2002, of the USDA's National Organic Program established for the first time consistent standards for how food must be produced to bear the "certified organic" label. Every day since, new organic food products have been introduced into supermarkets everywhere. The organic standards were an important first step, but they did not create a sustainable system. Many organic foods travel the same distance from field to market as any other product on grocery-store shelves.

Today, conscientious consumers seek out not only organic but also local sources for as much of their food as possible. The USDA reports that in 2006, 4,385 farmers' markets gave consumers the opportunity to buy locally grown foods, up 50 percent from 5 years earlier. In 2000, around 400 farms offered community-supported agriculture (CSA) programs, which allow consumers to "subscribe" to a weekly basket of food directly from a local grower. In 2008, more than 2,000 such farms operated nationwide.

Even school cafeterias—hardly known for a commitment to fresh, let alone local, food—are changing. Nearly 2,000 school districts around the country have linked up with local farms to serve fresh vegetables and fruit to children. At colleges and universities, students are not only pushing for local food but getting involved with campus gardens and composting projects, too. These students will be the driving force for a renewed food system.

On the supply side, the 2008 Farm Bill included $2.3 billion for farmers growing specialty crops, such as the eggplants or salad greens typically grown by small, mostly organic farmers. That's a major increase from the $100 million earmarked for small farmers in the preceding farm bill.

A hopeful vision of our future includes thriving diversified farms, raising a wide variety of plants and animals. The animals have generous access to pasture, and crops are grown without synthetic fertilizers and pesticides. Farmers earn fair wages. Currently, as little as 8 cents of a dollar that you spend on food at a supermarket may go to the farmer, according to the USDA. When farmers sell direct at a farmers' market or through a CSA, they get as much as 94 percent of the total price.

In a sustainable food system, you eat what is in season in your region, harvested fresh the same day you buy it. Many people have backyard gardens, and members of your community—consumers and producers—work together so that no one goes hungry. There is still a global marketplace (we will not see this disappear), but we are consciously consuming goods through careful Fair Trade certification.

Fresh and Fair

Some critics assert that sustainable food is "elitist," that it's too expensive and not widely available. As Anna Lappé, food activist and coauthor (with her renowned mother, Frances Moore Lappé) of *Hope's Edge: The Next Diet for a Small Planet*, points out, "food is not sustainable if it is not affordable." She believes that the current food system is elitist, with fresh, healthful food often more available in wealthy communities, while in many low-income neighborhoods, processed food from convenience stores is the ready option. The term *food desert* is often used to describe these areas. Fortunately, sustainable-food groups around the country are addressing this problem.

Change might not be happening fast enough for many of us, but we must recognize the tremendous progress that is being made. We each have a responsibility to our families, communities, and the future to bring about the change. And with simple steps, such as eating from our gardens and being conscious of where we spend our money, we can send a strong message to the industrial food system. None of us alone has the power to change the food system. But all of us together can.

GETTING STARTED

A garden is . . . a special place linking our way of thinking
with the nature of the earth itself.

—ROBERT RODALE, 1986

Whether you are new to gardening or new to gardening organically, you probably have an idea of what you hope to achieve in your garden. In your mind's eye, fix a vision of your gardening goals: abundant vegetables, sun-ripened fruits, colorful flowers, soothing shade. Decide where you want to go, then use this book as a guide to help you get there.

Water, sunlight, and healthy soil are all essential ingredients in a successful garden. Equally important is to begin modestly. If you're planning your very first garden, go easy on yourself and keep things simple. Better to enjoy modest success in your first gardening season than to overcommit and wind up overwhelmed before you've picked your first ripe tomato.

There are dozens of decisions to make at the outset of a new garden. Keeping even a few notes can help you stay on course when you're tempted to forego planning and preparation. Be patient. Learn from your mistakes. Take time to stop and smell the flowers.

Start small (but dream big). A large garden can be a lot of work, while a small one allows time for tending crops and getting the feel of the tasks that need to be done. A space that's 5 × 10 feet can be big enough for a first garden. Even if you're feeling ambitious, start no more than three or four 4 × 8-foot beds in your first season. But choose a site that has room for expansion.

Grow things you (and your family) like. There are no required crops— don't bother with spinach, for example, if no one will eat it. List favorite vegetables and flowers and choose from those when selecting what will go into your garden.

Start with the easy stuff. Some vegetables and flowers are easier to grow than others. Don't try to grow oranges in Ohio or tulips in South Texas. Stick with the tried-and-true flowers and produce that thrive in your area, and choose disease-resistant varieties whenever possible.

Good crops for beginners include green beans, cucumbers, and leaf lettuce and easy-growing flowers such as morning glories, nasturtiums, and zinnias.

10 STEPS TO GARDEN SUCCESS

Here are the basic steps to follow as you create and care for your garden.

1. **Choose a site.** Consider sunlight, space, soil conditions, convenience, and access to water.

2. **Prepare the site.** Decide if you will garden in containers, in raised garden beds, or in the existing soil. Plan to incorporate compost making into your garden to enrich and improve the soil. See Chapter 3 for specifics on soil care and composting.

3. **Select seeds and plants.** Choose the vegetables and flowers you want to grow and decide if you will grow them from seeds or from purchased plants. See Chapter 5 for a guide to growing the most popular vegetables and annual and perennial flowers.

4. **Start seeds indoors.** In places where the growing season is short, starting seeds of heat-loving crops like tomatoes and

peppers indoors is a way to ensure they have enough time to produce fruits before cold weather returns. But not everyone has the time, space, or interest to provide the conditions needed to start seeds during late winter—that's why garden centers sell transplants (garden-ready seedlings) of many popular flowers and vegetables. Chapter 4 will help you decide which method is right for you.

5. **Sow seeds and plant seedlings.** Some crops grow better from seeds planted right in the spot where they will grow to maturity. When the time is right, plant seeds and seedlings in the site you have prepared for them.

6. **Care for your plants.** Over the course of the growing season, they may need supplemental water and nutrients, help fending off pests or competition from weeds, pruning, trellising, and harvesting. Plant profiles in Chapter 5 include specific care information for each crop, and Chapter 6 covers basic garden maintenance. In Chapter 7, you'll find guidance on preventing and solving common problems. Chapter 8 offers tips for stretching the growing season and a month-by-month gardening guide.

7. **Harvest what you've grown.** Enjoy the fruits—and vegetables—of your labor, and the flowers and foliage, too. Check the plant profiles in Chapter 5 for crop-specific harvest information and Chapter 6 for general harvesting how-to.

8. **Extend the season.** It's not a stretch to squeeze extra time out of the growing season. You'll find techniques for producing earlier tomatoes, salad greens for the Thanksgiving table, and other beyond-the-usual-season pleasures in Chapter 8.

9. **Clean up and prepare for winter.** As the harvest winds down, gather up the fading plants and add them to compost piles to replenish the soil for next year's gardens.

10. **Repeat as desired.** We think you'll want to.

SITE SELECTION

Where will your garden grow? Picking the spot where your garden will put down its roots depends largely on where you have space for growing and what you want to grow.

Seek the sun. Walk around your yard at different times of the day and note where the sun shines brightly and for how long. Most food plants need at least 5 hours of full sun each day, and almost all vegetables will be more productive if they receive 8 hours of direct sunlight daily. Partially shaded sites are not a complete deal breaker—lettuce and other salad greens make do with just 4 hours of sun, and cool-season crops like cabbage, broccoli, and peas can benefit from a bit of shade when temperatures begin to climb in summer—but it's difficult to get tomatoes and peppers to grow well without plenty of sunshine. Ideally, pick a spot that gets light from the south or west to expose it to long hours of afternoon and evening sun during summer.

Plan for easy care—and dinner. Put your garden near your house or in a place you walk by every day so it's convenient to visit it daily to do a bit of weeding and check on the progress of your plants. A garden that's nearby also makes it easy to browse for fresh ingredients to add to your meals.

Check the drainage. Food crops do not grow well in consistently soggy soil. Avoid siting your garden where water doesn't drain away within a few hours after a rainfall. See Chapter 3 for easy tests to assess soil drainage and texture. If a wet site is your only gardening option, build raised beds to give your vegetables the improved drainage they need.

Build raised beds anyway. There are plenty of reasons beyond drainage for making a garden with raised beds. Even if you simply fluff up and amend the existing soil on your site to create mounded beds an inch or two above the original surface, you'll be creating better growing conditions for everything you plant. See "Raised Bed Benefits" starting on page 58 for more about the pluses of growing in raised beds and ideas for building your raised bed garden.

Keep airflow in mind. Good air circulation helps prevent disease and reduces the risk of injury from late spring and early fall frosts. Too much wind, however, can make plants dry out fast. A loose hedge or stand of trees can provide a partial windbreak for breezy sites (just be sure it doesn't cast too much shade on your garden).

talk the talk
Site Selection

EXPOSURE: Both the amount of light a garden receives and its directional orientation—which way it "faces," or which way the light hits it. Different exposures can create microclimates that make it possible to grow plants in places that otherwise would be inhospitable. A southern exposure, for example, offers maximum warming for crops such as eggplant and sweet potatoes in cool-summer climates.

FULL SHADE: Less than 3 hours of direct sunlight each day. Few food crops or flowers grow well in full shade.

FULL SUN: Six or more hours of direct sunlight each day. Most vegetables need full sun during their peak growing season.

HARDINESS: The measure of a plant's ability to tolerate frost and cold temperatures.

HARDINESS ZONES: The USDA divided the United States and southern Canada into 11 areas, or hardiness zones, based on average minimum winter temperatures. The hardiness zone indicates whether a perennial is likely to survive winter in your climate, and very little else.

Provide a water source. Make sure your garden is within hose range of a reliable water supply. Rainfall is unlikely to provide all the water a garden needs during the growing season, and hauling water by hand grows old rather quickly. See Chapter 6 for advice on how much water your garden will need, ways to measure the amount of water it receives from rainfall or a sprinkler, and how to use tools like soaker hoses and drip irrigation to reduce watering chores.

Consider containers. Don't have an ideal spot for a food garden? You can grow most vegetables and herbs in containers, which lets you turn almost any location—driveway, patio, balcony, rooftop—into an ideal spot for growing. If you'll need to move your containers to help your plants get the sunlight they need, think about keeping them in a wagon or cart. Large pots of moist soil can be heavy. See "Container Gardening" starting on page 64 for hints to help you make the most of gardening in pots.

Get to Know Your Place

Learn the right time to plant in your region. In south Florida, for example, folks are planting their "spring" gardens in fall. (Go to organicgardening.com to see *Organic Gardening*'s monthly zone-by-zone to-do list of region-specific advice.)

Obviously, gardening in Florida isn't the same as gardening in Maine because of the climatic conditions. That's why before you even start planning your garden, it helps to know what hardiness zone you live in.

COLD HARDINESS AND HEAT TOLERANCE

A plant's ability to withstand a given climate is called its hardiness. The USDA has developed a Plant Hardiness Zone Map (last updated in 2012) that divides North America into 11 numbered climatic zones. Zone 1 (Arctic regions of Alaska and Canada) is the coldest and Zone 11 (southernmost Florida) is the warmest. You can check which zone you live in by looking at the map. Hardiness zones are based on the average annual minimum temperature over a 30-year period. That means that temperatures lower than the ranges indicated on the map are entirely possible in any given year and should be considered if you want to experiment with plants rated for warmer zones. In the strictest sense, hardiness includes not only a plant's capacity to survive through winter but also its tolerance of all the climatic conditions characteristic of the area in which it grows. Still, most gardeners define a hardy plant as one capable of withstanding cold and a tender plant as one that's susceptible to injury from low temperatures and frost. Since most vegetable crops are annuals that complete their life cycle over a few months' time, hardiness considerations typically are more relevant when choosing perennials and woody plants, including fruit trees.

PLAN FOR LOCAL WEATHER PATTERNS

Climate factors other than frost dates and hardiness zones also play a role in determining when it's best to plant specific crops throughout the year. Look for the pattern that most closely describes the weather in your area.

Cold winters and hot, humid summers. In the northeastern, mid-Atlantic, and north-central states, the outdoor gardening season begins several weeks before the last expected spring frost. In the North, plant quick-maturing cultivars for summer crops and pay careful attention to hardiness of perennial crops. In all areas, look for cultivars that are resistant to

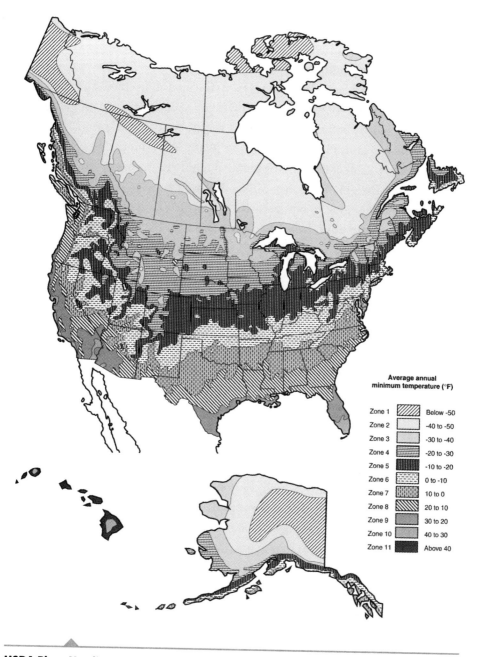

Average annual minimum temperature (°F)

Zone 1	Below -50
Zone 2	-40 to -50
Zone 3	-30 to -40
Zone 4	-20 to -30
Zone 5	-10 to -20
Zone 6	0 to -10
Zone 7	10 to 0
Zone 8	20 to 10
Zone 9	30 to 20
Zone 10	40 to 30
Zone 11	Above 40

USDA Plant Hardiness Zone Map This map is recognized as the best indicator of minimum temperatures available. Look at the map to find your area, then match its pattern to the key at right. When you've found your pattern, the key will tell you what hardiness zone you live in. Remember that the map is a general guide; your particular conditions may vary. To find an interactive version of this map, go to planthardiness.usda.ars.gov. There you can enter your zip code to find your precise location's hardiness zone information.

molds and mildews. The late season extends several weeks after the first fall frost and is ideal for cool-weather crops; it extends even longer for very hardy vegetables or those grown under cover.

Cold winters and hot, dry summers. In the mountain states, south-central states, and higher elevations of the Southwest and West, the outdoor gardening season begins shortly before the last frost. Early crops may need protection from occasional heavy snows late in the season. Plant quick-maturing cultivars in mountain states. Protect heat-loving plants if nighttime temperatures are quite cool—even in the height of summer. Mulch cool-weather crops to keep roots cool in the heat of the day. Look for cultivars that can withstand temperature extremes.

Mild winters and cool, humid summers. In the Pacific Northwest, where this type of weather is typical, frost-hardy and cool-weather crops can be grown year-round, but growing warm-weather crops is a challenge. Choose quick-maturing cultivars and cultivars with resistance to mildews and molds. Crops with high heat requirements, like lima beans, may not do well, but the long, cool springs favor substitutes like fava beans.

Mild winters and hot, humid summers. In the Southeast and coastal areas of the southwestern states, winters may be mild enough to grow even warm-weather crops. Grow cool-weather crops in late fall and winter months. To extend the harvest, protect cool-weather crops from the sun with shade cloth as temperatures rise in spring. Look for warm-weather crops that are resistant to mildews and molds. Look for cool-weather crops that are heat resistant. Choose perennial crops carefully. Rhubarb, asparagus, and many fruit trees require winter chilling, which your climate may not provide.

Mild winters and hot, dry summers. In the deserts of the Southwest and West, cool-weather crops grow best in late fall and winter. In this region, gardeners can set out warm-weather crops while northern gardeners are still waiting out winter. Heat tolerance is critical; look for crops and cultivars that can stand up to scorching weather. The extreme heat, low humidity, and desert winds can sap moisture from plants. Mulch plants to conserve moisture. Consider using sunken beds—the reverse of raised beds—to help conserve moisture and protect crops.

FIND YOUR FROST DATES

As you might conclude from all this talk of planting times and cool- and warm-season crops, planting a garden is not a once-and-done activity. After you've selected the things you want to grow and obtained seeds or plants, you'll need to

Deciding What to Plant When

Knowing what conditions your vegetables need will help you pick the best time to begin planting. Seed packets and seedling labels usually give recommendations on the best planting times, but here are some general guidelines.

COOL-SEASON CROPS. Also described as frost-hardy, leafy vegetables such as kale, spinach, chard, and lettuce; root crops such as radishes, turnips, beets, potatoes, onions, and carrots; cole crops (broccoli, Brussels sprouts, cabbage, and cauliflower); and peas all may be planted as soon as the soil has thawed and dried out enough for you to work it in spring. Some of these same crops that tolerate chilly early spring days also grow well at the end of the growing season and may actually do better than in spring because the days are growing shorter and cooler rather than longer and warmer. In addition to the vegetables already mentioned, fall crops include celery, leeks, and parsnips, all of which are planted along with warm-weather crops but don't mature until fall; garlic and shallots (plant in fall for harvest the following summer); and fall-planted spinach that overwinters to provide extra-early spring greens.

WARM-SEASON CROPS. Beans, cucumbers, melons, and squash won't grow well until the soil has warmed, so wait to plant them around the last spring frost date. (If you don't know your last frost date, contact your local extension office or ask a knowledgeable neighbor.)

COLD-SENSITIVE CROPS. Corn, eggplant, peppers, sweet potatoes, and tomatoes won't be ready to go in the ground until about 2 weeks after your last frost date. Rushing to plant these crops before the soil is warm and the danger of frost is past risks giving them a chill that can cause them to grow poorly for the rest of the season.

plant each crop when the weather conditions favor its success. While this does add a bit of complexity to the planning process, it also means you can maximize space in your garden by succession planting—planting a warm-season crop in the space left by a cool-season one that has finished its productive life, for example. Succession planting also refers to the practice of making multiple sowings, a week or two apart, of crops like radishes or beans or lettuce to keep a steady supply of those veggies coming from your garden to your table. You can also extend the harvest of a particular crop by planting varieties with different maturity times to make the harvest last longer.

When you're looking into the average last frost date for spring, be sure to find out the average date of the first frost in fall in your area as well. That date is useful for deciding what you can plant in midsummer as your spring crops are wrapping up. By knowing when nights are likely to turn frosty in fall, you can make midseason plantings of tender crops that will reach harvest before that date. The first fall frost date also provides a guide for timing cool-weather vegetables that will grow in the garden after low temperatures rule out less hardy crops. The plant profiles in Chapter 5 include timing tips for planting and identify those crops that you may want to sow more than once during the same growing season.

TIMING TIPS

To determine when it's time to sow seeds or set out transplants, you need to know the average date of the last spring frost for your area. While this date, which represents the *usual* end of frosty weather and thus the all-clear for planting frost-tender flowers and vegetables, is not hard and fast, it's a handy guideline as you plan your spring gardening schedule. You can find your area's average last frost date through your county extension office or Master Gardener program. Mark it on your calendar, then use the guide below (and the plant profiles in Chapter 5) to work out when to plant your favorites and whether you'll get them growing with seeds sown in the garden or from garden-ready transplants.

CROP	TIMING (RELATIVE TO LAST FROST DATE)	SEEDS OR PLANTS
Basil	2 weeks after	Plants
Beans	After	Seeds
Broccoli	2 weeks before	Plants
Carrots	2 weeks before	Seeds
Cucumbers	After	Seeds or plants
Lettuce	4 weeks before	Seeds
Peas	4 weeks before	Seeds
Peppers	After	Plants
Spinach	4 weeks before	Seeds
Squash	After	Seeds
Tomatoes	After	Plants

TOOL UP

Which tools are must-haves? Your soil type and the kind of gardening you do will determine which tools get used most often. The tools on this list are great for starters. A good rule of thumb is to buy the best tools you can afford. Not only will quality tools make the job easier, but they'll also last longer. The business end of digging and cultivating tools should be one solid piece of rustproof or rust-resistant metal, such as carbon steel. Heavy digging tools should have what's called solid-socket or solid-strapped construction, which places less stress on the tool head. Be wary of tools that have a blade attached to the handle by a single metal pin: These tools won't stand up to heavy use.

Keep your tools clean and their edges sharp, and you'll give out before they do. While experienced gardeners are likely to have many more tools in their collections—and definite favorites among them—the list below will give you a basic idea of the tools you'll need for tending your garden.

Good tools will give you a lifetime of good work if you give them a little bit of care. Try these tips to keep your tools in top condition:

- Clean, dry, and put away all hand tools after each use.
- Knock or wash off any clinging soil.
- Remove any rust with a wire brush.
- Sharpen your tools regularly to keep the proper bevel edge.
- Regularly sand and varnish wooden handles to protect them from moisture.
- At the end of each season, polish all metal parts of hand tools with steel wool, oil them to prevent rust, and store them in a dry place.

Different regions of the country also have their own specialized tools. In areas with heavy clay or rocky soil, for example, it sometimes takes a pick to break into the subsoil. In the Southwest, a tool called a caliche bar (also known as a crowbar) is used to poke holes in the concretelike caliche soil.

Getting the tools you need to start out with doesn't have to be a budget buster. Watch for neighborhood yard sales, moving sales, or estate sales, where it's possible to find good quality used tools at a fraction of their original cost. Online classified sites like Craigslist (craigslist.org) or the Freecycle Network (freecycle.org) may point you to people in your area with used tools for sale or to give away.

LONG-HANDLED TOOLS

garden shovel

wheelbarrow

spading fork

garden rake

stirrup hoe

collinear hoe

draw hoe

short-handled cobra head

GETTING STARTED

talk the talk
Long-Handled Tools

GARDEN SHOVEL: A garden shovel or spade gets top marks for versatility. It digs, edges, mixes, and cuts through sod. Look for a digging tool with a solid metal blade that is securely attached to the handle. Turned edges on the top of the blade let you use your foot to push the sharpened edge into the soil.

SPADING FORK: Sturdy, flat tines make a digging fork good for loosening soil, turning compost, dividing perennials, and distributing mulch.

GARDEN (OR BOW) RAKE: The rigid metal tines of a sturdy garden rake make it a gardener's best friend when it comes to clearing debris, spreading compost, shaping beds, and smoothing the soil surface before planting.

A WHEELBARROW has a single wheel, so you can dump a load by simply tipping it to one side. A garden cart has two (or three or four) wheels and is easier to maneuver. Each is very useful for moving compost, dirt, weeds, children, and just about anything else you can think of.

HOES are essential for weed control and come in dozens of blade shapes; many are available in both long- and short-handled forms. Some blades cut on the push stroke; others on the pull; and some whether pushing or pulling. Some popular blade types are stirrup, collinear, and draw, which all cover a lot of ground quickly and easily. A narrow blade on a short handle can be useful for both weeding and making furrows in compact garden spaces such as raised beds.

"Try on" long-handled tools before you buy. Hold tools like hoes and rakes the way you would during use. Check your posture. Is your back straight or do you have to bend as you work? Are the grips comfortably placed and smooth? If a tool forces you into an awkward position when you're using it, try a different size—or a different tool—to avoid post-gardening aches and fatigue. Good quality tools last longer, work better, and make gardening more enjoyable.

In addition to hand tools, you'll likely need a few more important things. Consider purchasing trellises, stakes, cages, or other plant supports, as well as plant ties. Invest in a good garden hose and adjustable nozzle and a quality watering can. Row covers (lightweight material used to protect plants from frost) will also serve as a barrier against pests and can be used to shade heat-sensitive crops in summer. And it's always handy to have a garden sprayer or trigger spray bottle.

SMALL HAND TOOLS

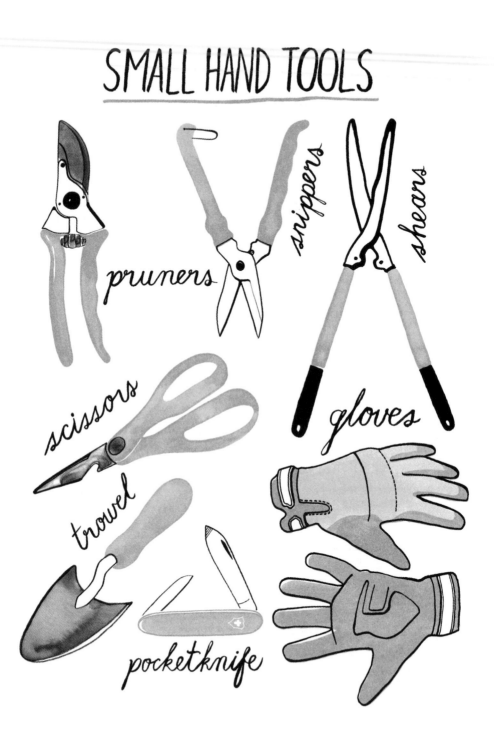

pruners

snippers

shears

scissors

gloves

trowel

pocketknife

talk the talk
Small Hand Tools

TROWEL: For transplanting seedlings, planting bulbs, and any close-up soil work, this little digger can't be beat. It will likely be your most used tool, so be sure to pick one with a comfortable handle.

POCKETKNIFE: A folding pocketknife comes in handy for cutting twine, opening bags (of peat moss, compost, potting soil, etc.), and slicing through the roots of potbound plants—plus any number of other tasks that come up as you garden. Choose one with a brightly colored handle to reduce the risk of losing track of it.

PRUNERS OR SNIPPERS: What you'll need in this grouping of cutting tools will depend on what you're growing in your garden. For roses, raspberries, or any trees or shrubs with woody stems, you'll want a pair of bypass (this means the blades cut like scissors) pruners. Lighter-weight snippers (or a sturdy pair of scissors) will do for removing faded flowers (known as deadheading), for cutting flowers for bouquets, and for harvesting peppers and eggplants. For cutting back ornamental grasses, long-handled garden shears with long, sharp blades are quite useful.

GLOVES: Many gardeners express a preference for gardening bare-handed, but there are plenty of tasks that call for the protection offered by a good pair of gloves. Leather (or a sturdy facsimile) is best for preventing blisters and protecting hands during encounters with pointy or prickly materials; cloth or rubber gloves typically offer more dexterity. Neoprene or nitrile or gloves that combine cloth and these materials are good for working in wet conditions. Long gauntlets that cover your forearms are useful when pruning roses or brambles.

Hand tools, including gloves, should fit comfortably in (or on) your hands. Watch out for seams or rough spots on handles that may rub during use and cause blisters. Choose top quality tools for the gardening chores you do the most—you may want a long, narrow, extra-sharp, and sturdy trowel specifically for planting hundreds of bulbs, for example. If pruning chores top your list, consider pruners or shears with ratcheted blades that minimize the amount of force needed to cut effectively.

GARDEN DESIGN BASICS

When it comes to garden design, the first rule is that there's no single correct method. Some gardeners thoroughly plan out their gardens on paper before they plant, while others seemingly tuck plants in at random yet still produce an attractive result. Whether a design is backed up by paper plans or just a knack for putting the right plant in the right place, basic aesthetic principles are the foundation of the best and most satisfying gardens.

There are two general types of garden design styles—formal and informal. Formal gardens exhibit classical symmetry. Garden beds and other features are generally rectangular and paths are straight. Or they may be round or oval with walks that curve around them.

Informal gardens include irregular shapes but tend to follow the features of the underlying site. Natural-looking woodland wildflower gardens and free-form island beds of perennials both are examples of informal style.

Regardless of style, all well-designed gardens make use of three essential principles—balance, proportion, and repetition—to blend the various parts of the garden into a harmonious whole. Even if your entire gardening effort is focused on edible crops, you can incorporate basic design principles to create a productive and visually attractive garden.

Balance. When elements on two sides of a central point are similar in size or visual weight, they are balanced. Balanced design gives the viewer a peaceful, restful feeling; unbalanced design is unsettling. Balance doesn't necessarily mean symmetry; you don't need mirror-image plantings to accomplish it.

Proportion. Garden features (plants, flowerbeds, structures, etc.) are in proportion when their scale is in pleasing relationship to their surroundings. For example, a large clump of 9-foot-tall bamboo planted in a bed with low-growing perennials creates a picture that is out of proportion. Similarly, a huge shed would be out of proportion in a small yard.

Repetition. Repeating an element—color, texture, shape, or even building materials such as the timber framing of garden beds—throughout a garden adds unity and harmony to a design, so the parts of the garden fit together more com-pellingly. For example, repeating the color red at intervals in a flowerbed leads the eye through the design and creates a feeling of wholeness and rhythm. You can repeat the same plant or use different species with similarly colored blooms to achieve the same effect.

talk the talk
Design and Planning Considerations

COLOR: Color can influence the mood of a garden. Hot colors—vibrant reds, oranges, and yellows—are cheerful and bright. They can make an object or area appear larger and closer. Cool colors such as greens, blues, and purples are serene and calming; they tend to recede visually and make objects seem farther away. This makes them useful for making a small garden appear bigger.

EDIBLE LANDSCAPING: Integrating food plants into a decorative landscape by planting fruit-bearing trees and bushes, ornamental varieties of vegetables and herbs, and edible flowers in plantings designed using principles of landscape design.

FORM: A plant's shape—round, vertical, creeping, or weeping, for example. Intersperse different plant forms throughout a design for balance and interest. Form may be used like color, although it's more subtle. Repeating a form at intervals in the garden strengthens unity and harmony. You don't have to repeat the same plant to achieve this effect; it works if you use different plants that have similar forms.

GARDEN "BONES": The structural elements of a landscape that are most often revealed in winter when many plants are dormant. A garden's "bones" may include dark tree trunks and branches, hardscape features like arbors and patios, and evergreen trees and shrubs that supply color, form and texture when other plants are visually absent.

HARDSCAPE: The nonplant constructed parts of a landscape, such as driveways, walls, fences, arbors, pathways, and patios.

SEASON OF INTEREST: The time when a plant, garden, or feature contributes visually in the landscape. A shade tree, for example, might make its biggest visual contribution in fall when it has brilliant foliage color, but it may also have an additional season of interest in winter when its textured bark is revealed and/or in spring when its young leaves emerge. Choosing plants with multiple seasons of interest helps to maintain visual appeal in the landscape year-round.

TEXTURE: Leaves can look coarse, crinkled, glossy, fuzzy, or smooth. Flowers may be feathery, airy, and delicate, or flashy and bold. Using plants with a variety of textures—and repeating noteworthy textures at intervals—adds interest and appeal. Like form, texture is a subtle design characteristic.

Patio Produce Garden

Bring dinner right to your door: Plant vegetables in pots on your patio or deck. A sunny spot to the south of your house will give your crops the bright light they need to produce their best harvest.

Plant pole beans to climb a tripod of bamboo poles in a half-barrel planter, with three or four plants at each leg of the tripod. You may need to attach the stems to the poles at intervals as they climb.

Install a sturdy stake or cage for each tomato plant at planting time. The eggplant and bell pepper also will benefit from a supporting stake or cage.

If the summer sun is strong where you live, you may need to cover the lettuce with shade cloth or a lightweight floating row cover during the hottest part of the day. Or position the lettuce planter box on one side of the garden instead of in the front.

Check daily—twice a day in hot weather—to see if the plants need water. Lettuce wilts easily, so don't let the soil or potting mix dry out.

Feed the plants once a week with a fish/seaweed fertilizer diluted according to label directions.

What's in the Garden?

1. **Beans, pole (12 plants)**
2. **Bell pepper (1 plant)**
3. **Carrot (8 plants)**
4. **Chard (3 plants)**
5. **Eggplant (1 plant)**
6. **Leaf lettuce (6 plants)**
7. **Parsley (3 plants)**
8. **Radish (8 plants)**
9. **Tomato, staked (2 plants)**

Helpful Growing Tips

Half barrels come in different sizes. Diameters can range from 18 to 25 inches. The one in this example has a 24-inch diameter. If your tub is smaller, use fewer plants than shown in this plan.

If you like arugula or the mixed baby greens called mesclun, substitute them for one or more of the lettuce plants.

When harvesting chard, you can cut the outer leaves individually and leave the inner ones to continue growing, or cut off the entire plant at once close to the ground and let it regrow.

Radishes grow quickly; when you harvest them, you can sow seeds for a second crop.

Choose a small-rooted carrot variety, such as 'Nantes' or 'Parmex', for container growing.

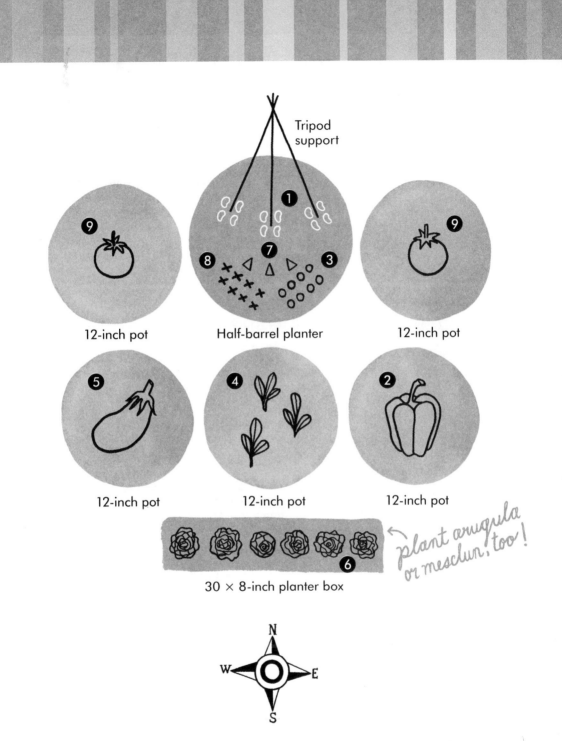

Tripod support

① ⑦ ⑧ ③

Half-barrel planter

⑨

12-inch pot

⑨

12-inch pot

⑤

12-inch pot

④

12-inch pot

②

12-inch pot

⑥

30 × 8-inch planter box

plant arugula or mesclun, too!

N W E S

Garden size: 4 feet deep × 6 feet wide

The Cook's Herb Garden

Once you've started cooking with fresh-from-the-garden herbs, you'll want them in your kitchen all the time. This compact herb garden would be perfect right outside the kitchen door, where you can harvest what you need in just a few quick moments. Use three small nursery starts of chives in this plan or one more sizable clump.

Herbs are easy to grow, and their flowers can attract bees and other beneficial insects. Watch for these helpers in your garden.

Give your herbs a sunny location. Position lower-growing thyme and cilantro to the south of taller plants like dill and sage.

What's in the Garden?

1. **Basil (3 plants)**
2. **Chives (3 plants)**
3. **Cilantro (6 plants)**
4. **Dill (4 plants)**
5. **Mint in container (1 plant)**
6. **Oregano (3 plants)**
7. **Parsley (6 plants)**
8. **Sage (1 plant)**
9. **Thyme (9 plants)**

Helpful Growing Tips

Give sage plenty of room—it grows into a sizable plant. Cut back the woody stems each spring to promote fresh green growth.

The flowers of chives, thyme, and oregano are tasty additions to salads and flavored butters.

Snipping off the flowers of dill before they develop can prolong the harvest of green leaves. Eventually the plants will bloom, no matter what. If you allow some of your dill to flower and set seed, the plants often will self-sow and regrow in fall or next spring.

Mint can be invasive, so be sure to plant it in a container. If you don't want to grow mint, place a birdbath or sundial in the center of your little garden.

Garden size: 4 feet × 4 feet

Summer Bounty Garden

Summer is the season of plenty, and this garden offers a bounty of warm-weather vegetables that capture its very essence. The plan shows four 4 × 5-foot beds with 3-foot-wide paths in between, but you can combine them into one larger garden if you like. Just remember to leave some space between different plantings to allow access for weeding, watering, and, of course, harvesting your home-grown abundance.

1. **Beans, pole (16 plants)**
2. **Beet (12 plants)**
3. **Bell pepper (3 plants)**
4. **Carrot (16 plants)**
5. **Chard (6 plants)**
6. **Cucumber (1 plant)**
7. **Edamame (24 plants)**
8. **Eggplant (3 plants)**
9. **Melon (2 plants)**
10. **Sweet corn (18 plants)**
11. **Tomato, determinate (3 plants)**
12. **Tomato, indeterminate (2 plants)**
13. **Zucchini (beneath corn) (2 plants)**

Helpful Growing Tips

In a south-facing vegetable garden, plant taller plants in back, on the north side of the garden, so they won't cast shade on shorter plants growing nearby.

For an early harvest, plant a spring crop of sugar snap peas on netting or a string trellis on the north side of the bed where the corn will be planted in summer.

Planting zucchini under the corn makes efficient use of space.

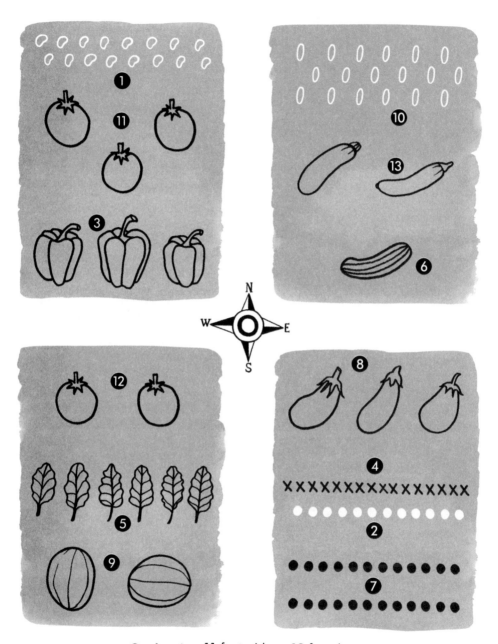

Garden size: 11 feet wide × 13 feet deep
Bed size: 4 feet wide × 5 feet deep

Gourmet Salad Garden

Salads are simple, and simply delicious, especially when you can pick the ingredients at their peak of perfection. The freshest, tastiest salad you can have is the one gathered right from your own garden.

Experiment with different varieties of lettuce in this garden, choosing loose-leaf, butterhead, and oak-leaf types for diverse flavor, appearance, and crunch. For this lettuce row, consider sowing six plants each of three different lettuces.

Most lettuce varieties bolt (send up flowerstalks and produce seeds) when the weather turns hot. They're still edible then, but the leaves can be bitter. Keep an eye on your lettuce and pick often, while the leaves are still tender and juicy. You can sow more seeds of lettuce, mesclun, and arugula again in late summer for a fall crop.

What's in the Garden?

1. **Arugula (9 plants)**
2. **Cherry tomato (1 plant)**
3. **Lettuce (18 plants)**
4. **Mesclun (16 plants)**
5. **Tomato, heirloom (3 plants)**

Helpful Growing Tips

Give this garden a location in full sun. If your summers are hot, you may want to cover the lettuce with row covers in the heat of afternoon. Also choose heat-resistant varieties such as 'Oak Leaf', which are slower to bolt when temperatures begin to climb.

Other good choices for a salad garden include sugar snap peas, bell peppers, and carrots.

You can substitute spinach for half of the lettuce, but be sure to plant it early in spring.

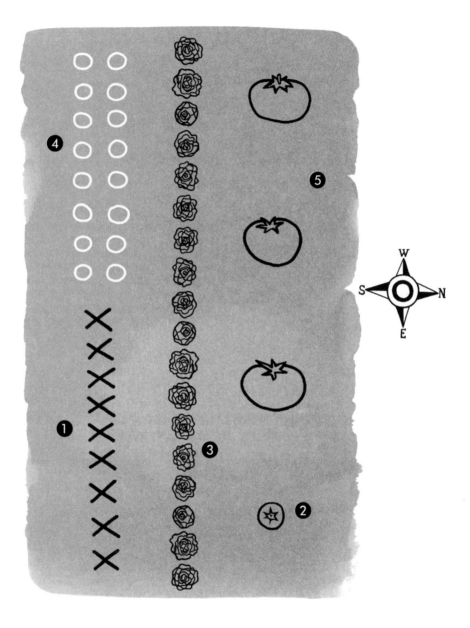

Garden size: 5 feet wide × 9 feet deep

Edible Ornamental Bed

If you have room for only a small garden, why not make it do double duty? You can grow vegetables, herbs, and edible flowers that are delicious and colorful, too. Purple pole beans such as 'Trionfo Violetta' and 'Amethyst' bear rich purple pods, as do 'Royal Burgundy' bush beans. Eggplant has purple blossoms, and some varieties produce colorful fruit, such as bright purple 'Neon' and 'Beatrice' and purple-and-white-streaked 'Fairy Tale' and 'Rosa Bianca'. Versatile, long-producing chard used to have green leaves and white stalks. More decorative varieties include 'Ruby Red', with bright red stems, and 'Bright Lights', with stems in shades of pink, orange, yellow, red, and purple.

What's in the Garden?

1 **Basil (3 plants)**

2 **Beans, purple-pod (18 plants)**

3 **Bell pepper (3 plants)**

4 **Chard (8 plants)**

5 **Eggplant (2 plants)**

6 **Nasturtium (12 plants)**

7 **Sage, variegated (2 plants)**

8 **Sunflower (2 plants)**

Helpful Growing Tips

Put a trellis or other supports for pole beans in place at planting time.

Nasturtiums bloom best in soil that's not too rich. If your soil is of average fertility, don't add fertilizer to the nasturtium area. The plants may quit blooming in summer heat, but they'll resume flowering when the weather cools in fall.

Other edible flowers to grow include anise hyssop, bee balm, borage, calendula, daylily (stir-fry the buds), clove pink (*Dianthus plumarius*), squash blossoms, flowers of culinary herbs, pansies, and violets.

Many benefits have been attributed to eating garden sage—whether traditional gray green or colorfully variegated—or drinking tea made from its leaves. However, health risks have been associated with eating large quantities of uncooked sage. As with most things, fresh sage from your garden is best enjoyed in moderation.

encourage the end bean plant to climb the sunflower stalk.

Garden size: 5 feet wide × 6 feet deep

A "Hot Tub" of Flowers

The bright colors of flowers are what summer is all about, and many annuals bloom all season long. You can create the look of a larger garden in a half barrel or a tub planter. Sizes vary, but most range from 18 to 25 inches in diameter. If your container is smaller than 25 inches, just subtract a few plants from what's recommended here.

The hot colors of these flowers bring the warmth of a summer sunset wherever you need it—on a sunny deck or patio, alongside the garage or driveway, or near a picnic table or outdoor seating area.

If your container garden will be visible from all sides, position the tallest plants in the center. If the container will be viewed primarily from one side (against the wall near the front door, for example), set the tallest plants at the back of the container.

If hot colors aren't your favorites, try this lineup of plants instead: pink or purple calibrachoa; pink and white cosmos instead of rudbeckia; hot pink geranium; red-violet or lavender New Guinea impatiens; white or pink nicotiana; and pink or magenta Wave petunia.

What's in the Garden?

1. **Yellow or terra-cotta calibrachoa (5 plants)**

2. **Salmon geranium (4 plants)**

3. **Red or lime green nicotiana (4 plants)**

4. **Dark purple 'Blue' Wave petunia (5 plants)**

5. ***Rudbeckia hirta* 'Irish Eyes' or 'Gloriosa Daisy' (1 plant)**

6. **Red salvia or yellow and orange American marigold (8 plants)**

Helpful Growing Tips

Regular deadheading is important for annuals, especially geraniums, nicotianas, and salvias. The plants look better and will keep blooming when you clip off the old flowers.

An old gardener's rule of thumb is that you can't overfeed an annual. That may or may not be true, but annuals do need regular nourishment to fuel their season-long bloom. Feed your annuals every week or two with fish/seaweed fertilizer or fresh compost tea, if you have it, to keep them blooming. Or feed them with every watering, diluting the fertilizer to one-half or one-quarter the strength usually recommended.

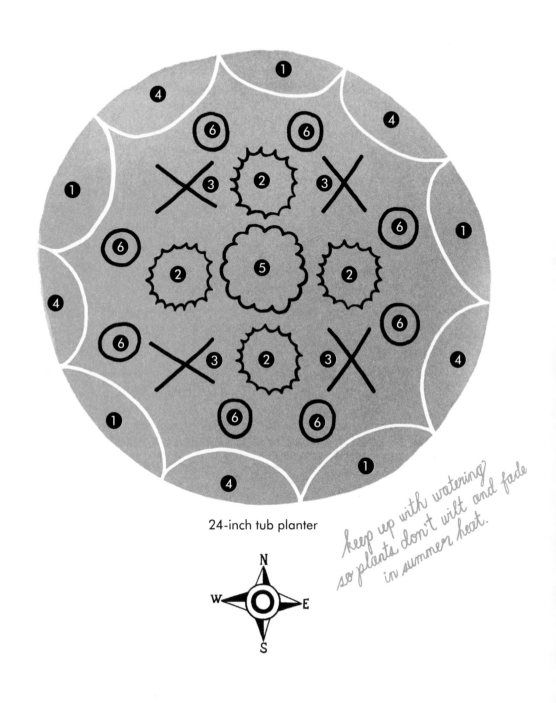

24-inch tub planter

keep up with watering so plants don't wilt and fade in summer heat.

Garden for a Shady Spot

As human habitation replaces more of their natural habitat, deer are an increasingly common sight in gardens. Except for the hostas, the plants in this garden are reasonably unattractive to deer—a big plus if you live where deer are active. If you have deer in your neighborhood, skip the hostas in this plan and plant more of the hellebores, geraniums, ferns, and bleeding hearts instead. Astilbe, another lovely shade perennial, used to top the list of deer-resistant plants but now appears on the growing menu of things deer occasionally dine on. Before planting any, ask your neighbors, the local garden club, or your county extension office to determine if deer are known to nibble on astilbe in your area.

The plants in this plan will thrive in partial to light shade. A location just to the south of a deciduous tree with small leaves (such as a locust) would suit them well. Large-leaved trees such as oaks and Norway maples cast deeper, denser shade that is less hospitable to flowering plants.

What's in the Garden?

1. **Cinnamon fern (6 plants)**

2. **Fringed bleeding heart (*Dicentra eximia* 'Luxuriant') (5 plants)**

3. ***Geranium* 'Johnson's Blue' (4 plants)**

4. ***Geranium* 'Wargrave Pink' (4 plants)**

5. **Hellebore (8 plants)**

6. ***Hosta* 'Aureomarginata' (3 plants)**

7. ***Hosta* 'Gold Standard' (3 plants)**

8. ***Hosta* 'Krossa Regal' (3 plants)**

9. **Japanese painted fern (2 plants)**

Helpful Growing Tips

If your shade tree is a large-leaved oak or maple, place the garden closer to the edge of the canopy (the tree's leafy reach), where the shade isn't as dense.

Hellebores start blooming in late winter or early spring and continue for 2 months or more, getting this garden off to an early start. They make good companions for daffodils and narcissus, too.

The hardy geraniums and bleeding heart in this garden are long bloomers, often continuing through much of summer or resting during the hottest times and reblooming in late summer or fall.

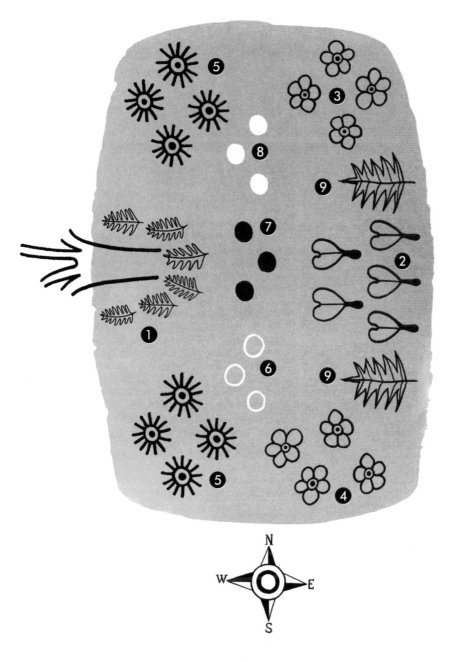

Garden size: 4 feet wide × 12 feet deep

Grandma's Cottage Garden

A cottage garden is a place for old-fashioned flowers like the ones our grandmothers grew in their gardens. This charming assortment of easy-care annuals will be colorful from spring to fall. Petunias, sweet alyssum, and nicotiana offer gentle fragrance—nicotiana releases its scent in the evening. Zinnias and sweet alyssum are attractive to bees and other beneficial insects. Sunflowers and marigolds, if you don't deadhead them completely, will produce seeds for local birds.

Surround the garden with a low picket fence to add to its charm, but let the plants within its borders tumble about in happy profusion. Cottage gardens are all about informal, rustic appeal.

1. **Black-eyed Susan (3 plants)**

2. **Celosia (18 plants)**

3. **Cosmos (4 plants)**

4. **French marigold (16 plants)**

5. **Nicotiana—a tall variety (3 plants)**

6. **Pansy (32 plants)**

7. **Petunia (6 plants)**

8. **Portulaca (32 plants)**

9. **Salvia, blue, such as 'Victoria' or 'Blue Bedder' (4 plants)**

10. **Salvia, red (9 plants)**

11. **Sunflower (3 plants)**

12. **Sweet alyssum (32 plants)**

13. **Zinnia (4 plants)**

Helpful Growing Tips

A cottage garden is a place for serendipity. Some of the flowers in this garden may self-sow and spread, although not aggressively enough to be considered invasive. Sweet alyssum, cosmos, portulaca, and petunias all may come back next year (petunias may revert to the color of their parent plants).

Pansies love cool temperatures and will flop and fade when the weather heats up. If you plant new pansies in fall, they will bring color to the late-season garden, and they'll come back and bloom again early the following spring. In warm climates, plant pansies for winter flowers.

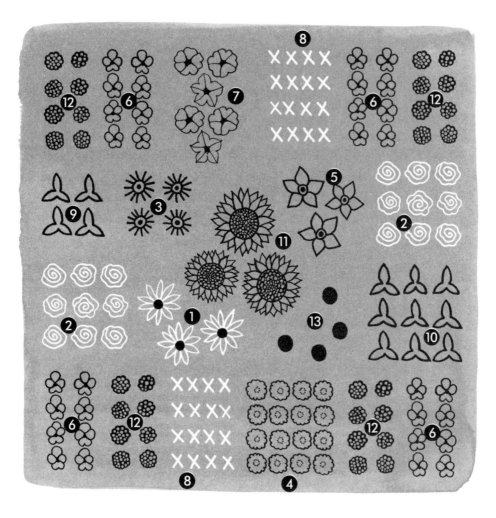

Garden size: 8 feet × 8 feet

Multiseason Perennial Border

This triangular bed fits neatly into a sunny corner. By rounding off the corners and curving the straight edges, you can bring this garden out of the corner and turn it into a kidney-shaped island bed.

The flowering begins with 'Stella de Oro' daylilies, which start opening their golden trumpets in midspring and keep on blooming through summer. Siberian iris flowers in late spring to early summer. Nepeta blooms in early to midsummer over several weeks. Cut back the plants by half when they finish flowering to stimulate another round of blossoms. Salvia, too, begins flowering in early summer, and some varieties will rebloom if you remove the old flowers regularly. 'May Night', 'East Friesland', and 'Blue Hill' are three salvias that will bloom all summer until fall if you deadhead them faithfully.

Tidy up coreopsis when its old flowers turn brown to keep it in bloom all summer. Cut back each long stem of golden *Coreopsis grandiflora* to the basal leaves near the bottom of the plant to encourage new flowering stems to grow.

What's in the Garden?

1. **Coreopsis (4 plants)**
2. **Daylily 'Stella de Oro' (10 plants)**
3. **Echinacea (4 plants)**
4. **Nepeta (8 plants)**
5. **Salvia, dark blue (6 plants)**
6. **Sedum 'Autumn Joy' (4 plants)**
7. **Siberian iris (3 plants)**

Helpful Growing Tips

Remember to cut off flowering stems of 'Stella de Oro' when the last flower has bloomed. The plant will send out new stems of flowers all summer long.

To deadhead blue salvia, cut back each flower stem to the nearest pair of leaves on the stem; two new flower stems will grow from that point. If you continue to regularly deadhead the varieties mentioned here, the plants will bloom all summer.

Purple coneflower loves sun but doesn't generally do well in moist, humid conditions, where it is prone to mildew. If you use automated overhead sprinklers, run them early in the morning rather than overnight, and not so often that the soil remains constantly moist. Purple coneflower is native to the prairie and needs little fussing. Its flowers attract butterflies.

Threadleaf coreopsis, with its many thin stems, takes ages to deadhead, but you can cut back the entire plant with hedge shears when blooming slows to promote new growth and flowers.

Purple coneflower (*Echinacea* spp.) thrives in summer sunshine and blooms in mid- to late summer. Clipping off old flowers encourages more to appear.

Sedum has presence in the garden all summer, but it bursts into colorful bloom late in the growing season.

use stakes and twine to lay out this garden with straight edges or use rope or a garden hose to create a curvy outline.

Garden size: 10 feet × 10 feet

3-Year Rotation Garden

Rearranging the crops in your garden from one growing season to the next helps maintain healthy soil, cut down on disease and pest problems, and keeps nutrients balanced. For example, fruiting crops (such as broccoli, corn, and tomatoes) are heavy feeders that rapidly use up nitrogen. Root vegetables (like carrots and beets) are light feeders. To keep soil nutrients balanced, avoid planting the same type of crop—leafy, fruiting, root, or legume—in the same place 2 years in a row. Alternating different types of crops lets the soil naturally balance and replenish its store of nutrients—especially if you add organic matter each year.

Rotating crops also helps prevent many diseases and pests that affect only a certain plant or family of plants. Although it can be difficult to do in a small garden, try to avoid planting the same crops or ones in the same plant family in the same location year after year. Crop rotation to build the soil doesn't always combine readily with rotations meant to deter problems. Even though it seems logical from a soil-care standpoint to rotate tomatoes (a fruiting crop) with potatoes (a root crop), for example, this is not a good plan from a plant health perspective. Tomatoes and potatoes both belong to the Solanaceae family and are susceptible to some of the same diseases.

You can use cover crops in a rotation plan to discourage specific types of pests and improve the soil. Beetle grubs—the larvae of many garden pests— thrive among most vegetables but not in soil planted in buckwheat or clover.

This simple, 3-year rotation plan includes cover crops in years 1 and 3 to build the soil and moves crops to different locations to prevent buildup of disease organisms and pests. It also takes sunlight into account, positioning taller plants (and trellised crops) to the north side of the garden to avoid shading lower-growing vegetables. To make this garden even more productive, incorporate succession planting in early spring and late summer into the plan, preceding tomatoes with an early crop of peas, for example, interplanting carrots with radishes, or following summer squash with late-season greens.

Rotation Rule #1: Follow heavy feeders with light feeders or soil builders.

Rotation Rule #2: Follow shallow-rooted vegetables with deep-rooted ones.

Rotation Rule #3: Place tall plants to the north of shorter plants.

Rotation Garden in Year 1

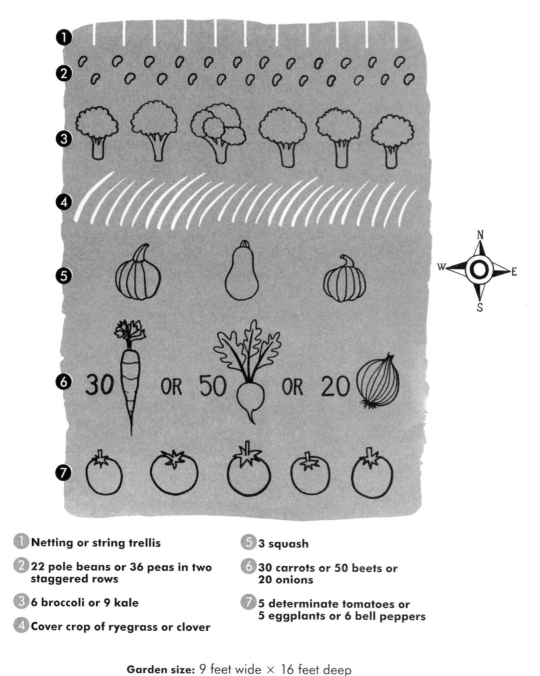

1. **Netting or string trellis**
2. **22 pole beans or 36 peas in two staggered rows**
3. **6 broccoli or 9 kale**
4. **Cover crop of ryegrass or clover**
5. **3 squash**
6. **30 carrots or 50 beets or 20 onions**
7. **5 determinate tomatoes or 5 eggplants or 6 bell peppers**

Garden size: 9 feet wide × 16 feet deep

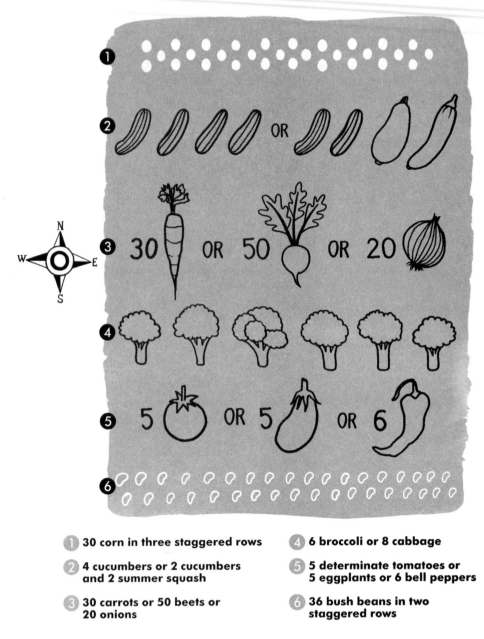

1. **30 corn in three staggered rows**

2. **4 cucumbers or 2 cucumbers and 2 summer squash**

3. **30 carrots or 50 beets or 20 onions**

4. **6 broccoli or 8 cabbage**

5. **5 determinate tomatoes or 5 eggplants or 6 bell peppers**

6. **36 bush beans in two staggered rows**

Garden size: 9 feet wide × 16 feet deep

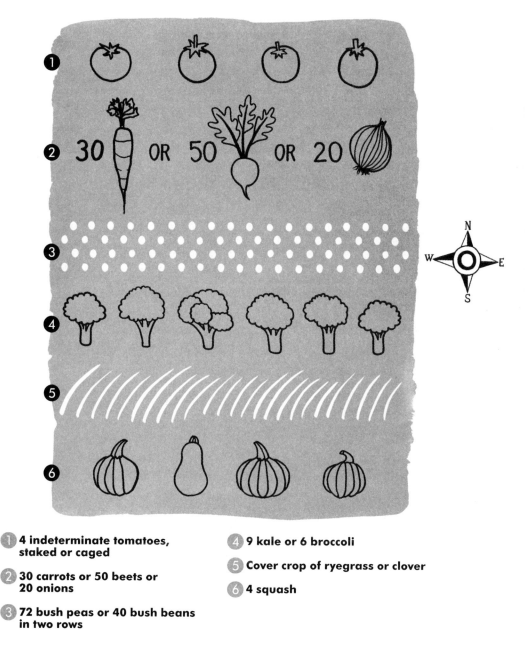

1. **4 indeterminate tomatoes, staked or caged**

2. **30 carrots or 50 beets or 20 onions**

3. **72 bush peas or 40 bush beans in two rows**

4. **9 kale or 6 broccoli**

5. **Cover crop of ryegrass or clover**

6. **4 squash**

Garden size: 9 feet wide × 16 feet deep

Once you've identified a suitable location for your garden and acquired the necessary tools and equipment, it's time to prepare the site for planting. Chapter 3 contains everything you need to know about soil evaluation and care, including techniques for building your soil with compost. But what sort of garden will you make—a basic bed in the soil, a raised bed, or a garden in containers? Here are some bed preparation pointers to help you get started, then turn to the next chapter for more about tending the soil that will support your plants.

Preparing a Garden Bed

If you've inherited a recently abandoned garden plot, you'll probably only have to pull out the dead crop plants and weeds. If your site is now a lawn, you'll need to cut the turf out using a spade (a flat-edged, barely curved digging tool). Slice under the turf with the spade, and lift it in thin slabs. Pile the cut turf, grass side down, a foot or two high. Keep the pile of removed sod moist, and next year it will be a great soil amendment to add to your garden. Now you're ready to start making the bed.

Begin with cultivating. Cultivating your garden soil is important because it can improve aeration and drainage, allow the roots of your plants to spread more freely, and help break up compacted soil.

- *Digging or tilling.* You can dig or till your garden site a couple of days or a couple of months before you intend to plant. Just make sure the soil isn't too wet when you go to work or you may end up with large, hard-packed clods of earth that will be impossible to plant in. The soil should be just dry enough to crumble easily in your hand and slide off your spade or fork without sticking. If the soil seems very dry and hard, water the area deeply and wait 2 or 3 days before turning it.

- *Starting a new site.* If you're just starting out in a new garden site, hand-tilling offers a big advantage over using a rotary (mechanical) tiller to work the soil. Digging by hand allows you to carefully remove roots, runners, or other parts of perennial weeds as you work. (Using a tiller can make weed problems worse by chopping weed roots into small pieces. Each little piece may then resprout to make a new weed!)

Top with compost. Use a garden rake to spread a 1-inch-deep layer of compost over the surface of the soil, then use a shovel or digging fork to loosen and turn the soil, mixing the compost in as you work. A digging fork is the best tool for this task if you're removing weedy roots, since it is less likely to slice them into pieces that will grow up to infest your garden. A fork is also easier to use in rocky soil.

Work your way through. As you dig, work from one end of the bed to the other, turning over the soil to the depth of your shovel or fork. Break up large clods, and remove rocks and weed roots as you go.

Watch your step. Don't stand on the freshly turned soil as you work, and don't walk on the bed after you've finished. Walking on the soil will destroy the loose, fluffy texture you've worked so hard to create. For this reason, it's helpful to limit the width of garden beds to 3 to 5 feet so you can reach into the middle of the beds from the sides to plant and weed and harvest without stepping on the bed itself.

When Space Is Tight—Grow Up or in a Pot or on a Community Plot

If inground space for a garden is limited, you can still grow vegetables and flowers. The most important point to remember is to find the sunniest spot you can. Then plant vegetables such as cucumbers, squash, peas, and beans that you can grow vertically onto trellises. If possible, prepare raised beds with extra-rich soil so you can pack more plants into a small space. Growing vegetables in containers on a deck, patio, balcony, or roof is also an option. Good choices for growing in pots or planters include salad greens, pepper plants, and compact tomato varieties (known as determinate tomatoes) developed for container growing.

If you have no space of your own for growing, not even a spot where you can place a container or two, explore your area's community gardening options. A community garden is a shared plot of land on which members of a community collectively maintain individual gardens. The members of the American Community Gardening Association (communitygarden.org) can help you locate a gardening group near you or, if there are none in your neighborhood, help you start a community garden.

Raised Bed Benefits

Although your plants will thrive in traditional, organically tended ground-level beds, they may do even better if you grow them in raised beds. Typically, raised beds have better aeration and drainage than ground-level beds because the soil is deeper, looser, and more fertile.

For space efficiency and high yields, it's hard to beat a vegetable garden grown in raised beds. Raised beds can improve production as well as save space, time, and money. They also are the perfect solution for dealing with difficult soils such as heavy clay. In addition, raised beds improve your garden's appearance and accessibility.

Raised gardening beds are higher than ground level and consist of soil that's mounded or surrounded by a frame to keep it in place. Plants cover nearly the entire surface of the bed areas, while gardeners work from the paths that separate the beds. Limiting the beds to no more than 3 to 5 feet wide allows easy access from the paths. You can grow any vegetable in raised beds, as well as herbs, annual or perennial flowers, berry bushes, or even roses and other shrubs.

Plants benefit from the improved soil drainage and aeration of a raised bed's loose, fertile soil, and plant roots penetrate readily. Since gardeners stay in the pathways, the soil is never walked on or compacted. Soil amendments and improvement efforts are concentrated in the beds and not wasted on the pathways, which can be covered with mulch or planted with grass or a low-growing cover crop.

Raised beds save time and money because you need only dig, fertilize, and water the beds, not the paths. You don't need to weed as much when crops grow close together, because weeds can't compete as well. (Weeds that do manage to squeeze in are easier to pull out of the loose soil.) Gardeners with limited mobility find raised beds the perfect solution—a wide sill on a framed raised bed makes a good spot to sit while working. A high frame puts plants in reach of a gardener using a wheelchair. For best access, make beds 28 to 30 inches high and keep the beds narrow—no more than 4 feet wide—so it's easy to reach to the center of the bed.

MAKE A SIMPLE MOUNDED BED

The quickest way to make a raised bed is by mounding. After removing weeds or sod from your garden site, work the soil with a fork to loosen it, then heap compost and well-rotted manure on top and rake it together to create a mounded bed. Shape the soil in an unframed bed so that it is flattopped, with sloping sides (this shape helps conserve water), or it forms a long, rounded mound. The soil in an unframed bed will gradually spread out. You'll need to periodically reshape the bed to maintain its mounded form.

FRAME IT

A frame around the outside edge of the bed prevents soil from washing away and allows you to add a greater depth of improved soil. Wood, brick, rocks, or cement blocks are popular materials for framing. Choose naturally rot-resistant woods such as cedar, cypress, or locust or long-lasting planks made of recycled plastic. Avoid commercially pressure-treated wood because it contains toxic materials that may leach into the soil.

Why Garden in Raised Beds?

There are good reasons to plant in raised beds.

- **The soil can be liberally supplemented with compost and other organic amendments, creating a rich and porous root zone that nurtures plants.**
- **Soil doesn't become compacted, because you don't step on the growing area.**
- **The bed sides act as an edging, helping to keep out weeds and turfgrass.**
- **Raised beds offer easier access for planting, thinning, weeding, and harvesting.**
- **Many gardeners, including those of restricted mobility, find that the slightly higher soil level makes gardening tasks easier.**
- **The elevated soil of raised beds drains quickly and doesn't become waterlogged, and it warms earlier in spring. (Although those two characteristics are beneficial in cool, rainy climates, gardeners in hot, dry regions may consider them to be negatives.)**

Build a Raised Bed

When it comes to framing your garden beds, there's more than one way to lift your loam. Here are directions for making a simple wooden frame. This design uses four pieces of untreated framing lumber, with not a scrap of waste.

Each bed requires:

Three 2 × 12 boards, 8 feet long

One 2 × 4 board, 8 feet long

2½-inch galvanized deck screws (approximately 28 screws)

1 When purchasing lumber, inspect it for straightness. Straighter boards will result in tighter corners.

2 Cut one of the 2 × 12 boards in half to make two 4-foot lengths; these will be the two end pieces.

3 Cut the 2 × 4 board into one 4-foot length, to serve as a center brace, and four 1-foot lengths for corner supports. The two uncut boards will become the sides of the raised bed.

4 After drilling pilot holes, attach one of the side boards to an end board with three evenly spaced screws.

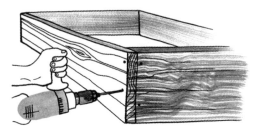

5 Place one of the corner supports in the angle between the boards and attach it to the side board with three screws.

6 Repeat for the remaining three corners.

7 Attach the center brace to join the two sides at their midpoints. Use a square to position the brace at a right angle to the sides. The brace prevents the sides from bowing outward when the bed is filled with soil.

8 The finished bed measures 4 × 8 feet—a size that makes seed sowing, weeding, and harvesting easy—and raises the planting level by almost a foot. The wood can be stained or painted, if desired.

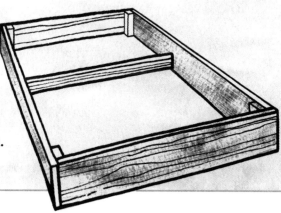

Once you've shaped up a mound of soil, you can frame it with just about any-thing. Wooden frames look tidy and are easy to work with, but all sorts of materials may be used for corralling raised beds, depending on what you have available and the limits of your time, imagination, and resources. Here are five nonlumber frame ideas to get you started. Perhaps one will catch your fancy or prompt you to think of your own raised bed frame material.

Each of the beds described below is meant to measure about 4 × 8 feet. You can adjust the dimensions to suit your needs (or materials), keeping in mind that anything wider than 4 feet will be more difficult to maintain.

Wattle

Hammer 2-foot lengths of rebar into the ground around the perimeter of the bed, spacing them about 16 inches apart and leaving 10 inches of the rebar exposed above ground. Cut long, straight lengths of tree or shrub branches, up to $\frac{1}{2}$ inch in diameter and at least 2 feet long. Weave the sticks or "wattle" through the vertical rebar, basket style; trim the ends at the bed corners as needed.

Once the bed sides have reached the top of the rebar, bend 2-foot sticks in half and poke them into the ground over the woven wattle, holding the sticks in place. Pin the sides in this manner every few feet. Line the sides of the bed with burlap to keep soil from sifting through the wattle.

To build a bed 4 × 8 feet, you'll need 18 pieces of rebar 24 inches long; 8 yards of burlap about 18 inches wide; and about 100 long, flexible sticks.

Logs

Choose straight logs about a foot in diameter to create the bed edges. Logs of smaller diameter can be stacked. To avoid having to move massive logs, line up shorter firewood-length sections.

To build a bed 4 × 8 feet, you'll need two 7-foot logs for the sides and two 4-foot logs for the ends.

Concrete Blocks

Place concrete blocks with open ends facing up to outline the raised bed. The open-ings can be filled with soil and used as planting pockets for small herbs or edible flowers. To build a bed 4 × 8 feet, you'll need 16 blocks, 8 × 8 × 16 inches each.

Planks and Rebar

This bed can be constructed of leftover lumber of almost any dimension, so long as the wood is untreated. Hold the planks on edge with short lengths of rebar pounded into the ground every 2 to 3 feet. To build a bed 4 × 8 feet, you'll need two 2 × 12 planks 8 feet long, two 2 × 12 planks 4 feet long, and 12 pieces of rebar 24 inches long.

Straw Bales

Bales of straw are great for framing a bed on a new site that you are converting to garden space. The bales will serve as a frame during the growing season and then can be broken up and composted when the garden is done for the winter. The soil under the bales will also be improved, so your growing space can expand outward in future seasons.

Standard bale sizes are roughly 24 inches wide by 16 inches high by 48 inches long or 18 inches wide by 14 inches high by 36 inches long. You'll need six of the larger bales or eight smaller ones to frame a bed that's about 4 × 8 feet.

FILL IT

If your garden soil is difficult—heavy clay, very alkaline, or full of rocks—you may want to mix your own soil from trucked-in topsoil, organic matter, and mineral amendments. Then you can build beds up from ground level, without disturbing or incorporating the native soil. You may also need to add extra materials to raised beds if you want them to be tall enough for a gardener in a wheelchair to reach easily.

Before installing any frame, cultivate the site 6 to 8 inches deep and amend it with compost. Once the frame is in place, thoroughly mix the purchased topsoil and compost together and then fill the frame right up to the rim. The soil will settle slightly over a period of a few weeks.

Fill the bed with a mix of about two-thirds high-quality topsoil and one-third compost. Look for topsoil that is fine, loose, and granular; watch out for subsoil that has a lot of clay in it.

Purchase soil and compost (or make your own—see Chapter 3 for details) from a reliable local retailer and inspect it prior to delivery or pickup to make sure it is free of rubble, clods, clay, or inert material.

Lasagna Gardening

"Lasagna gardening," so called for its layering approach, is a no-till option for building raised beds and great soil. Also referred to as "sheet composting," it allows you to build raised beds without stripping grass or weeds off the site. You can also build a lasagna garden on top of an existing vegetable garden site.

If you are starting on a new site, first cut the grass as short as possible and/or scalp the weeds at ground level. Next cover the bed with a thick layer of newspaper (at least 6 to 10 sheets) to smother existing vegetation. Use sheets of cardboard or flattened cardboard boxes if there are vigorous perennial weeds on the site. Either wet down the newspapers as you spread them or weigh them down with handfuls of soil or mulch as you spread. Overlap the edges of the newspaper or cardboard as you work to avoid leaving spaces where weeds or grass might poke through.

After that, begin layering organic matter on top of the site. Combine materials as you would in a compost pile, by mixing "browns" and "greens." Add layers of organic materials such as grass clippings, finished compost, chopped leaves, kitchen scraps, coffee grounds, seaweed, shredded mail or newspaper, garden trimmings, used potting soil, sawdust, and weeds (don't add weeds that have gone to seed or perennials with vigorous rhizomes, which will spread and grow in the bed). You can also add topsoil, which will help speed things along. Make a pile that is 1 foot or more deep, and top it off with a layer of mulch to keep weeds from getting a foothold. Then wait several months for materials to decompose.

You can build a lasagna garden any time of year. Building one in fall to plant in spring is a good idea, and there are plenty of leaves available for chopping and adding to the mix. If you're building in spring or summer, you can speed up the time when it will be ready to plant by adding extra compost and topsoil in the mix. Top the bed with 2 to 3 inches of topsoil and/or compost for annual crops (more for perennial plants) and then plant seedlings directly into the topsoil/compost mix. You can also sink containers into the layers of a newly made lasagna bed and grow vegetables or flowers in the pots while the lasagna layers "cook" into a welcoming growing medium for future crops.

Container Gardening

Gardening in containers is ideal for those with little or no garden space. If your potential growing area is limited to a balcony, a small yard, or only a patch of sun on the driveway, you still can produce a wide variety of vegetables and flowers in containers. Basil, chives, cilantro, parsley, thyme, and other herbs also are quite happy growing in pots, which can be set in a convenient spot right outside the kitchen door for quick meal-time picking.

CHOOSING CONTAINERS

Pots and planters come in a wide range of sizes, shapes, materials, and styles. You can also modify everyday containers such as bowls or barrels to be planters.

Size. When choosing a container, keep in mind that it's easier to grow plants in large containers than small ones. That's because large containers hold more soil, which stays moist longer and is less subject to rapid temperature fluctuations. Small hanging baskets are especially prone to drying out, and during hot summer weather, you may have to water them twice a day to keep plants alive.

It's also important to decide what plant you want to grow in each container. Several factors help determine how large and deep the container must be. Consider the size and shape of a plant's root system; whether it is a perennial, annual, or shrub; and how rapidly it grows. Rootbound plants, which have filled up every square inch of the soil available, dry out rapidly and won't grow well. Choose a large pot or tub for a mixed planting, one that will offer enough root space for all the plants you want to grow. Light-colored containers keep the soil cooler than dark containers.

In general, shallow-rooted plants, such as lettuce, spinach, radishes, and most herbs, need only 6 to 8 inches of soil depth to grow well, while deeper-rooted plants, such as tomatoes and squash, need 12 inches of soil. Terra-cotta pots, wooden boxes, and even 5-gallon buckets make great containers. Just make sure your containers have drainage holes, are not translucent or clear (sunlight will fry plants' roots), and are big enough to support the plants growing in them.

The maximum size (and weight) of a container is limited by how much room you have, what will support it, and whether or not you plan to move it. If your container garden will sit on a balcony, deck, or roof, be sure to check how much weight the structure will safely hold.

Drainage. Whatever container you choose, drainage holes are essential. Without drainage, soil will become waterlogged and plants may die. The holes need not be large, but there must be enough so that excess water can drain out. If a container has no holes, try drilling some yourself. A container without holes is best used as a cachepot, or cover, to hide a plain pot. Cachepots (with holes and without them) are useful for managing large plants and heavy pots: Grow your plant in an ordinary nursery pot that fits inside a decorative cachepot so you can move them separately.

Self-watering double-walled containers, hanging baskets, and window boxes are available. These are a useful option for dealing with smaller plants that need frequent watering.

Materials. Each type of container has merits and disadvantages.

- Clay or terra-cotta containers are attractive but breakable and are easily damaged by freezing and thawing. In northern areas, most need to be stored in a frost-free location to prevent cracking and are not suitable for hardy perennials or shrubs that will be kept outdoors year-round.

- Cast concrete is long lasting and comes in a range of sizes and styles. These can be left outside in all weather. You can even make attractive ones yourself. Plain concrete containers are very heavy, so they are difficult to move and not suitable for using on decks or balconies. Planters made of concrete mixed with vermiculite or perlite or of a blend of concrete and fiberglass are much lighter.

- Plastic and fiberglass pots and planters are lightweight, relatively inexpensive, and available in many sizes and shapes. Choose sturdy and somewhat flexible containers and avoid thin, stiff ones—they become brittle with cold or age.

- Containers made of polyurethane foam weigh up to 90 percent less than terra-cotta or concrete containers, yet they look remarkably like their much-heavier cousins. Polyurethane foam containers resist chipping and cracking and also can insulate roots against both hot and cold temperatures, making them a good choice for potting up plants that will stay outside year-round.

- Wood is natural looking and protects roots from rapid temperature swings. You can build wooden planters yourself. Choose a naturally rot-resistant wood such as cedar or locust, or use pine treated with a nontoxic preservative. (Don't use creosote, which is toxic to plants.) Molded wood-fiber containers are sturdy and inexpensive.

- Metal containers are strong, but they conduct heat, exposing roots to rapid temperature fluctuations. Metal must be lined with plastic for growing edibles.

- Grow bags made of heavy-duty plastic or air- and water-permeable polypropylene fabric are available in many sizes and shapes to suit different crops. Filled with potting soil or soilless mix, these flexible containers allow you to put a garden anyplace where there's a suitably sunny spot—on a concrete patio or on the steps leading to your front door, for example. At the end of the growing season, you can empty the bags and fold them flat for easy storage until the next year.

PREPARING YOUR CONTAINERS

Since containers are heavy once they are filled with soil, decide where they will be located and move them into position before filling and planting. If keeping them watered during the day is a problem, look for sites that receive morning sun and are shaded during the hottest part of the day, even if you are growing plants for full sun. Afternoon shade will reduce the amount of moisture plants need. Consider putting heavy containers on casters or grouping containers in a wagon or cart that can be moved to sunnier or shadier locations as needed.

While your containers must have drainage holes, it's not necessary to cover the holes with pot shards or gravel before you add potting mix. The covering won't improve drainage, and pot shards may actually block the holes. Instead, prevent soil from washing out by placing a layer of paper towel or newspaper over the holes before adding mix. If your container is too deep, you can put a layer of gravel or Styrofoam in the bottom to reduce the amount of potting soil required.

Fill your containers with a well-draining potting mix (topsoil will compact in containers) that has some compost or an organic granulated fertilizer mixed in. Plain garden soil is too dense for container plantings.

You may want to mix in one of the special superabsorbent polymers—synthetic substances that hold large amounts of water available for plants. They will improve water availability without making the soil soggy. While these products are not naturally occurring substances, they appear to be inert and to have no toxic breakdown products.

Premoisten the potting mixture either by watering it before you fill containers or by flooding the containers with water several times and stirring. Be sure the soil is uniformly moist before planting—it can be very difficult to adequately moisten the growing medium after your plants are in place. Plant in containers as you would in the garden. If you are planting a mixed container, ignore spacing requirements and plant densely; you may need to prune plants once they fill in.

SELECTING PLANTS

Almost any vegetable, flower, herb, shrub, or small tree can grow successfully in a container. Dwarf and compact cultivars are best, especially for smaller pots. Select plants to suit the climate and the amount of sun or shade the container will receive. If you are growing fragrant plants, place containers in a site protected from breezes, which will disperse the aroma.

Use your imagination and combine upright and trailing plants, edibles, and flowers for pleasing and colorful effects. Container gardens can be enjoyed for one season and discarded, or they can be designed to last for years. When designing permanent containers, remember that the plants will be less hardy than usual because their roots are more exposed to fluctuating air temperature. Nonhardy plants will need to have winter protection or be moved to a sheltered space. So consider how heavy the container will be and decide how you will move it before choosing a nonhardy plant.

Here are some suggestions to get you started.

Vegetables and herbs. Almost all vegetables grow well in containers, but choosing the right variety helps. 'Window Box Roma' tomato, for instance, stays a size that's manageable for pots, and 'Tumbler' tomato vines spill nicely out of hanging baskets. Beans, peas, and even squash can be grown up trellises set into a larger container. Try the compact 'Sunburst' yellow scalloped squash and 'Spacemiser' zucchini. 'Miniature White' cucumbers have small vines and unusual white fruit. Carrots such as the heirloom 'Oxheart' and the miniature 'Kinko' grow to only 4 to 6 inches long. You can grow vegetables in individual containers—from large pots to 5-gallon buckets or half barrels, the largest of which will accommodate a single tomato plant or several smaller vegetables such as broccoli or cabbage. Dwarf or bush forms of larger vegetables such as tomatoes, pumpkins, and winter squash are most suited to container culture. Theme gardens also are fun to try. Plant a salad garden with colorful lettuces, dwarf tomatoes, chives, and parsley. Or perhaps try a pizza garden, with different types of basil, plus tomatoes and peppers. Or plant a container with edible flowers such as marigolds, pansies (*Viola ×wittrockiana*), and nasturtiums (*Tropaeolum majus*).

Annuals. For containers that remain attractive all summer long, look for warm-weather annuals that bloom all summer or have foliage that remains attractive. Geraniums, marigolds, wax begonias, coleus (*Solenostemon scutellarioides*), scarlet sage (*Salvia splendens*), and flowering tobaccos (*Nicotiana* spp.) are all good choices, but you will find many, many more in garden centers and seed catalogs. Experiment. If one plant doesn't work out, don't worry about it—just cut it down and try something else. For large containers, dwarf cannas and dwarf dahlias also make satisfying additions.

Perennials and shrubs. Containers planted with hardy perennials and shrubs can be grown and enjoyed from year to year. Hostas and daylilies are great container plants, but many other perennials work as well. Try ferns, European wild ginger (*Asarum europaeum*), sedges (*Carex* spp.), lavender, lamiums (*Lamium maculatum*), sedums, and lungworts (*Pulmonaria* spp.). Ornamental grasses are great in containers, too, as are dwarf conifers and small shrubs.

SOIL CARE BASICS

The soil is not, as many suppose, a dead, inert substance.
It is very much alive and dynamic.

—J. I. RODALE, *PAY DIRT*, 1945

*P*ay Dirt*, published in 1945, was J. I. Rodale's first book, elaborating on his views and observations about the connections between soil health and human health. In 1980, Robert Rodale's article "Soil Is Better Than Gold" appeared in *Organic Gardening* magazine, extolling the advantages of healthy, productive soil as an investment for the future. And in 2010, third-generation soil enthusiast Maria Rodale's *Organic Manifesto* reported new research showing that one of the many benefits of organically managed soil is its ability to sequester carbon—making it a practical tool in the fight against global climate change.

Healthy soil = healthy plants = healthy people. It's as simple—and enduring—as that. But what is healthy soil, and how do you know if you have it? Use this chapter to learn the fundamentals of soil care and composting, the ultimate soil-building technique. Build your garden on a foundation of vibrant, well-tended soil and your success is virtually guaranteed.

First, do no harm: Don't hurt the dirt. Before you start digging and fertilizing and adding and planting, learn what's going on down in the ground. Your awareness of the characteristics of your soil will help you care for it to produce long-term benefits for your garden. At the root of every healthy plant is healthy soil, so pay attention to it. Plants get their nourishment from the soil, and good nutrition—much as it does for people—supports plants' ability to combat disease, pests, and other stresses of life.

GET TO KNOW YOUR SOIL

Far from being an inert substance—a mere holder for plants' roots—soil is wonderfully alive. Beneath the surface, healthy soil is full of organisms that interact in a finely tuned living system. Once you start digging around, you'll find there's more to it than meets the eye. Healthy soil contains lots of life, a good balance of nutrients available for plants' use, and a loose, open structure. The way you manage and work the soil affects all these aspects of soil health.

This chapter introduces some of the organisms you may find when you take a closer look at your soil. It also explains how to do a few simple tests that can tell you a lot about what's happening beneath your gardens, lawn, and landscape.

Unless you live in a place where previous occupants have tended the soil, you may not have great soil in your yard and garden to start with. The soil around many homes is in trouble, either because of damage caused during construction or neglect by past owners. But how do you decide what your soil really needs? What would be most beneficial for the plants you want to grow? And where do you begin?

What Soil Is Made Of

On a percentage basis, soil consists mostly of minerals (45 percent), followed by air (25 percent), and water (25 percent). That leaves just 5 percent for soil's biological component—organic matter—but it's a very important 5 percent.

Minerals. Tiny particles of rock, categorized by their size as sand, silt, or clay, make up the mineral portion of the soil. The percentages of each of these particle types vary from place to place and can have a significant effect on soil drainage and fertility. The proportions of the different sizes of mineral particles in the soil determine its texture, which may be described by terms such as *sandy, loamy,* or *clayey.*

Of the particle types, sand particles are the biggest. Sand particles don't adhere, or stick together, when wet. Sandy soils often drain too quickly and don't hold enough water for good crop production. They also tend to be lower in natural fertility.

Silt particles are smaller than sand particles. They will adhere when wet. Soils that have moderate amounts of sand, silt, and clay are called loam soils. They generally are considered the best soils for gardening.

Clay particles are extremely tiny, and they adhere very tightly when wet. Clay soil can be slow to dry out after rains. It tends to form heavy clods and surface crusts. It may hold nutrients so tightly to the surfaces of its particles that it doesn't easily supply enough nutrients for healthy plant growth.

coarse sand

fine sand

silt

clay

Air and water. The spaces, or pores, between soil particles are filled with air or water. Soil structure, the arrangement of soil particles, determines the size and quantity of pore spaces in the soil. Many factors contribute to the creation of soil structure. Water in the soil freezes and thaws, plant roots grow and die, and earthworms move through the soil. All of these processes contribute to the formation of soil pores and soil clumps, or aggregates. Soil structure also is affected by soil pH, the amount of humus in the soil, and the combination of minerals. Ideal soil is described as friable—the soil particles clump together in clusters with air spaces between them.

Pore spaces are important because they enable plants' roots and soil organisms to get the air and water they need. Ideally, pore spaces should vary in size and be evenly distributed throughout the soil. Large pore spaces let water drain through the soil to make room for soil air. Smaller pores hold water in the soil for plant roots.

Air in the soil supports both soil organisms and plant roots. Plant roots "breathe" and need air exchange between the soil and the atmosphere to grow. Many beneficial soil organisms cannot live without the oxygen in soil air, and nitrogen-fixing bacteria use the nitrogen in soil air as a raw material. These bacteria "fix" nitrogen into proteins that are later broken down into nitrogen compounds called nitrates, which plants can absorb.

Roots take up water from the soil and pass it on to leaves and stems, where it serves as a nutrient, a coolant, and an essential part of all plant cells. Many mineral nutrients also are transported into roots and through plants in water.

If soil doesn't drain well, water fills up all of its pore spaces. This prevents roots from getting the air they need, suffocating the plants. Walking on the soil, driving power equipment over it, or digging in it when it's wet all destroy soil structure, causing these important pore spaces to collapse.

Organic matter. Once-living material in the soil is termed organic matter. It includes plant residues (raw or partially decomposed organic matter) and humus, the dark-colored, stable form of organic matter that remains after most of the plant and animal residues in it have decomposed.

Organic matter has different sizes of particles and pore spaces, which help retain air and water in the soil. It also provides a good environment for root growth and many of the nutrients plants need to grow. When clay, raw organic matter, and humus bind together in the soil, they form tiny, sticky particles called colloids. Colloids act like minute, negatively charged magnets. They attract nutrient particles that have a positive charge, such as potassium, magnesium, and calcium.

A soil's capacity to hold positively charged particles (cations) is called the cation exchange capacity (CEC). A high CEC means soil can hold on to lots of the nutrients plants need to grow.

talk the talk
Soil Properties

ACID SOIL: Soil with a pH lower than 7.0; sometimes described as "sour" soil.

AERATION: The exchange of air in the pore spaces of the soil with air in the atmosphere. Good aeration is necessary for healthy plant growth.

ALKALINE SOIL: Soil with a pH value higher than 7.0; sometimes described as "sweet" soil.

DRAINAGE: The movement of water through the soil, resulting from a combination of soil texture and structure and the effects of soil management or mismanagement.

HUMUS: A dark-colored, stable form of organic matter that remains after most of the plant and animal residues in it have decomposed.

MICRONUTRIENT: A nutrient required in small amounts for healthy growth and development. For plants, soil needs to contain micronutrients such as boron, copper, and zinc for best growth. Where a soil test shows deficiencies in micronutrients, fertilizers can be applied to supply them.

MYCORRHIZA: A symbiotic association of plant roots and fungi in which the roots supply a protected environment and secrete sugars as an energy source for the fungi and the fungi help extract nutrients and water from the soil to nourish the plants.

NEUTRAL SOIL: Soil with a pH of 7.0—that is, neither acidic nor alkaline.

NITROGEN: One of the three major nutrients needed by plants, nitrogen promotes the growth of foliage.

Another benefit of organic matter is that as it decomposes, it is transformed into vitamins, hormones, and substances that stimulate plant growth. Decomposing organic matter also produces certain toxins that suppress weeds and plant disease organisms (pathogens). Organic matter also provides a favorable environment for beneficial organisms that prey on pathogens.

Living organisms. Earthworms, insects, mites, soil-dwelling mammals and reptiles, nematodes, bacteria, fungi, and other microorganisms live in the soil. As they move through it, they contribute in different ways to decay and nutrient cycles. Most of the animals and microbes in the soil are beneficial to the soil and to plants. They cause organic matter to decompose into humus, and

ORGANIC MATTER: Materials that are derived directly from plants or animals. Organic gardeners use plant and animal by-products to maintain soil and plant health and don't rely on synthetically made fertilizers, herbicides, or pesticides.

PHOSPHORUS: One of the three major nutrients needed by plants, phosphorus facilitates the transfer and storage of energy through plants. Phosphorus is important to seed production (and thus, flowers), root growth, stem strength, and other functions.

POTASSIUM: One of the three major nutrients needed by plants, potassium does not have a clearly understood role. It is known to be associated with the transport of water and nutrients through plant tissues and is important for healthy growth and good crop yields. Potassium deficiency leads to stunted growth.

SOIL PH: The soil's alkalinity or acidity is a critical measurement of its hospitability to plants. Most vegetables grow best in slightly acidic (pH 6.5 to 7.0) soil.

STRUCTURE: The balance of soil aggregates (clumps) and pore spaces.

SYMBIOTIC RELATIONSHIP: An interaction between two different biological species in which the two are interdependent, and one needs the other to survive. There is increasing evidence that almost every plant species has corresponding soil microorganisms with which it forms symbiotic relationships in the soil of its native environment.

TEXTURE: The relative amounts of the different-size mineral particles (clay, silt, sand) in the soil.

---

they transform some plant nutrients into forms plants can absorb. Some even prey on pests and disease organisms that are harmful to plants. Mycorrhizae help plant roots take up nutrients and water.

WHO'S WHO DOWN IN THE DIRT

If you keep the beneficial organisms in the soil happy and productive, much of your job as a gardener will be done for you. Think of the beneficial organisms as your "microherd" and treat them well. While many of your subterranean helpers (and foes) are too small to be seen, here are a few that you may encounter when you sink your trowel into the soil.

GOOD GUYS

millipede

Slow moving despite their many legs, millipedes range from ½ to 1½ inches long. Most species feed on decaying plant material, breaking it down into organic matter for the soil, while some millipedes are predators that feed on many kinds of soil insects.

earthworm

As they tunnel, earthworms break up compacted soil so air and water can move more freely. They feed on organic matter in the soil and produce nutrient-rich droppings, called castings, that improve soil texture and provide nourishment for plants.

ground beetle

Many of North America's 3,000-plus species of ground beetles prey upon slugs, snails, cutworms, and caterpillars as they scurry about the garden. Don't be startled when you encounter one of these large, dark-shelled beetles—it's likely on the hunt for pests.

BAD GUYS

beetle grub

No one refers to "baby" beetles when they use the expression "cute as a bug." The soil-dwelling grubs (beetle larvae) of June beetles and Japanese beetles are pale, fleshy, C-shaped pests that feed on the roots of strawberries and potatoes, and turfgrasses, respectively. If you unearth one while digging, toss it onto a hard surface where a hungry bird may find it.

symphlan

Symphylans look like tiny (¼-inch-long) centipedes with 12 pairs of legs but are pests that eat the roots of asparagus, cucumber, lettuce, radish, and tomato seedlings. Their damage can be puzzling because they are so hard to see, unlike larger, darker, predatory true centipedes that have 15 or more pairs of legs. Symphylans are common, but populations in the soil rarely reach damaging levels.

cutworm

Cutworms are inch-long, gray green caterpillars that feed just below—or just above—the soil surface, severing the stems of seedlings and transplants. These nocturnal pests can fell an entire bed of unprotected young plants overnight.

Soil pH describes the acidity or alkalinity of the soil. It is a measure of the concentration of hydrogen ions in soil water and is expressed as a number between 1.0 and 14.0. Soil pH is important because it affects whether plants can absorb the nutrients in the soil through their roots. Although some plants have specific soil pH preferences, most will tolerate a fairly wide range of soil pH. To find out your soil's pH, you can have a sample tested by a laboratory. Or buy a home pH test kit and do it yourself.

Soil Tests and What They Tell You

It's entirely possible to have a successful garden without performing a single soil test. But your chances of succeeding are much greater if you take the time to find out a little bit about the soil your plants will grow in. Especially if you are gardening for the first time or planting your garden in a new location, it's worth conducting a few simple tests on your own. To get a thorough evaluation of your soil's quality and suitability for the things you want to grow, plan to send in a sample for laboratory testing.

Besides visual inspection, you also can do your own tests for texture and drainage. For a few dollars, you can buy a kit that will let you test your soil's pH; for a few dollars more, you can get a test kit that delivers somewhat more accurate pH readings. And if you send your soil to a lab for testing, you will get an even more accurate pH assessment along with lots of other useful information.

Drainage test #1. With a shovel, a watch, and your garden hose or a big bucket of water, you can get a reasonably clear picture of how well your soil drains. Dig a hole 6 to 12 inches deep and 6 to 12 inches wide. Fill the hole with water and note the time as the water seeps into the soil. Soil with good drainage should absorb the water in 15 to 30 minutes. If the water drains faster than that, your soil doesn't hold water well and probably has a lot of sand in it. If it drains more slowly, your soil has poor structure and/or a lack of pore spaces between soil particles—it probably has a lot of clay in it. Both too-rapid and too-slow drainage can be improved by the addition of organic matter. Making raised beds helps to solve problems caused by poor drainage.

Drainage test #2 (visual exam). The color of the soil in your garden can give you some useful clues about water drainage. Dig a hole at least 2 feet deep and 2 feet wide so you can see down into it. Look at the color of the soil as you dig.

- Tinges of blue and gray indicate poor aeration, which often results from inadequate water drainage.
- Brown soils generally drain much better than gray-colored soils.
- Browns and reds indicate the presence of oxidized iron, which means there's both air and water in the soil pores.

Worm math. While you're digging to examine soil color and drainage, take stock of the earthworm population. Count the worms you find in a hole that's 8 to 10 inches deep and a foot wide. More than 10 worms is great; 6 to 10 indicate moderately healthy soil. Less than 5 earthworms may be an indication of low organic matter, pH problems, and/or poor drainage.

Hands-on texture test #1. When the soil is moist but not wet, pick up a loose ball of soil (about the size of a golf ball) in the palm of your hand. Squeeze the ball in your hand and release. If it crumbles, it has a reasonably balanced texture. If the ball holds its shape, it has a substantial percentage of clay.

Hands-on texture test #2. Using the same ball of soil as in the previous test, squeeze gently so it starts to come out between your thumb and forefinger. Use your thumb to press the soil out into a ribbon shape over the side of your finger. The longer the ribbon of soil, the more clay content the soil has. If the soil is too crumbly to form a ribbon, it has a good balance of sand, silt, and clay particles.

READING SOIL RIBBONS

Sandy loams and silty loams are light-textured soils. Silty clay and clay are heavy-textured soils. Everything else is considered medium texture. Texture tells you how well your soil will drain in wet seasons, how well it will hold water during dry conditions, and how easy it will be for plants to grow healthy root systems in it. To some extent, texture also indicates soil fertility (in the ability to form colloids that will hold nutrients in the root zone).

RIBBON LENGTH	FEELS MOSTLY GRITTY	FEELS MOSTLY SMOOTH	FEELS BOTH GRITTY AND SMOOTH
Shorter than 1"	Sandy loam	Silty loam	Loam
1"–2" long	Sandy clay loam	Silty clay loam	Clay loam
Longer than 2"	Sandy clay	Silty clay	Clay

Soil Test in a Jar

Dig a representative sample from the top 8 inches of soil. Dig soil from several spots in your garden and mix the samples in a bucket. Remove stones, roots, mulch, and other chunks of organic matter. Break up clods.

1 Put about 2 inches of soil in a straight-sided, flat-bottomed quart jar. Add 1 teaspoon of powdered dishwasher detergent to help disperse the soil particles. Add water to within 2 inches of the top. Screw on the lid tightly and shake the jar for 5 minutes or until the soil is thoroughly liquefied.

2 Place the jar in a spot where it can remain undisturbed for several days. After 1 minute, use a wax pencil to mark the level of sediment in the jar; this represents the sand in the soil sample. Make a second mark after 1 hour; the sediment between the two lines is silt. Clay particles will settle to the bottom last, taking up to a week. Some organic material may remain floating after all the mineral particles have settled out.

3 Use a ruler to measure the depth of sand, silt, and clay as well as the total soil depth in the jar. (If the silt layer has become more compressed as the clay settles, measure by observing the slight variations in color instead of the wax pencil marks.) Use the measurements to calculate the percentage of each soil component.

For example, the jar above shows $\frac{1}{2}$ (0.5) inch of sand, $\frac{5}{8}$ (0.625) inch of silt, and $\frac{3}{8}$ (0.375) inch of clay, for a total of $1\frac{1}{2}$ (1.5) inches. Divide each particle depth by the total soil depth to get the percentages:

0.5—1.5 = 0.333, or about 33 percent sand

0.625—1.5 = 0.417, or about 42 percent silt

0.375—1.5 = 0.25, or 25 percent clay

If one type of particle in your test makes up more than half of the total amount of soil in the jar, that is your dominant soil type. If the three layers are relatively equal, your soil is probably loamy—the best texture for gardening.

How to Get an Accurate Soil Test

One of the best deals for gardeners is a soil test, available through local Cooperative Extension offices (csrees.usda.gov/Extension/) or private laboratories. In most areas, you can get a fairly comprehensive and informative test done for $5 to $10—less than you'd spend for a bag of fertilizer. And that soil test may tell you that you don't even need that fertilizer.

When you send your soil for testing, ask the lab to tailor any recommendations for a garden. Lab recommendations for remedying soil deficiencies are typically designed to serve farmers and thus are given in terms of pounds of the proposed remedy per acre of land unless you request otherwise. (If you don't mind or have to do that math yourself, just divide "pounds per acre" by 43 to convert the recommendation to "pounds per 1,000 square feet.")

Also note on the paperwork accompanying your soil sample that you would like any remedies proposed to be in the form of organic soil amendments, as opposed to agricultural chemicals.

WHAT IS THE TEST FOR?

Laboratories test the soil's pH level, nutrient content, and percentage of organic matter. Most garden vegetables and flowers prefer slightly acidic soil, about pH 6.2 to 7.0. This is the range where nutrients are most available for uptake by plants' roots.

If your soil is too acidic, your soil test report will probably tell you to add lime to raise the pH. But another portion of the test results should determine what kind of lime you choose. If your soil's magnesium levels are okay, the lab will probably tell you to add calcitic lime. But if your soil needs magnesium, you'll probably want to add dolomitic lime (also called magnesium lime) to correct both problems.

If your soil is too alkaline, the test results may tell you to add sulfur to lower the pH. Choose pelleted or granular sulfur, which is also known as garden sulfur. Stay away from ground sulfur—it is so finely ground you need to wear protective gear to handle it safely.

The nutrients most commonly tested for are phosphorus, potassium, calcium, sulfur, and magnesium. Most labs don't include nitrogen as part of their basic test. That's because the nitrogen content of your soil can change dramatically and quickly. If you want a test of the nitrogen in your soil, you usually have to request it; you'll pay a few dollars more for this test.

Micronutrients are essential to plant health but, as their name implies, plants use them in very small amounts. Zinc, iron, and copper are all micronutrients, and the best sources of these and other micronutrients are compost and other organic materials. If you haven't been amending your soil with compost and your garden has visible problems, a micronutrient deficiency could be the cause. If you suspect this problem, ask that your soil be tested for micronutrients when you send in a sample. It will probably cost more than a standard soil test, but the resulting information will tell you just what your garden needs and how much of each to add.

SIX STEPS TO A SUCCESSFUL SOIL SAMPLE

1. Get a trowel and a bucket. Be sure neither is rusty or made of galvanized (zinc-coated) metal, which could skew your results.

2. Scrape mulch and leaf litter from the soil surface. Dig out a wedge of soil about 6 to 8 inches deep, and set this wedge aside.

3. Now dig out a half-inch piece of soil from the hole and pour it into your bucket.

4. Repeat steps 2 and 3 at least a half-dozen times in different parts of the garden so that the soil sample represents your whole garden when mixed.

5. Use your trowel to mix the soil together thoroughly.

6. Fill the soil sample bag or container with the mixed soil, complete the paperwork, and mail it all off to the lab.

DIGGING IN

Once you've learned a little bit—or a lot—about your soil, it's time to get it ready to become the foundation of your garden. Whether you're improving the texture with soil amendments or adding fertilizer to correct deficiencies identified by a soil test, it's far easier to incorporate these things into the soil *before* your garden is planted. Adjustments to soil pH, for example, may take a few months to produce the desired effect, and some forms of organic matter can cause nutrient imbalances as they decompose.

talk the talk
Amendments and Fertilizers

FERTILIZER: A natural or manufactured material added to the soil that supplies one or more of the major nutrients—nitrogen (N), phosphorus (P), or potassium (K)—to growing plants.

NPK RATIO: A recognized abbreviation that refers to the ratio of the three major nutrients—nitrogen (N), phosphorus (P), and potassium (K)—in fertilizer, such as 5-5-5 or 10-2-2.

SOIL AMENDMENT: A material that improves soil condition and aids plant growth.

Use your observations and the results of any testing to give your soil what it needs. Begin as far in advance of your intended planting time as possible, and cultivate (dig or till) the soil, incorporating compost, soil amendments, and fertilizers as you prepare your garden beds for planting.

You may hear experienced gardeners talk of "double-digging" a garden bed, a term that refers to a labor-intensive process of removing and setting aside the upper 12 inches of soil from a 12-inch-wide trench and using a digging fork to loosen the soil in the bottom of that trench another 12 inches. A second trench is dug next to the first one, with that soil being used to fill the first trench, and the process is repeated until the entire bed is dug up and aerated to a total depth of 24 inches. The soil removed from the first trench is used to fill the last one.

While gardeners who use this method report dramatic improvements in yields over beds prepared with other methods, double-digging is not for everyone. It is undoubtedly hard work and can be nearly impossible in rocky or heavy clay soil. In those cases, it's better to spare your back and choose an alternative:

- Build raised beds.

- "Single-dig" amendments into the topsoil just one spade deep. This is especially true if the only crops to be grown will be shallow-rooting leaf crops, beans, and so on.

- Mulch repeatedly with decomposable materials. This will eventually generate a deep tilth, which, if not walked on, will remain open and free draining.

Building up, rather than digging down, when preparing a new garden is particularly good advice in places where a scant few inches of loamy topsoil cover heavy clay subsoil. Double-digging in such conditions risks incorporating the nutrient-poor subsoil into the upper layer. Better to actively incorporate organic matter on the surface, building up the topsoil to a depth that is sufficient for most flowers and vegetable crops.

"SINGLE-DIGGING" A BED

1. Mark the borders of your bed. Stakes and string work well for straight edges; use a rope or a line of flour or chalk dust to mark out curved or irregularly shaped beds.

2. Remove sod or existing vegetation. Cut sod carefully, loosening with a digging fork and slicing underneath the roots if you want to use pieces of it to patch other spots in your lawn. Otherwise, lift chunks and shake as much soil as possible from the roots of sod, then pile it upside down to compost.

3. If removing the sod is too daunting, cut the turf as close to the soil as possible (scalp it) and cover the area with several layers of wet newspaper or corrugated cardboard, followed by 8 to 10 inches of organic matter. This type of "lazy" bed is best prepared in late summer for planting the following spring, since the organic material needs time to break down. You can tuck containers of flowers or vegetables into the layer of organic matter to enjoy this sort of garden right away.

4. Top the exposed soil with 1 to 2 inches of compost and any other amendments or fertilizers recommended by soil testing.

5. Use a shovel, digging fork, or rotary tiller to loosen the soil at least to the depth of your shovel blade, mixing the amendments into the upper layer of the soil as you work.

6. When the soil is light and fluffy and the amendments are mixed in, grab a garden rake and level the surface of the soil with the tines. Then flip the rake over and smooth the soil with the back of the rake. Now your bed is ready to plant.

SOIL CARE BASICS

Don't Till Too Much

Many a new garden bed has been created through the efficient soil-churning efforts of a gas- or electric-powered rotary tiller. Rotary tillers are great for saving time and your back. They can make short work of sod busting and are tops for turning under cover crops (see page 94). But overusing them in the garden is harmful to your soil.

Too many tiller turns around the garden pulverizes the soil and destroys its structure. Tilling also reduces the organic matter content of your soil by speeding up decomposition of the soil's organic reserves. Tilling is also hard on earthworms—the whirling tines chop up some worms and leave others exposed to drying sun and wind. And if you have perennial weeds like pokeweed or Canada thistle that have spreading root systems, dig them out of your beds before you till. If you don't remove these weeds first, the tiller will chop the root systems into small pieces, each of which is capable of sprouting into a new plant pest in your lovingly prepared garden bed.

Use a rotary tiller for big soil-turning tasks, but avoid the temptation to apply those whirling blades to every soil-related chore. For example, a garden rake is better for mixing in soil amendments, and a sharp hoe is the tool of choice for routine weed removal and cultivation.

COMPOST: THE SECRET TO SOIL SUCCESS

You've already seen the word *compost* countless times in this book, for the good reason that compost and compost making are the heart and soul of organic soil care and organic gardening. While the soil testing and turning methods described up to this point in this chapter are highly desirable and beneficial, you can ignore pretty much all of them if you only make and apply copious amounts of compost to your garden beds.

Compost is the best way to ensure good, healthy soil. You can buy it or make it. By using compost, you are providing your plants with optimal nutrition naturally. By making it, you are keeping your organic refuse out of already overburdened landfills. (About 75 percent of American household garbage is suitable for composting.) One to 2 inches of compost mixed into your garden beds your first year, followed by a ½- to 1-inch layer each year thereafter, will provide all the nourishment most flowers, fruits, and vegetables need. (Use the higher amounts in southern regions or if you have sandy soil.)

There are at least as many ways to make compost as there are ways to garden, and each method has its advantages and purposes and both fans and detractors. The key, when starting out, is to use a technique that serves your garden's needs, whether it's a loose, casually tended pile; a closely managed closed-system tumbler; a multiple-bin compost complex; or some other method.

Compost Happens (with Your Help)

Neither gardening nor composting is a truly natural process, although both incorporate elements found in nature. Like the controlled growing of plants in a garden, compost making involves controlling the natural process of decomposition to make it happen more quickly and with more predictable results. To make compost, you simply need to create optimal conditions for the breakdown of organic material: air + water + carbon + nitrogen = compost.

Air. Like most living things, the bacteria that decompose organic matter, and the other creatures that make up the compost ecosystem, need air. Compost scientists say compost piles need porosity—the ability for air to move into the pile. Think of porosity in terms of fluffiness. A fluffy pile has plenty of spaces—or pores—for air to move about. A flat, matted pile of grass clippings, for example, does not. Even fluffy piles compress during the composting process. Occasionally turning your pile refluffs the material, moves new material into the center, and helps improve airflow into the pile.

Water. Compost microbes also need the right amount of water. Too much moisture reduces airflow, causes temperatures to fall, and can make the pile smell; too little water slows decomposition and prevents the pile from heating. Conventional wisdom says that compost should be about as moist as a wrung-out sponge.

Carbon ingredients. The microbes that break down organic matter use carbon as an energy source. Ingredients with a high percentage of carbon are usually dry and brown or yellow in color. The most common high-carbon ingredients are leaves, straw, and cornstalks. Sometimes people call these ingredients "browns."

Nitrogen ingredients. Microbes need nitrogen for the proteins that build their tiny bodies. Ingredients high in nitrogen are generally green, moist plant matter (such as leaves) or an animal by-product (such as manure). These ingredients are often referred to as "greens," but in reality they can be green, brown, and all colors in between. Household kitchen scraps typically function as a nitrogen source in the compost pile.

C/N ratio. In order for a compost pile to decompose efficiently, you need to create the right ratio of carbon (C) to nitrogen (N) (C/N). Piles with too much nitrogen tend to smell, because the excess nitrogen converts into an ammonia gas. Carbon-rich piles break down slowly because there's not enough nitrogen for the microbe population to expand. An ideal compost pile should have a 30:1 C/N ratio. Grass clippings alone have about a 20:1 C/N ratio. Adding one part grass clippings, or other green matter, to two parts dead leaves, or other browns, will give you the right mix.

Compost. Compost is a mix of decomposed and partially decomposed organic matter (such as kitchen scraps, leaves, grass clippings, and dead plants) that is dark in color and crumbly in texture. Used as an amendment, compost increases the water-holding capacity of the soil and is an excellent nutrient source for microorganisms, which later release nutrients to your plants.

HOW TO BUILD A COMPOST PILE

Following are the fundamentals of compost making. There are many variations on the process, but at its heart, composting is simply a matter of combining organic materials and encouraging them to decompose.

HERE'S WHAT YOU NEED

- Carbon-rich "brown" materials, such as fall leaves, straw, dead flowers from your garden, and shredded newspaper or cardboard.
- Nitrogen-rich "green" materials, such as grass clippings, plant-based kitchen waste (vegetable peelings and fruit rinds, but no meat scraps or dairy products), or barnyard animal manure (even though its color is usually brown, manure is full of nitrogen like the other "green" stuff). Do not use manure from carnivores, such as cats or dogs.
- A shovelful or two of garden soil.
- A site that's at least 3 feet long × 3 feet wide.

1. Start by spreading a layer that is several inches thick of coarse, dry brown stuff, like straw or cornstalks or leaves, where you want to build the pile.

2. Top that with several inches of green stuff.

3. Add a thin layer of soil.

4. Add a layer of brown stuff.

5. Moisten the three layers.

6. Continue layering green stuff and brown stuff with a little soil mixed in until the pile is 3 feet high. Try to add stuff in a ratio of three parts brown to one part green. (If it takes a while before you have enough material to build the pile that high, don't worry. Just keep adding to the pile until it gets to at least 3 feet high.)

7. Every couple of weeks, use a garden fork or shovel to turn the pile, moving the stuff at the center of the pile to the outside and working the stuff on the outside to the center of the pile. Keep the pile moist, but not soggy. When you first turn the pile, you may see steam rising from it. This is a sign that the pile is heating up as a result of the materials in it decomposing. If you turn the pile every couple of weeks and keep it moist, you will begin to see earthworms throughout the pile, and the center of the pile will turn into black, crumbly, sweet-smelling "black gold." When you have enough finished compost in the pile to use in your garden, shovel out the finished compost and start your next pile with any material that hadn't fully decomposed in the previous one.

You don't need a compost bin to make compost. You simply need a pile that is at least 3 × 3 × 3 feet. A pile this size will have enough mass to decompose without a bin. Many gardeners buy or build compost bins, however, because they keep the pile neat. Some are designed to make turning the compost easier or protect it from soaking rains. A bin also may be desirable to keep pets and wild animals from digging in the compost in search of tempting kitchen scraps, or for aesthetic reasons.

Composting Cold or Hot

How much—or how little—you manage your compost pile will affect how quickly or slowly the assembled materials break down and become the compost you desire. Nearly any discussion of composting includes the terms "hot" and "cold" composting; these two approaches may also be characterized as fast or slow. Both will get you to a similar end result, but the amount of time and effort involved can differ considerably.

Cold black gold. Even acknowledged experts admit that they do this type of composting in their own backyards because it's easy. Here's how to make cold compost: Mix together yard wastes, such as grass clippings, leaves, and weeds; place them in a pile; and wait 6 to 24 months for the microorganisms, earthworms, and insects to break down the material. Add new materials to the top of the pile. You can reduce the waiting period by occasionally turning the pile and monitoring and adjusting the pile's moisture level. The compost will be ready when the original ingredients are unrecognizable. Generally, compost on the bottom of the pile "finishes" first. You may not want to include woody material, because it breaks down too slowly.

Pros: Takes little effort to build and maintain; can be built over time. Conserves some beneficial microorganisms that cannot survive the higher temperatures of a hot compost pile.

Cons: Takes up to 2 years to produce finished compost; doesn't kill pathogens and weed seeds; undecomposed pieces may need to be screened out.

Some like it hot. Hot, or fast, composting takes more work and the right combination of ingredients, but you can get high-quality compost in under 2 months. Here's how: Wait until you have enough material to create compost critical mass (27 cubic feet), which is the minimum volume for a pile to hold heat. Then mix one part green matter with two parts brown matter. Bury any vegetative food scraps in the center to avoid attracting animals. Check to make sure the mixture has the ideal moisture level. Continue adding mixed greens and browns and checking the moisture until you've built a pile that is 3 × 3 × 3 feet or 5 feet wide at the base and 3 feet wide at the top. The microorganisms will immediately start decomposing, and their bodies will release heat. The pile will insulate the heat, and the temperature of the pile's interior will reach 120° to 150°F. Turn the pile weekly (or as often as every 2 to 3 days to really speed things along) and regulate moisture levels. After about a month, the hot phase will be done, and the pile will finish decomposing at temperatures between 80°

and 110°F. The compost will be ready to use when it no longer heats and all of the original ingredients are unrecognizable.

Pros: Produces high-quality compost within 2 months (and sometimes as soon as a few weeks); can kill weed seeds and pathogens. (The best approach is to avoid adding weeds with seeds, diseased plants, or manures that may contain human pathogens to compost—hot or cold—because uniform heating is difficult to achieve in home compost piles.)

Cons: Time consuming and labor intensive; requires careful management of moisture, air, and C/N ratio.

COLD-WEATHER COMPOSTING

When the weather turns cold in fall, you can still keep your compost pile working by insulating it. Gather bags of fallen leaves and heap them in a circle about 4 feet in diameter around a low compost pile. The bags will provide some heat and insulation, the contents of the bags will decompose slightly, and the center of the circle should stay unfrozen all winter, so you can keep dumping your kitchen scraps there.

You can also insulate a pile or bin by surrounding it with straw bales and covering the whole thing with a sheet of heavy-duty plastic or landscape fabric.

A compost pile enclosed by a bin made from straw bales and covered with a tarp, heavy plastic sheeting, or landscape fabric may be insulated enough to continue decomposing through the winter months. When spring arrives, mix some of the straw from the bin into the compost pile and use the rest as mulch.

Leave It Out!

Most kitchen and garden wastes make good compost pile fodder, but there are specific materials you should never add to your compost pile:

- **Meat, dairy products, or grease.** These animal products may attract rodents. Don't use kitchen scraps that are heavy with oil because oils are slow to decompose.

- **Droppings from cats, dogs, or any other carnivores,** because they could contain disease organisms that are harmful to humans.

- **Diseased plants or weeds that have produced seeds.** Your compost pile may not heat up enough to kill disease organisms and weed seeds. The same rule applies to perennial weeds with spreading roots, such as Canada thistle or field bindweed.

Pens made of wire fencing are good for stockpiling ingredients such as dry leaves and grass clippings until they're needed in an active compost project, but the open sides let the outer materials get too dry for effective decomposition. Enclosed bins made of plastic or wood may become overly soggy without adequate ventilation and/or turning, but they're useful for keeping critters from raiding the compost pile.

Examples of Compost Ingredients

Carbon/Dry Browns

Dry leaves

Dry weeds

Straw

Hay

Chopped
cornstalks

Aged sawdust

Nutshells

Paper
(moderate amounts)

Nitrogen/Wet Greens

Vegetable
scraps

Fruit scraps

Coffee grounds
(with or without
filter)

Tea grounds
or bags

Fresh grass
clippings

Fresh leaves
(avoid walnut
and eucalyptus)

Freshly pulled
weeds

Hair
(pet and
human)

Manure
(cow, poultry,
horse, rabbit,
sheep)

Seaweed

ADVANCED SOIL MANAGEMENT: COVER CROPS

You can help keep your soil healthy and your plants happy by planting cover crops in your vegetable and annual flowerbeds. Cover crops, sometimes also called green manures, are crops grown to protect and enrich the soil and to control weeds. You "harvest" organic matter and nutrients from cover crops by tilling the plants back into the soil. The optimum plan is to have a vigorous cover crop growing whenever you're not growing vegetables or flowers. In most areas of the United States, that means late fall through early spring, although in some southern areas, it may mean growing your cover during summer months.

Here are eight great reasons to include cover crops in your garden plans:

- Cover crops provide nitrogen.
- Cover crops add organic matter.
- Cover crops protect against erosion.
- Cover crops catch nutrients.
- Cover crops break up compacted soil.
- Cover crops control weeds.

- Cover crops attract beneficial organisms.
- Cover crops can be effective mulches.

COVER CROP HOW-TO

1. **Sow it.** Seeds left on top of the soil may dry out, wash away, or be eaten by birds. Covering the seed with a bit of soil gives it a much higher chance of success. A well-prepared seedbed is ideal, of course, but when that's not possible—if you want to sow a cover crop between established rows of vegetables, for example—just rake the seed gently with a hand tool. This is especially important for large-seeded covers such as fava beans or cereal rye.

2. **Water it.** Give your garden a good soaking after planting a cover crop. Another watering soon after the cover comes up will give it a competitive edge.

3. **Dig it.** What you do with your finished cover crop depends on what you grow in your garden. If you've planted a legume cover to provide nitrogen for a crop like tomatoes, turn the cover under about the time it flowers (that's when nitrogen levels peak). Winter annual legumes typically flower between mid-April and late June.

   If the cover crop hasn't bloomed, but you're ready to sow or transplant some vegetables, dig it in anyway. You can plant right after turning under a legume, unless it has added a lot of bulky material to your soil. In that case, let it decompose and settle a bit.

   If your cover is not a legume, wait 2 to 3 weeks after you turn it under to plant. Decomposition can tie up available nitrogen in the soil for a while.

   How should you turn it under? That depends on how tall it is. The average "tiller"—either a machine with tines or a gardener with a turning fork—can easily handle a low-growing cover crop such as clover.

4. **Or mow it, then dig it.** If your cover crop is on the tangled, jungly side, mow it first and let it dry out for a few days before turning it under. If your lawn mower can't do the job, try using a string trimmer or a scythe.

   Once the cover is cut, you can also consider setting aside the trimmings for use as a weed-smothering mulch or as green matter to add to your compost pile.

CHOOSE YOUR COVER CROP

Consult the listings below to decide which cover crop will work best for you. For example, fast-growing cover crops are good for filling beds between plantings of vegetable crops. Winter annuals serve well as a winter groundcover to prevent runoff. Check the "comments" column for special hints on how to use each crop.

SPECIES	TYPE	NORTHERN LIMIT (BY USDA ZONE)	
LEGUMES			
Common/white vetch (*Vicia sativa*)	WA	7	
Purple vetch (*Vicia benghalensis*)	WA	8	
Red clover (*Trifolium pratense*)	SLP	5	
White clover (*Trifolium repens*)	P	5	
Crimson clover (*Trifolium incarnatum*)	WA	6	
Berseem clover (*Trifolium alexandrinum*)	WA/SA	7	
Subterranean clover (*Trifolium subterraneum*)	WA	7	
Fava beans (*Vicia faba*)	SA	8	
Alfalfa (*Medicago sativa*)	P	5	
Yellow-blossom sweet clover (*Melilotus officinalis*)	B	5	
Hubam white sweet clover (*Melilotus alba*)	SA	8	
Cowpeas (*Vigna sinensis*)	SA	10	
NONLEGUMES			
Buckwheat (*Fagopyrom esculentum*)	SA	10	
Cereal/winter rye (*Secale cereale*)	WA	3	
Annual ryegrass (*Lolium multiflorum*)	WA	4	
Oats (*Avena sativa*)	SA	8	

KEY

GROWTH RATE	COMMENTS
F	Flowers in early May in most regions
F	Good winter-kill mulch in areas with hard frost
M	Not recommended for flooded soil; shade tolerant
M	Low growing; good living mulch; shade and drought tolerant
VF	Reseeds itself; flowers mid-May in most zones; some shade tolerance
VF	Fast growth in cool and warm weather
M	Reseeds by burrowing seed into ground; some drought tolerance
F	Can also produce edible bean crop
S	Has deep taproot; won't grow in wet soils; low shade tolerance; high drought tolerance
S	Has deep taproot; low shade tolerance; some drought tolerance
F	Rapid growth in warm weather; some drought tolerance
VF	Rapid growth in hot weather; prefers well-drained soil
VF	Good nutrient-catching and weed-smothering crop; low drought tolerance
VF	Can be planted later in fall than other covers; some drought and shade tolerance
VF	May tie up nitrogen temporarily when turned under; shade tolerant; some drought tolerance
VF	Very rapid growth in cool weather; low drought tolerance

CONTAINER GARDEN
GROWING MEDIUM

Of course, if your garden will be confined to containers, all this talk of soil tending and building may be moot. (You still can and should make compost to enrich the growing medium in your containers.) You can buy organic potting mix to fill your planters or you can mix up your own custom blend. If you shop for potting soil to put in your containers, be sure it says "organic" on the label. If it doesn't, the mixture may include synthetic fertilizers and very little organic matter.

The more planters you have to fill, the more economical it may be to make your own mix, especially if you have homemade compost to blend in.

For containers up to 1 gallon in size. Use a mixture suitable for houseplants. Combine one to two parts commercial organic potting soil or good garden soil; one part builder's sand or perlite; and one part coir fiber or peat moss, compost, or leaf mold. Add 1 tablespoon of bonemeal per quart of mix.

For larger containers. Use a relatively coarse soilless planting mixture to maintain the needed balance of air and water in the root zone. To make your own, combine equal parts of compost, pulverized pine or fir bark, and perlite or vermiculite. For each cubic foot of mix, add 4 ounces of dolomitic limestone, 1 pound of rock phosphate or colloidal phosphate, 4 ounces of greensand, 1 pound of granite dust, and 2 ounces of bloodmeal. (See Chapter 6 for descriptions of the organic fertilizers and amendments.)

Many of the components of potting soil are lightweight, dust-producing materials that can irritate your eyes, skin, and lungs. In particular, vermiculite can contain low levels of asbestos; compost and peat moss can contain mold spores. When you mix potting soil, take the following precautions:

- Work outdoors or in a well-ventilated garage or garden shed.

- Wear a dust mask.

- Dampen individual ingredients before mixing them together to minimize the amount of dust released.

- When finished, wash your hands thoroughly. If you've been working with vermiculite, be aware that the dust can cling to your clothing. Remove and wash dusty clothing as soon as possible to avoid dispersing asbestos inside your house.

STARTING SEEDS, TENDING TRANSPLANTS

Many [of *Organic Gardening*'s readers] have also written to their
local newspapers, describing how the organic method has produced fabulously
bountiful growth in their vegetables and flowers.

—J. I. RODALE, "WHY I STARTED *ORGANIC GARDENING*,"
ORGANIC GARDENING, 1971

G rowing plants from seed is as simple as putting the seed in conditions favorable for growth and letting it do what comes naturally. Everything else—which can turn out to be quite a lot or almost nothing at all—is finesse.

Your role in sowing and growing seeds is to provide the conditions that favor successful germination and subsequent growth and maturation. From seed and site selection to soil preparation, timing, and tending, gardening involves managing the natural process to produce the desired result: beautiful flowers, juicy tomatoes, crisp carrots, and everything else you choose to grow.

Once you've selected a spot, enriched the soil, planned the layout, and prepared the beds, the next step toward creating your beautiful, productive, organic garden is to plant it with healthy transplants or seeds. In this chapter, you'll learn what to look for when buying seeds or plants, along with everything you need to know about getting them off to a good start in your garden.

BUYING SEEDS AND PLANTS

You can fill your gardens either by planting seeds directly into the prepared soil or by planting transplants (purchased plants or ones you've started indoors from seed). Seeds cost less than transplants, but they need more care and more time to grow before they can fill your borders with flowers or your plate with fresh vegetables. Purchased plants cost more but come closest to delivering instant gratification once they're tucked into your gardens, and transplants you've started yourself give you the greatest amount of control over every aspect of the growing process. Most vegetable gardens start out as a combination of direct-sown seed crops and transplants, while ornamental gardens may rely more heavily on purchased plants for speedier visual impact. Following are some hints to help guide your decisions, whether you're shopping for seeds or for plants.

Why Grow from Seed?

In spring, when packs and flats of flowers and vegetable are plentiful, it's easy to wonder why anyone would go to the trouble of starting plants from seed. Just head to the store and pick up a garden already in progress; take the plants home and tuck them into the soil.

While the garden center's sturdy tomato plants and bud-laden flowers may be tempting, it's not usually economical or logical to rely solely upon purchased plants. Many gardeners start the growing season with a combination of home-grown and store-bought plants, but there are good reasons for bypassing the flats of plants at the home center and starting your own from seed instead.

Sometimes seeds make more sense. Seeds are inexpensive, and they offer a significant return on your initial investment. For the price of a single potted tomato plant, you can buy a packet that contains enough seeds to grow a gardenful of tomato plants.

When direct-sow is the way to go. Tomatoes, peppers, and other heat-loving crops typically enter the garden as transplants that have been started indoors. But not all crops need an indoor head start to make it to maturity before the close of the growing season. Quick-growing greens, short-season peas, and speedy radishes go from seed to supper so quickly that there's little need to get them growing ahead of the time when they can safely be sown directly into the garden.

Crops that have fragile or fleshy roots or stems that are prone to injury during transplanting also are good candidates for sowing directly in the garden. Beans, carrots, and cucumbers are among those garden crops that don't take kindly to having their roots disturbed and are usually sown where they will grow to maturity. Such crops can be started indoors to get a jump on a short growing season, but they need special care to get them into the garden without injury to their fragile, fleshy roots or stems.

VEGETABLES COMMONLY PLANTED IN THE GARDEN AS SEED

Beans	Peas	Sweet corn
Beets	Radishes	Turnips
Carrots	Salad greens	
Cucumbers	Squash	

Go organic all the way. Unless you're buying transplants directly from a grower who follows organic practices, there are no guarantees about what's been sprayed on the young plants you purchase to tuck into your carefully tended organic plot. If you want to ensure that your food crops grow from start to finish without exposure to pesticides and chemical fertilizers, begin with certified organic seed and raise them, organically, yourself.

Plant when the time is right. Plants' arrival on store shelves in late winter and early spring is no guarantee that the weather will be favorable for putting them in your garden. Starting transplants from seed lets you get the timing just right for each crop and for the local climate and weather conditions. It also means you can have transplants ready to plant in late summer for a fall garden—even if local stores are filling their shelves with back-to-school items and snow shovels.

Avoid what's going around. The perennial and woody plants sold at chain stores may be shipped from distant growers in other parts of the country, occasionally bringing pests and problems with them to their new home. Vegetable transplants typically come from large growers that supply all of the stores in a particular region. This widespread distribution of a few varieties of plants can set the stage for widespread disease problems, too. Growing crops from seed lets you choose cultivars that are resistant to pests and diseases that are prevalent in your area. It also avoids bringing home problems that may have originated at the grower or developed in transit or at the point of sale.

Enjoy the greatest variety of plants. In the absence of a really great local grower, the number of varieties available as transplants tends to be quite limited. The garden center may offer one kind of broccoli, two or three types of cabbage, four pepper varieties—two hot and two sweet, and five or six kinds of tomatoes. Compare that to the pages of choices in a seed catalog, and it's easy to see what's missing—a rainbow of colors, a wealth of shapes and sizes, and long- and short-season crops to suit any gardening condition. Stores selling vegetable transplants have to play it safe and offer only standard-issue stuff that will yield a standard-issue harvest. Starting from seed opens the door to new varieties and old ones. And because the initial investment is small, trying new and different crops poses very little risk and has the potential to produce outstanding results.

Preserve the past and plan for the future. Modern agriculture and food processing are not well suited to the quirks and irregularities of beloved flavorful crops that produce monster fruits or beautifully speckled beans. Heirloom crops endure because they have qualities that are prized by the gardeners who have grown them and passed them from one generation to the next, not because they hold up well in shipping or yield a large crop all at once for easy harvesting. By saving seeds of their favorite crops, our gardening forebears ensured that those crops would be around for the next season and for subsequent generations. Seeds of heirlooms may be found listed in the pages of most major seed catalogs as well as from seed companies such as Seeds of Change (seedsofchange.com) and Baker Creek Heirloom Seeds (rareseeds.com) that specialize in heirloom varieties. The Seed Savers Exchange (seedsavers.org) is a nonprofit organization that promotes the saving and sharing of heirloom seeds; they sell hundreds of heirloom varieties and offer guidance on saving and storing seeds for the future.

Smart Shopping for Seeds

Shopping for seeds requires the imagination to "see" what those seeds might become and the commitment to starting and sowing and tending to make those dreams a reality. Use these tips to make the most of your seed shopping:

- Browse several seed catalogs or seed company Web sites to compare availability of the seeds you want and prices. It's easy to buy much more than you need, however. While most seeds will keep from one season to the next, fresh seeds typically offer better results, so it's best to avoid having lots of "leftovers."

- Whether you're perusing the pages of a seed catalog or buying seeds "off the rack" at a garden center, shop with a plan and a list in hand. Begin with at least an idea of what you want to grow and how much space you have in your garden.

- If you're new to gardening or to the area where you'll be planting your next garden, talk with other gardeners and the local extension agent. Ask what crops grow best in your area, and start with those. Most extension service offices also provide lists of recommended cultivars. Get recommendations for favorite nurseries, garden centers, and seed sources, too. Seek out catalogs and plant lists offered by seed companies that specialize in regionally adapted selections.

- Read descriptions and choose varieties with qualities that are important to you. Match varieties to your garden's conditions and potential problems. Look for varieties that are resistant to disease organisms that may be widespread in your area, such as VF tomato cultivars, which are resistant to verticillium and fusarium fungi. A seed catalog or Web site usually has a key to help users interpret the letters that indicate disease resistance for each crop.

- Be aware of how much seed of any one variety you are buying. If you buy seeds by the packet, take note of how many seeds it contains. Seed quantity per packet varies widely. Some packets of new or special varieties may contain fewer than 20 seeds. Some companies offer small seed packets at reasonable prices; these can be a great way to try growing something new without buying a lot of seed.

- Seed mixtures, such as mesclun mixes of salad greens or flower samplers, offer variety from a single packet.

- Take advantage of all the information that's available. The best seed catalogs (and their online counterparts) are packed with helpful guidance on how many seeds are in a pound or packet, how many seeds to plant per row, days to germination and/or maturity, and even pictures or illustrations of what the seedlings look like when they germinate. If your questions aren't answered in the pages of the catalog or on the company's Web site, give a call to the customer service number—often these phones are staffed by extremely knowledgeable and experienced gardeners who are there to help.

- Some seed is routinely treated with synthetic chemical fungicide. Specify untreated seed if you prefer to avoid it, or buy from companies that sell only untreated seed. Reputable companies will identify treated seeds to make it easy for organic gardeners to remain so.

- Seeds identified as All-America Selections grow and produce well over a wide range of conditions.

Smart Shopping for Plants

Be a savvy consumer when buying plants for your garden. If possible, shop at a local garden center or nursery rather than a mass-market retail chain. The odds of finding a good selection of healthy plants are better if you start by looking someplace where plants and related products are the primary business. Wherever you wind up shopping for plants, here are some hints to help you make smart selections.

Get a good first impression. Are the plants and flats crowded together? Do the plants generally appear healthy and well cared for? If your first impression is of sickly, spindly, floppy, or dried-out plants, or if there are obvious signs of pests or diseases, take your business elsewhere.

How to Read a Seed Packet

The back of a seed packet contains valuable growing information about the plant. Here's how to decipher it. (Keep in mind that packets of organically grown seed—that is, seeds produced in accordance with the standards of an organic certification organization—will be labeled as such on the packet.)

Planting Information

This may include advice on how deep to plant the seed, suggestions for spacing or thinning, whether to start indoors or direct-sow in the garden, how long it will take to germinate, and how long from germination to harvest.

Variety Name

Crop and cultivar name usually appear at the top, along with a brief description of the cultivar's characteristics.

Package Date

This date indicates that the seed met or exceeded the federal standards for minimum germination when tested for that year.

Planting Map

A planting map gives a general guide to when to sow seed outdoors in broad regions of the country. Combine this information with climate data and observations specific to where you live.

Number of Plants or Seeds

Some packets have specific seed counts, while others list the approximate number of plants you should be able to grow from the amount of seed in the packet. Some may simply indicate the weight of the seed the packet contains.

talk the talk
Seeds, Seed Starting, and Transplants

BROADCAST PLANTING: To sow seeds evenly across an area by hand or with a spreading tool.

COTYLEDON: Also called a *seed leaf*, a cotyledon is the first leaf to emerge when a seed sprouts. It does not generally look like the leaves typical of the plant (called its *true leaves*).

CROSS-POLLINATION: The transfer of pollen from the stigma of a male flower to the pistil of a female flower, resulting in the production of seeds.

CUTTING: A piece of stem or root from an existing plant, collected and prepared to grow into a new plant.

DIRECT SEEDING: Planting seeds outside directly into the garden.

DISEASE RESISTANT: The characteristic of a plant variety that allows it to avoid or withstand infection by common disease organisms. A variety that is resistant may still be infected by disease—resistance is not immunity—but the infection may be less severe than in more susceptible varieties.

DIVISION: A method of propagation by which a plant clump is separated or split apart into two or more plants.

GERMINATION: The beginning of growth of a seed.

HARDENING OFF: Gradually exposing tender seedlings to the outdoors in a protected area for a week prior to transplanting them into the garden.

HEIRLOOM PLANTS AND SEEDS: Plants and seeds grown in earlier times and still preserved by gardeners but which are no longer widely used in agriculture. Heirloom varieties are generally open pollinated (see below).

HORTICULTURAL HEAT MAT: A flat, waterproof heating pad made specifically for creating warm conditions for seed starting. The best ones have thermostats that let you adjust the temperature. Heating pads and electric blankets meant for warming people are not suitable for seed starting.

HYBRID: A plant that was produced by crossing parents of different species.

INOCULANT: A powder containing cultures of beneficial bacteria applied to seeds of legumes (peas and beans) to enhance their ability to develop nodules on their roots that fix nitrogen in the soil and result in better plant growth. Inoculants expire and must be purchased fresh each year.

LIFE CYCLE: The germination, growth, flowering, seed production, and death of a plant.

NODE: An area on a stem, branch, or root where new branches or buds develop.

OPEN POLLINATED: The term used to describe a plant that will remain true to type as long as it is fertilized with pollen from the same species.

PERLITE: An ingredient of potting mixes added to lighten and aerate texture; it's a type of volcanic glass and appears in potting mixes as little white balls.

POLLINATION: The transfer of pollen from a male flower to a female flower. Pollination can be carried out by insects, water, wind, or the gardener's hand.

PROPAGATE: To make new plants from existing ones. Some methods of propagation include saving seed from plants and then planting the seed, taking cuttings from plants, and dividing clumps of plants.

SEEDLING: A young plant grown from seed. Plants grown from seeds are commonly termed *seedlings* until they are first transplanted.

THINNING: Removing some of the young plants from a row of seedlings to create the proper spacing for the remaining plants.

TRANSPLANT: Moving a plant from one location to another. For gardeners, transplanting often means moving a seedling from a small container or flat into the garden or a larger container.

TRUE LEAVES: Plant leaves that have the form characteristic of the mature plant, usually all leaves that form after a germinating seed's first one or two leaves, which are called *seed leaves*.

VERMICULITE: A mineral derived from silica that's included in potting mixes for its ability to retain water and aerate the soil.

Germination

The germination process varies among different species, but the overall result is the same: a dry, inert seed awakens and becomes a green, growing plant.

As a seed absorbs moisture, its internal pressure rises and ruptures the seed coat. Hormones within the seed stimulate the growth of new tissue. The first root, called the radicle, emerges and starts to grow, the stem elongates, and the seed leaves unfold.

Seed Parts

Flowering plants are classified as either monocots or dicots, based on whether they have one or two cotyledons, or seed leaves.

Corn seed

Plants in the grass family, which includes all of the grains, are termed monocots (short for monocotyledonous), meaning they produce just one seed leaf when they germinate. In corn and other grains, the developing seed's nourishment comes from the pericarp, which is fused to the seed.

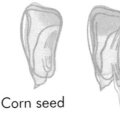

Bean seed

Most garden seeds are dicots (short for dicotyledonous). Perhaps the best known example of a dicot is a bean seed with its two fleshy seed leaves. Particularly among dicots, the seed leaves often bear little resemblance to the true leaves that follow.

Question the keepers. Ask if the transplants you're buying have been hardened off yet, so you know how to handle them when you get them home.

Examine plants carefully. Seedlings should have short, thick, sturdy stems and uniformly green foliage. Avoid plants with leaves that are (unnaturally) yellow or pale, curled, mottled, dry, or misshapen.

Size matters. Be wary of big transplants in very small containers—their roots may have suffered from overcrowding to the point of being unable to recover. This applies to perennials and woody plants, too.

Don't fall for flowers. Retailers know that color sells, and it's much more appealing to buy a flat of plants with brightly colored blooms than one that's leafy and green. But plants that are already flowering—annuals, vegetables, or perennials—won't survive the shock of transplanting as well as younger plants will.

Look under the leaves. Check the undersides of foliage and along stems for insect eggs, webbing, and small pests such as aphids, whiteflies, and spider mites. While a stray insect here and there need not be a deal breaker, you don't want to bring home an infestation that could spread throughout your garden.

Review the roots. Take a plant gently out of its container—ask for help if you need it—and look at its roots. The soil mass should retain its shape out of the container but not consist entirely of roots. Look for white tips on the roots—they're an indication that the roots are healthy and growing.

Help them feel at home. If you can't plant right away, place containers in a shady spot and keep them well watered. Check them daily and get them in the ground as soon as you can.

PLANTING SEEDS

For things that grow best when sown directly into the garden, planting is a simple matter. Once the seedbed is prepared and the conditions are right, follow these steps in the next section to give your seeds the best possible beginning.

Direct Seeding Outdoors

Weather is the biggest variable seeds face when you plant them in the garden. Good soil preparation, proper planting depth, and careful watering will help them thrive even when Nature turns fickle.

- *Make a furrow—or not.* If you like symmetry and order, carve out a shallow trench with a hoe or hand trowel, following the planting depth listed on the seed packet. But you don't have to plant in rows, and you may want to sow flower seeds in a less rigid arrangement. You can organize your garden as a grid, with plants at the four corners of each square, or you can broadcast seeds evenly over a prepared planting bed.

- *Water lightly.* Moisten but don't soak the soil. Watering before rather than after planting the seeds protects them from being swamped or washed up and out of the soil.

- *Sow the seeds.* Sprinkle small seeds through the trench or drop larger seeds at the spacing recommended on the seed packet. Don't worry about sowing seeds too closely; you can thin them after they come up and, in many cases, eat the thinnings.

- *Cover with soil.* As a rule of thumb, bury seeds only about as deep as their diameter. Sprinkle soil on top of the seeds, pressing gently to ensure they have contact with the soil. A few seeds, such as lettuce and dill, need light to sprout, so press them into the soil surface rather than covering them up. (Seed packets tell you if they need light to germinate.)

- *Keep the soil moist.* Sprinkle water on the seedbed whenever the surface is dry until all the seeds have sprouted.

Starting Seeds Indoors

Starting seeds indoors gives you a jump on the gardening season because you can get plants growing while it's still too cold to plant them outside. In addition to extending the gardening season, indoor seed starting gives you control over crop timing and offers a greater selection of varieties (including many heirlooms that are not often sold as transplants). Organic gardeners take advantage of the opportunity to begin the growing process with certified-organic seeds. Success with indoor seed starting requires a suitable light source and a careful eye toward the seedlings' temperature, moisture, and nutrient needs.

Here are the basics of indoor seed starting:

- *Start with a light growing mix.* Seeds contain their own food supply, so they don't need rich soil right away. What they do need to grow into strong seedlings is moisture, air, and a loose planting medium so their tender roots can easily stretch and grow. A commercial seed-starting mix will do the trick, or you can make your own by mixing equal parts vermiculite, milled sphagnum moss (or screened compost), and perlite—all available at garden supply stores.

• *Choose a container that drains well.* Seed-starting containers should have drainage holes in the bottom so seedling roots don't get waterlogged. Shallow containers with drainage holes also work in the other direction—they let you water your newly sown seeds from the bottom to avoid washing them away with streams of water from above. Recycled cell packs (like the containers transplants are sold in) and many other recycled containers work well, as long as they have drainage holes. If you recycle cell packs, wash them thoroughly with soap and hot water to kill disease-causing organisms before reusing the packs for seed starting.

Presprouting Seeds

Sprouting seeds before you plant them can boost germination rates and give you more control when working with expensive or scarce seeds. Here's how to presprout seeds:

1. Spread a double layer of damp paper towels on a flat surface.
2. Evenly space seeds 1 inch or so apart on the moist towels.
3. Roll up the towels, being careful to keep the seeds from bunching up.
4. Label the seed roll and enclose it in a plastic bag. Close the bag loosely—germinating seeds need some air. You can put several rolls in one plastic bag.
5. Put the seeds in a warm place—near a water heater or on top of a refrigerator. Make a note on your calendar to check them in 2 to 3 days.
6. After the first inspection, check the seeds daily for signs of sprouting.
7. As soon as seeds begin sprouting, remove them from the toweling and plant them. If they remain in the paper towels too long, their roots will grow tangled together and into the towels and will break when you try to remove them.

Plant the sprouted seeds in individual containers in fine, loose potting mix, or plant them directly in a prepared garden bed. Handle them gently. The fleshy roots and stems are easily broken. Then treat as you would any newly germinated seedlings.

Seedling Troubleshooting

What if no seedlings appear, or the ones that do seem fine at first and then begin to die? Use the following information to help you troubleshoot if a problem threatens your tiny charges.

LOW OR NO GERMINATION. If your containers fail to fill with seedlings after ample time has passed, one or more of these things may have happened: Temperatures were too low or too high, planting depth wasn't correct, seeds were old, or you let the growing mix dry out. Sow more seeds or change the conditions and wait a little longer.

LEGGY SEEDLINGS. Tall, leggy stems mean seedlings are struggling to get enough light, are too crowded, or are kept too warm. Supplement windowsill lighting with fluorescent shop lights, or thin crowded seedlings. If you think they're too warm, move them to a cooler spot. Plant leggy seedlings deeper than usual when transplanting them into larger pots or outdoors.

DISCOLORED LEAVES. If your seedlings outgrow the nutrients stored in their seeds and seed leaves, their foliage may turn colors, depending on the nutrients they lack. (Yellow leaves, for example, are usually a sign of nitrogen deficiency, while bronze leaves indicate a need for potassium.) Water with a half-strength solution of liquid fertilizer to prevent deficiency woes.

SHRIVELED SEEDLINGS. Seedlings that look fine one day but are keeled over the next are victims of damping-off. If the stems have shriveled and collapsed at the point where they touch the soil, the culprit is probably the kind of soilborne fungi that thrive in damp, poorly ventilated spaces. To spare yourself damping-off disappointment, keep your planting flats clean and use fresh seed-starting mix for each batch of seeds. Avoid overwatering and be sure your containers are well drained. Thin seedlings so air can circulate between them (you can even use a fan to keep air flowing in your seed-starting area). And keep the soil level in flats and containers high so that the sides don't block air currents.

- *Prewet the mix.* It's important to plant seeds in moist mix because if you try to water newly planted seeds (especially very tiny ones), you'll probably wash them to one corner of the container or bury them too deeply. Also, dry growing medium is hard to wet thoroughly once it's in a container. To moisten dry mix, put it in a bucket, add some warm water, and stir. Keep adding water until the mix is evenly moist—only a few drops of water should ooze out when you squeeze a handful.

Hardening Off

Starting about 2 weeks before you plan to transplant the seedlings into the garden, move them to a sheltered spot outdoors for a few hours at a time. This process, called hardening off, allows the seedlings to adjust gradually to outdoor conditions such as wind and sun. Stop fertilizing the seedlings and water less frequently. Avoid putting them in direct sunlight right away; start in a shaded location, leaving them out for just an hour the first day. Gradually increase their time outdoors and light exposure until they are spending full days outdoors, but bring them in at night.

After about a week, start leaving the seedlings outdoors overnight. Protect frost-tender crops such as tomatoes by hardening them off on a porch or in a cold frame. Once they become accustomed to the outside world, they're ready to transplant into the garden.

Transplanting to the Garden

Transplanting simply means moving a rooted plant from one place to another. If you prick out tiny parsley seedlings from a flat into individual pots, you're transplanting. If you move tomato plants from your windowsill into the garden, you're transplanting. And if you decide to move the big forsythia in the backyard, that's transplanting, too.

If you miscalculated the seed-starting date or if the weather turns nasty, you may need to transplant your seedlings (or purchased plants) again to larger containers so they won't stop growing and become stunted. Roots pushing through drainage holes are a clue that it's time to transplant.

- *Dig the hole.* Transplant on a cloudy or drizzly day or in early evening to spare transplants from the sun's heat. Water the plants before you start—

(continued on page 114)

Planting a Seedling Flat

Follow these steps for sowing seeds and tending seedlings. This technique works for many vegetable crops (broccoli, cabbage, eggplant, lettuce, onion, pepper, and tomato) as well as for many annual flowers and herbs.

1   To sow the seeds, fill a flat with moist seed-starting medium. Level the medium and use a ruler or piece of lath to press shallow rows about ¼ inch deep and 2 inches apart.

2   Sprinkle seeds into the depressions. Space seeds about ½ inch apart. If planted too closely, the seedlings will be more difficult to separate at transplant time. Label each row.

3   Once all rows are planted, gently scatter more of the seed-starting medium to cover the seeds (unless the packet specifies leaving the seeds uncovered). Water the surface with a gentle mist and cover the flat with a plastic dome or sheet of clear plastic to maintain moisture.

    Some seeds germinate best in cool soil, and others in warm; check the seed packet for temperature requirements. If the seeds need warmth, place the flat near a heat vent, on top of a refrigerator, or on an electric heat mat to warm the soil. Watch daily for emerging seedlings. As soon as they appear, remove the plastic cover and place the flat in a sunny window or under grow lights. At this point, many types of seedlings prefer cool growing temperatures around 65°F.

4 When seedlings have grown their second set of leaves, they are ready to be transplanted to individual containers. Use a narrow blade like a letter opener to lift and loosen the soil beneath a row of seedlings. Gently tug the seedlings apart. Hold the seedlings by their leaves instead of their stems, which are more easily damaged by rough handling.

5 Add some potting mix to the bottom of a container—a cell pack or 3-inch square pot, for example. Center the seedling in the pot, then add more soil around the roots to fill. Press lightly to firm the soil around the roots.

6 Using a rose (or water breaker, a device to moderate the flow of water) on the watering can, soak thoroughly.

Seedlings grown in a mix that includes compost won't require fertilizer. In compost-free mixes, feed the seedlings lightly every 2 to 3 weeks after moving them to individual pots, using liquid kelp and fish emulsion, mixed at half the recommended rate.

until the roots start growing, they can't draw water from the soil. Dig a hole slightly wider than and of the same depth as the container. (Plant tomatoes deeper, so that roots form along the stem.)

- *Remove the plant from its container.* Place your hand on top of the growing medium, with your fingers around the plant's stem. Turn the pot upside down and gently squeeze it or push the plant out from the bottom with your other hand. If you must tug it out, pull it by its leaves rather than the stem (if a leaf comes off, no harm done; damage the stem, and the plant will not survive). Plants in peat or paper pots can be planted pot and all.

- *Check the roots.* If the roots have wrapped around and around in the container, gently pull a few loose with your fingers.

- *Plant the plant.* Gently place the plant in the hole and spread out the roots of plants that aren't in pots. Slit the sides of peat pots to open them up for better root penetration after planting. Stripping away the top rim of the pot above the soil line is also important, because if even a small piece of peat pot is exposed after transplanting, it will draw water from the soil surrounding the transplant's roots, leaving the plant in danger of water stress. Set the plant in the hole at the same depth it was in its pot, generally where the stem meets the roots. Tomatoes are an exception to this rule—plant them deeper.

- *Replace the soil and then water.* Backfill the hole with the soil you removed and press gently to ensure that the roots have solid contact with the soil. Be sure the soil stays consistently moist until you see the plant start to grow.

SAVING SEEDS

Saving seeds is an easy way to multiply most garden vegetables, many herbs and flowers, and some nut trees. Seed saving is fun and can be a money saver, too—any seeds saved from this year's crop to sow for the next season are essentially free. Saving seeds avoids chemical treatments that are commonly applied to commercially produced seeds, and it helps ensure that favorite cultivars can be part of your garden each year, even if they disappear from the pages of every seed catalog.

You can save seeds from individual plants with desirable traits such as earliness, disease resistance, high yield, or flower color. By carefully selecting exceptional plants each year and saving their seed, you can develop strains that are uniquely suited to your growing conditions. Seed saving also is an important way to perpetuate heirloom varieties that are in danger of becoming extinct.

Not every plant in the garden can be perpetuated by saving seeds. Some do not bear seeds readily; others are hybrids that yield seeds that are not genetic equals to the parent plant. And seeds gathered from fruit tree or berry cultivars rarely grow into plants that produce high-quality fruit. But many common vegetables, flowers, and herbs, like lettuce, tomatoes, hollyhocks, marigolds, basil, and dill, are good candidates for home seed saving.

Plant Parenthood and Pollination

To decide whether a particular plant would be a good "parent" for future generations, start by identifying its life cycle: Is it annual, biennial, or perennial? Annual and perennial crops generally are easy to save seeds from. Saving seeds of biennials can be trickier.

Next, find out whether the plant is stable, meaning its seedlings will be similar to the parent plant, or if it is a hybrid. Seeds from hybrid plants produce seedlings that are quite different from each other—and in most cases, not as good as the parent. For saving seeds, stick with stable cultivars and avoid hybrids.

Finally, it's important to know if the plant can pollinate itself or if it needs a partner. This helps guide the arrangement of crops in the garden. Different cultivars of self-pollinated crops can be close together and their seedlings will still look like the parent plant. But cross-pollinated crops need to be separated by space or barriers to avoid seeds that contain an unwanted genetic jumble.

HOW LIFE CYCLES AFFECT SEED SAVING

Annuals generally are the easiest plants to save seeds from. They are predisposed to produce lots of seeds to ensure the survival of the species. Just plant the crop, let it go to flower, and then collect the seeds.

Many perennials also are simple to gather seeds from. Growing perennial crops from seeds often is a long-term prospect, though, since it can take a few years for a seedling to grow to flowering or fruiting size. Some named cultivars don't "come true" (don't resemble the parent plant) from seed. And a few, like French tarragon, rarely set seed. These plants must be reproduced by asexual methods, such as divisions or cuttings.

Biennials can be the most difficult plants to collect seeds from. Some biennials, such as parsnips, carrots, and beets, overwinter well in the garden if covered with a thick layer of mulch. In cold climates, though, getting biennials to produce seeds requires digging them up and storing them packed in leaves or sand in a cool root cellar over the winter, then replanting them in the garden in spring so they can flower and set seed.

POLLINATION PATTERNS

Understanding how each crop is pollinated and how pollination shapes the next generation of plants is central to choosing which seeds to save from year to year and which to buy each season. Most commercial seeds are from stable, open-pollinated crops. This means they consistently produce plants that are very similar. First-generation (F1) hybrids are not stabilized. Seeds collected from F1 plants will produce seedlings that are unlike the parents.

Seed catalogs or packets usually identify hybrid seeds. Look for the symbol F1 following the cultivar name or in the description. If there's no mention of the word *hybrid,* a cultivar most likely is open pollinated. Most heirloom crops are open pollinated.

To get reliable results from saved seeds year after year, stick with collecting from open-pollinated plants. There's no harm in experimenting by sowing seeds collected from hybrids if there's space in the garden. The resulting plants likely will be duds, or at least not as good as the plant the seeds came from. But seeds collected from hybrids occasionally produce seedlings that have desirable traits such as bigger fruits or earlier ripening. By saving seeds from the best of any crop, you can try to preserve or improve on positive genetic combinations.

Self-pollinated crops. All self-pollinated crops have perfect flowers (possessing both female and male parts). Each flower can be fertilized by pollen from itself or from another flower on the same plant. Since the mother plant usually fertilizes itself, its genetic material basically remains the same year

116   STARTING SEEDS, TENDING TRANSPLANTS

after year. The resulting seeds, therefore, will produce plants that look just like the parent.

This means it's reasonably safe to plant bush beans, for example, close to snow peas without having to worry that the seeds saved from either crop will turn out to be genetic mix-ups of the two crops. Beans, tomatoes, lettuce, endive, barley, oats, and wheat are examples of crops that usually self-pollinate. These are all good candidates for beginning seed savers.

A note of warning: Just because plants are *usually* self-pollinated doesn't mean they are *always* self-pollinated. Sometimes wayward insects can transfer a bit of pollen from one cultivar to another, and the seeds from that flower will be different from all of the other seeds produced by that plant. To be safe, separate rows of the same self-pollinated crops with a row of a different, fairly tall, crop. For example, a row of tomatoes or corn would be good insurance against chance crosses between rows of bush beans and snow peas. To virtually eliminate any chance of crossing for more susceptible plants like beans, separate different cultivars by about 150 feet.

Cross-pollinated crops. Most other garden crops, including broccoli, cucumbers, and peppers (to name a few), are cross-pollinated. Cross-pollinated plants can have either perfect or imperfect flowers. Unlike self-pollinators, though, the flowers of cross-pollinators can be fertilized by pollen from a different plant in the same species or genus. The resulting seeds contain genetic material from each of the parent plants. Depending on the pollen source, the seedlings may look quite different from the plant that produced the seeds.

To collect seeds that come true from a cross-pollinated plant, you must ensure that no pollen from a different cultivar can reach its flowers. The easiest way to avoid mongrel seeds is to grow only one cultivar of each crop and to make sure that your garden is several hundred feet away from any neighboring gardens. Keep at least 200 feet of space between different cultivars of the same crop.

Squash, cucumbers, and melons need a half-mile or more between crops of the same species. For home gardeners, a more practical approach is to grow a few plants of the desired cultivar under row cover or insect-proof screens and pollinate them by hand. Or cover the flowers you plan to save seeds from with bags before they open, and dust them with pollen from another flower from the same cultivar. This technique also works well for wind-pollinated crops like corn; just slip a bag over the ear to protect the silks from wayward pollen.

Start Saving Seeds

Good candidates for initial seed-saving ventures are self-pollinated annuals such as beans, lettuce, peas, and tomatoes. With experience, consider trying more challenging crops, like squash and melons.

When selecting plants to save seed from, choose those that are vigorous,

Heirlooms: Seeds from the Past

Old-time varieties of vegetables that come true from seed often are described as heirloom plants. That means that they're open pollinated, so their seeds can be saved from one season to plant in the following year's garden. In addition to wonderful heirloom vegetables, most cottage-garden flowers and herbs fall in this category, too. Of course, even the hybrids that replaced many open-pollinated plants in commerce now boast some old "heirloom" cultivars of their own. But usually, "open pollinated" continues to be the hallmark of herbaceous heirloom plants.

Some famous heirlooms have been sold and passed down in families or communities for hundreds of years; others date just to the early 1900s. What they all have in common is that backyard gardeners have prized them for their beauty, flavor, fragrance, or productivity. Because home gardeners thought highly enough of these plants to save seed from them year after year, we can still enjoy them today.

CHARACTERISTICS. Heirlooms are often ideal for home gardeners. Many heirloom crops have a more pleasing flavor or texture than their hybrid replacements, and many spread their harvest over a longer period so families can enjoy picking just what they need for each day's meals rather than having to harvest a bumper crop all at once. If grown for years in one locality, the heirlooms have adapted to the climate and soil conditions of that area and may outproduce modern cultivars. Others may be less productive than today's hybrids but offer greater disease and insect resistance, which is invaluable to organic gardeners. (On the other hand, some heirlooms are less resistant than hybrids bred specifically to resist particular diseases.) Heirloom plants also add interest to garden and table, with a wide range of shapes, colors, and flavors unavailable in modern cultivars.

disease free, and outstanding in qualities you wish to encourage, such as the earliest fruit or the best cold or heat tolerance. Mark chosen plants with a stake or colored string so you won't forget and harvest them for other purposes by mistake. Selecting for special characteristics is a form of plant breeding. By propagating only the best plants each year, you'll gradually develop crop strains that are uniquely adapted to your garden.

GENETIC DIVERSITY. As fewer seed companies remain in existence and those that survive offer a dwindling number of cultivars, there's an even more vital reason for growing old cultivars: These open-pollinated heirloom plants represent a vast and diverse pool of genetic characteristics—one that will be lost forever if these plants are allowed to become extinct. Even cultivars that seem inferior to us today may carry a gene that will prove invaluable in the future. One may contain a valuable but yet undiscovered substance that could be used in medicine. Another could have the disease resistance vital to future generations of gardeners and plant breeders.

The federal government maintains the National Seed Storage Laboratory in Fort Collins, Colorado, as part of its commitment to maintaining genetic diversity, but the task of preserving seed is vast. Heirloom gardeners recognize the importance of maintaining genetic diversity, and many feel a real sense of urgency and importance about their own preservation work. Thanks to them, to seed companies that remain committed to offering open-pollinated heirlooms to the public, and to organizations like Seed Savers Exchange that are dedicated to maintaining diversity in the garden, the future of heirloom plants looks bright.

GETTING STARTED. To start growing heirloom plants in your garden, try ordering seed from small specialty seed suppliers that carry old cultivars. You'll find several seed companies that specialize in heirloom varieties listed in the Organic Gardener's Resource Guide, beginning on page 306. Contact nonprofit organizations that work with individuals to preserve heirloom plants, such as the Seed Savers Exchange (seedsavers .org). Some gardening publications also have a seed swap column.

HARVESTING SEEDS

Seeds are everywhere in the garden—at the tops of lanky radish flower stalks, in the berries decorating ferny asparagus plants, and below the fading petals of marigold blossoms. The edible parts of peas, corn, and beans are the seeds, and the fruits most of us think of as vegetables—cucumbers, eggplant, melons, peppers, squash, and tomatoes—hold seeds within their interiors.

Seeds that are borne in loose clusters are the fastest and easiest to harvest. Keep an eye on the plants until a few of the seeds begin to drop; then collect whole seed heads or clusters. If seeds are ripening unevenly, cover them with paper bags fastened with ties to trap seeds that fall early.

Seeds borne in pods, like beans and peas, take a bit more work to harvest and clean. Leave pods on the plants until they are overripe, but pull up the plants before the pods open. Let the plants dry out, then pick off the pods and shell them or thresh them by putting them in a pillowcase and beating the pillowcase with a stick. Clean away the chaff by pouring the seeds from one container to another in a light breeze.

To save corn seeds, leave a few ears unpicked until the husks begin to get brown. Pick and open them, but leave the husks attached. Use the husks to hang the corn in a warm, dry place. Shell the ears after the kernels turn hard and separate easily from the cob.

Allow fleshy fruits like squash and cucumbers to get a little overripe on the plant before harvesting them, but don't let them start to rot. Separate the seeds from the flesh and wash them clean in water. Tomato seeds are covered with a thick, jellylike coating. Pick the best ripe fruits to save for seeds. Cut open each fruit and squeeze out the seeds and juice into a jar. Add some water—about half as much as the amount of tomato juice—and stir this mixture twice a day for 3 days. A thick layer of white or gray mold will form on top of the liquid. Add more water and stir vigorously. Pour off the mold and any floating debris and seeds; the good seeds will sink. Add more water and repeat the process until only clean seeds are left. Pour off the liquid and any remaining pulp and dry the seeds.

DRYING SEEDS

Drying seeds is a snap. An excellent way to dry large seeds, like peas and beans, is to spread them on a fine-mesh wire screen. Support the screen a few inches

Know Before You Sow

Don't throw away those half-full seed packets. Many seeds stay viable for several years if stored in a cool, dry place. If you're unsure about the age or viability of saved seeds from seasons past, conduct a simple test to see if you should plant them or pitch them.

Before planting, spread 10 seeds from each packet on a wet paper towel, fold it, and then place it in a plastic bag, seal, and label it. Allow it to remain at room temperature for a week or more. If all 10 seeds sprout, you're definitely in business. If six or seven sprout, you can still use them—just sow more thickly to allow for duds.

The life expectancy for most vegetable seeds ranges from only 1 year to up to 6 years.

Beans: 3 years	Corn: 2 years	Peppers: 2 years
Beets: 4 years	Cucumbers: 5 years	Radishes: 5 years
Broccoli: 3 years	Eggplant: 4 years	Spinach: 3 years
Cabbages: 4 years	Lettuces: 6 years	Squash: 4 years
Carrots: 3 years	Onions: 1 year	
Cauliflower: 4 years	Peas: 3 years	

above a table or lay it over sawhorses so air can circulate beneath it. Spread fine seeds on newspaper or paper towels and let them air-dry for about a week. Write seed names on the newspaper so you don't get them confused. One to 2 weeks in a warm, airy place usually is enough to dry most seeds. Once seeds are dry, brush away or screen out any debris.

STORING SEEDS

In 2005, scientists in Israel germinated a date palm seed that was nearly 2,000 years old when archaeologists found it in the desert near the ancient fortress of Masada. Even though most gardeners are not considering planting seeds that date to the time of Jesus, there's a lesson to be learned from this feat: Store seeds in a dry place.

In storage, a seed's worst enemies are heat, humidity, sunlight, and hungry rodents. Here's the proper way to preserve viability.

- *Start with dry seeds.* Make sure harvested seeds are totally dry before storing (see "Drying Seeds," above). If they're not, they can develop mold, which will make them unusable. Purchased seeds are already dry and should be kept that way until planting time.

- *Pack 'em up.* Put collected seeds into envelopes, seal them, and clearly mark the envelopes with variety names and dates.

- *Leave purchased seeds in the packets they came in, taped shut.* Place the envelopes into a plastic zipper bag, a glass jar, a plastic storage container, or some other resealable container—anything that will seal out humidity and keep the seeds safe from rodents. Don't use cloth, paper, or thin plastic bags that cannot be made airtight. Place some dry milk powder or a desiccant such as silica gel at the bottom of the container as added protection from dampness.

- *Keep them cool, dry, and dark.* A dark basement corner—or any cool, dry room—is a good place for storing seeds. With some exceptions (such as aquatic and tropical plants), seeds remain viable longer if stored at constant temperatures of 40°F or lower, making a refrigerator a better choice for long-term storage. To prevent moisture from condensing on seed packets that have been refrigerated, allow the storage container to warm to room temperature before opening it.

EASY-GROWING PLANTS FOR EVERY GARDEN

The best crop of a garden, year after year, is hope.

—ROBERT RODALE, *ORGANIC GARDENING*, 1987

The rewards of growing your own vegetables, herbs, and flowers are many. From savoring the flavor of a freshly picked tomato or seasoning your sauce with homegrown basil to gathering bouquets of bright flowers or relaxing in a landscape enhanced by long-blooming perennials, your gardening efforts can produce nourishment for both body and spirit.

In this chapter, you'll find descriptions and complete how-to-grow guidance for dozens of plants to get you started on the path to gardening success. Planting-to-harvesting information for 30 vegetable garden crops tells you when to plant, whether to grow from seeds or transplants, how to plant, any special care or conditions needed, and when and how to harvest each crop. Profiles of 10 favorite herbs make it easy to enjoy fresh flavors and fragrances unlike any found in a supermarket spice jar. Tips for getting the most out of 20 easy-to-grow annuals include ways to keep them looking great all season long and which ones to grow from seeds and which to buy as transplants in spring. Adding perennials to your garden can bring color to your landscape year after year. Here you'll find everything you need to know to grow more than 20 popular perennials, with hints on where to plant them in your yard and how to enjoy them season after season.

In addition to the crop- and plant-specific profiles, this chapter includes glossaries of helpful terms to help you navigate seed and plant catalogs like a pro. A table of 10 more perennials (page 228) offers a quick-care guide to some additional garden-worthy plants that often appear in garden centers, and a table of flowering bulbs (page 230) gives you the basics on adding those popular plants to your gardening repertoire.

CHOOSING THE RIGHT CULTIVARS

For the most part, the growing information for the vegetables, herbs, and flowers in the pages ahead refers broadly to each species (or group of species) rather than to the many cultivars of those species. Once you've identified the kinds of plants you want to grow, you'll need to select the varieties and cultivars that have the features you want and that will perform well in your garden.

Flavor, hardiness, disease resistance, plant habit, yield, fruit or flower type, flower and/or foliage color, and days to maturity all are options to consider as you browse seed catalogs and Web sites. For the most productive garden, you'll also want to take planting time into account and how your cultivar choices can help you extend the harvest or the duration of bloom. Here are some factors to keep in mind as you make your selections.

Seasonal Suitability

Many cultivars have been developed to be suited for growing in certain seasons and regions. For example, some lettuce cultivars are ideally suited to early spring. They germinate well in cold soil and grow rapidly while the weather is cool, but they may fail to germinate in warm soil and hot weather may cause them to bolt quickly. If you live where spring temperatures can be quite warm, you may get better results with a cultivar that has been selected for its heat resistance.

Choosing a cultivar that's suited to your region and climate helps ensure healthy plants and good yields. In fact, it's one of the best defenses against pest and disease problems. Seed catalogs that cater to specific regions of the country are a good source of suitably adapted cultivars.

Time to Maturity

Catalog descriptions generally include the approximate number of days it will take a cultivar to be ready for harvest (or to start blooming, in the case of flowers). This figure can vary depending on the date of planting and growing conditions, but it is useful in planning for a steady supply of vegetables from the garden or a continuous display of blooms in the flowerbeds.

Full-Size or Fun-Size?

Plant breeding programs have produced compact cultivars that are more in scale with small-space gardens. From "bush-type" beans, cucumbers, peas, and squash to determinate "patio" tomatoes, these scaled-down crops may lend themselves to container culture or save you the trouble of putting up a trellis.

Compact cultivars make it possible to grow vegetables that otherwise might be passed over for lack of space. Many mature earlier than their full-size counterparts, although smaller plants typically produce smaller yields overall.

Maximize a Mini Garden

In addition to choosing compact cultivars, here are a few other strategies for getting the most out of a small garden space:

- Plant vertical crops that grow up rather than out. Use trellises for peas, pole beans, and cucumbers.

- Interplant quick-growing salad crops such as lettuce, radishes, spinach, and beets in 2-foot-square blocks. Make additional plantings every 2 weeks in early spring and early fall to keep the salads coming.

- Avoid overplanting any single vegetable, especially rampant producers like summer squash. Two plants each of zucchini and yellow-neck summer squash will yield plenty for most households.

- Try out unusual vegetables like kohlrabi and bok choy that are naturally compact.

- Choose medium- and small-fruited cultivars of tomatoes, peppers, and eggplant. The smaller the fruits, the more the plants tend to produce.

- Maintain permanent clumps or plants of perennial vegetables such as hardy scallions, and perennial herbs like chives, sage, and thyme. Even a small garden should always have something to offer.

PLANT PARTS

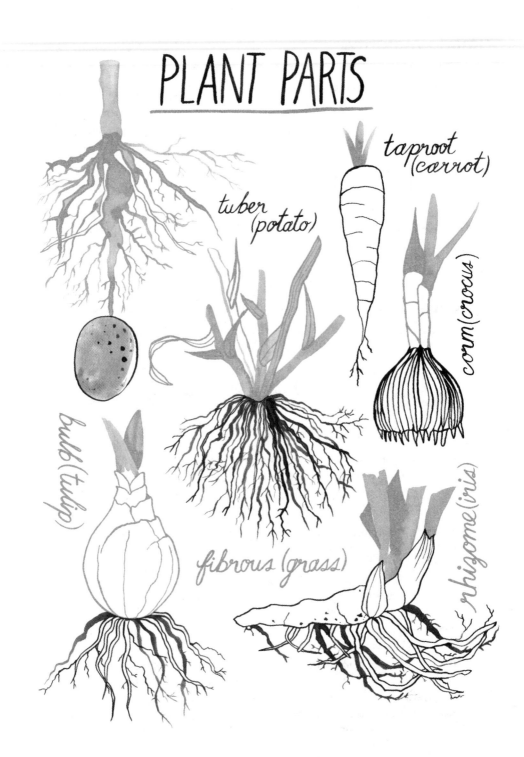

taproot (carrot)

tuber (potato)

corm (crocus)

bulb (tulip)

fibrous (grass)

rhizome (iris)

talk the talk
Plant Parts and Processes

BOLTING: Producing a flowerstalk, blooming, and developing seeds; also termed "going to seed." For many garden crops, bolting marks the end of their productivity, as their energies go into seed production and their leaves (or roots) become bitter and tough. Some plants bolt in response to hot or cold temperatures or to drought. Lettuce, for example, will bolt when the weather gets too hot.

BULB: A plant storage structure, usually underground, that consists of layers of fleshy scales (modified leaves). The term *bulb* is also used to describe a diverse group of perennial plants including those that grow from true bulbs and bulblike structures including corms, rhizomes, and tuberous roots.

CORM: A rounded, swollen stem covered with a papery tunic. Unlike true bulbs, corms are solid, with a bud on top that produces leaves and flowers.

CROWN: The part of a plant where the stem meets the roots, usually at or just below the soil line. Also, a 1- or 2-year-old root of asparagus sold for planting.

RHIZOME: A horizontal underground stem modified and often enlarged for food storage.

SELF-SOWING: When plants drop seeds that germinate and grow—either right away or in the subsequent growing season—where they land. Gardeners often refer to the resulting seedlings as "volunteers." Depending on where they are, how many there are, and their quality, self-sown seedlings may be a happy surprise (an early crop of arugula in spring from last summer's plants) or a weedy nuisance (seedlings produced by hybrid flowers that are inferior to the parent plants in color and form but extremely prolific).

SUCCULENT: Having thick, fleshy, water-holding leaves or stems.

TAPROOT: A central, often thickened, plant root that grows deeply into the soil—as opposed to fibrous roots, which typically are fine textured and branching.

TUBER: An enlarged area of an underground stem that includes eyes, or dormant buds, from which new plants can grow.

The variety of forms seen in plants' aboveground parts—from tiny creeping thymes to towering oaks, for example—is similarly represented in their roots. Some are fine textured and threadlike, while others are thickened into stubby rounded shapes where plants store moisture and nutrients. Many garden crops and flowers, such as potatoes, garlic, onions, tulips, crocuses, and daylilies, are commonly grown from specialized root structures instead of from seeds.

30 VEGETABLES ANY GARDENER CAN GROW

Although the crops in a vegetable garden are a diverse group, representing many plant families, they share broad general requirements. Most will thrive in a sunny garden that has moist but well-drained soil (able to retain moisture long enough for plant roots to absorb what they need, but allowing excess moisture to drain off easily) with a pH of 6.5 to 7.0 and average fertility (neither deficient in the nutrients plants need to grow nor overly rich with them). Some crops can tolerate frost; while others need hot days and warm nights to reach peak productivity. A garden site that receives full sun is optimal for most vegetables, but some crops—especially those that prefer cool temperatures—can grow well in light or partial shade. If you pick an appropriate site, prepare the soil well, and keep your growing crops weeded and watered, you should have little trouble growing vegetables successfully.

The 30 vegetables profiled in this chapter are popular, easy-to-grow choices. Use the information for each crop to guide you through planting, growing, and harvesting your favorites.

Six Speedy Vegetables

While gardening tends to be a patient process that can't be hurried, some vegetables reach harvest size more rapidly than others. Besides getting you to salads sooner, quick crops are good choices for inclusion in a children's garden, serving up some positive reinforcement along the way to ripe tomatoes and lessons on the rewards of patience. Here are six crops to plant if you have both the urge to garden and a need for speed:

1. **Arugula: 21 days for baby leaves**
2. **'Cherry Belle' radish: 22 days for $3/4$- to 1-inch-round red roots**
3. **'Black Seeded Simpson' lettuce: 28 days from seed to salad**
4. **Spinach: 35-40 days for baby leaves**
5. **'Contender' bush beans: 49 days for stringless, 6- to 8-inch pods**
6. **'Sugar Ann' snap peas: 56 days to sweet, edible $2^1/_2$-inch pods**

Arugula

Easy to grow and quick to harvest, arugula adds a distinctive, nutty, aromatic note to salads. Also called salad rocket or roquette, arugula grows easily from seed and may be planted in window boxes or containers as well as in a garden bed. Garden centers and nurseries sometimes offer starter plants of arugula.

Soil: Any well-drained soil of average fertility.

Temperature: Grows best in cool weather. Arugula bolts (flowers and goes to seed) in hot weather, and its flavor becomes spicier. The leaves, stems, and flowers are edible.

Time to harvest: Leaves are fully grown in 40 to 50 days but may be picked while smaller for baby greens.

How to plant: Plant in early spring when the soil temperature is about 60°F. Arugula grows best in full sun, as long as temperatures are cool. In hot weather, provide afternoon shade or grow arugula where it will be partially shaded by taller crops. Broadcast the seeds over moist soil, scattering them as evenly as you can. Press them gently into the soil surface, then cover with $\frac{1}{4}$ inch of soil. Water with a fine mist from a hose or a watering can with a rose attachment. To enjoy an ongoing harvest of arugula, plant more seeds every 2 to 3 weeks until early summer; then sow again in late summer for a fall crop.

Care: Seeds are tiny, and you may find a crowd of seedlings coming up close together. You'll have to thin the seedlings to spread them out. This takes patience. Use cuticle scissors to snip off stems at ground level to leave the remaining seedlings 6 to 10 inches apart. Water the plants during dry weather. Use floating row cover over arugula to provide light shade and to protect it from pests. Slugs may be a problem in wet weather, particularly if the plants are overcrowded. Use ground-level traps filled with beer to catch these slimy pests.

How to harvest: Pick individual stems by pinching them off with your fingers, or use a sharp knife to cut off whole plants at ground level.

Tips for success: If you love arugula and want to have it in your garden next year, allow some of your plants to flower and produce their own seeds. When the plants die back and dry out in fall (or sooner, depending on when you planted them), the seeds will fall to the ground and self-sow to give you a head start on next spring's garden.

Asparagus

Asparagus is a long-lived perennial that bears feathery foliage resembling the asparagus fern houseplant, to which it is related. The edible part of asparagus is the growing tip that pushes up through the ground in spring. Asparagus is one of the garden's great rewards, but it takes care and patience.

Soil: Well-drained, sandy loam is ideal, but asparagus adapts to a range of soils as long as the drainage is good. Prepare the soil by removing all weeds, along with their roots, and digging in plenty of compost or composted manure.

asparagus crown

Temperature: Survives cold winter temperatures in USDA Zones 2 to 9 to re-emerge the following spring.

Time to harvest: Begin harvesting after two or three seasons of growth to allow the plant time to produce edible spears.

How to plant: You can grow asparagus from seed, and you'll have a bigger choice of varieties that way, but it's easier to buy crowns (1- or 2-year-old asparagus roots) at a local nursery or from an online garden supplier. Plant crowns 2 to 4 weeks before the average date of the last spring frost in your area.

Asparagus needs a permanent bed so you can plant it once and then let it grow. The traditional way to make an asparagus bed is to dig a trench 12 to 15 inches wide and about 18 inches deep. Put a couple of inches of compost in the bottom and work it in with a garden fork or spading fork. Sprinkle some bone meal and potassium fertilizer, such as greensand or kelp meal, into the bottom of the trench. Make a mound of soil (or compost) every 24 inches along the bottom of the trench. Set one crown atop each mound so the eyes (small bumps that are dormant buds) are facing upward, and fan out the roots over the mound. Cover the crowns with 2 inches of soil.

As the plants sprout and grow, add more soil to the trench, 1 to 2 inches at a time, until the top of the trench reaches ground level, which should happen around the middle of the growing season.

Care: Water deeply during prolonged dry spells. Keep the bed weeded. Apply 6 to 8 inches of compost or composted manure in fall. Leave foliage in place over winter.

How to harvest: Harvest spears when 8 to 10 inches tall and less than 1 inch around, while the tip is still tightly closed. To avoid injuring the crowns, break off the stem at ground level rather than cutting it.

Tips for success: Because an asparagus bed can be in place for 20 or more years, take the time to prepare the soil well before planting the crowns.

Beans

Versatile in the kitchen and easy to grow, beans belong in every garden. Try an heirloom variety or two for especially great flavor. Grow snap, or string, beans for their long, slender pods and pick them before the seeds inside mature. Other varieties are grown for the plump seeds that grow inside the pods. Some of these shell beans, such as limas, are eaten fresh, while black beans, pinto beans, navy beans, and others may be dried for long-term storage.

Beans grow on two types of plants: bush and pole. Bush beans grow on short plants that are usually self-supporting. Tall, vining pole beans need to climb a trellis, tepee, or other vertical support. Bush beans remain productive for about 3 weeks in summer. You can keep picking pole beans until the first frost.

Soil: Beans need a sunny, well-drained area rich in organic matter. Lighten heavy soils with extra compost to help seedlings emerge.

Temperature: In general, beans are very sensitive to frost. (The exception is fava beans, which require a long, cool growing season.) Pole beans, and especially limas, are most sensitive to cold. Most types grow best when air temperatures are 70° to 80°F; the soil temperature should be at least 60°F at planting. Seeds tend to rot in soggy, cold soil.

Time to harvest: 48 to 60 days for bush beans; 62 to 68 for pole beans; 75 to 100 days for dry beans.

How to plant: Grow your beans from seed; they don't transplant well. Don't plant a first crop of bush beans until a week or two after the date of the last expected spring frost. Pole beans require only one planting at the beginning of the season. They take longer to mature than bush beans but produce about three times the yield in the same amount of garden space.

Plant seeds directly in the garden, 1 inch deep in heavy clay soil or 1½ inches deep in light-textured soil. Drop each seed into its hole and firm the ground over it to ensure soil contact. Plant most bush beans 3 to 6 inches apart in rows 2 to 2½ feet apart. They produce the bulk of their crop over a 2-week period. For a continuous harvest, sow bush beans every 2 weeks until about 2 months before you expect the first killing fall frost. Bush beans germinate in about 7 days, pole beans in about 14. Plant pole beans 2 inches deep and 10 inches apart in rows 3 to 4 feet apart.

Care: Water as needed to maintain even soil moisture during germination and also when the plants are about to bloom. If the soil dries out at these times, the harvest may be significantly reduced. Water deeply at least once a week when there is no rain, being careful not to hose off any of the blossoms on bush beans.

Apply several inches of mulch (after seedlings emerge) to conserve moisture, reduce weeds, and keep the soil cool during hot spells (high temperatures can cause blossoms to drop off).

Provide a trellis or other support for pole beans when you plant them, or as soon as the first two leaves of the seedlings open. Planting pole beans around a tepee support is a fun project to try with children, but it will be more difficult to harvest the beans than from a simple vertical trellis.

How to harvest: Pick snap beans as soon as the pods are large enough to make picking worthwhile but before seeds have begun to fill out the pods. Keep picking to prolong the harvest. Pole beans will produce all summer if kept picked. Harvest green shell beans when the seeds have reached full size but before the pods begin to deteriorate.

Pull up entire plants of dry beans when about 90 percent of the leaves have dropped and the pods are dry. Finish drying them under cover (where rain cannot touch them). Shell the beans when they are completely dry. Store dried beans in airtight containers in cool, dry conditions for up to a year. Tuck a small envelope of powdered milk into each container of beans to absorb moisture.

Tips for success: Bean seeds usually show about 70 percent germination, and the seeds can remain viable (able to sprout) for 3 years. Don't soak or presprout the seeds before sowing. If planting in an area where beans haven't grown before, help ensure that the bean crop will fix nitrogen in the soil by dusting seeds with a bacterial inoculant powder for beans and peas (available from garden centers and seed suppliers).

Beets

Delicious beets are among the easiest vegetables to grow. Both the roots and leaves are tasty. In addition to the familiar deep red, round roots, seed catalogs offer beet varieties with purple, gold, white, or bicolored roots, in oval or cylindrical shapes. Choose a variety that produces small, rounded roots if pickling whole beets is your goal. For a sweet treat, drizzle a panful of beets with olive oil and roast them in the oven until soft.

Soil: Beets grow best in a sunny site in soil that is loose textured, well drained, and free of rocks.

Temperature: Beets are adapted to grow in cool weather, making them a perfect vegetable to plant both in spring and late summer. Where summers are extremely hot, plant beets as an early spring, fall, or winter crop. They grow best in temperatures averaging 60° to 65°F. Beets can tolerate cold and some frost but not a hard freeze.

Time to harvest: 50 to 70 days.

How to plant: Plant beets in the garden a month before the last spring frost date. Plant seeds ½ inch deep and 2 inches apart in rows 1 foot apart. For a fall crop, sow seeds about 4 to 7 weeks before the average date of the first fall frost in your area.

Care: Beet seeds are compound: Each seed is actually a small fruit that contains up to eight seeds. When seedlings come up, you will need to thin the clusters of seedlings, removing or snipping off excess seedlings with nail scissors to space out the remaining seedlings to 2 inches apart. You can eat the thinnings in salads if they are big enough. When the plants are 2 to 3 inches tall, thin them again to leave the remaining plants 4 to 6 inches apart. Weed around beets by hand; a hoe may damage the roots and cause them to "bleed." Water as needed to keep the soil evenly moist. Beets that are thinned properly and weeded and watered regularly are usually pest and disease free.

How to harvest: Dig the roots before the first expected fall frost.

Tips for success: A steady supply of moisture promotes rapid growth, which helps ensure flavorful beets. Lack of water during warm weather causes beets to bolt and the roots to crack or become tough and stringy. Be sure to water your beets when the weather is dry.

Broccoli

Supernutritious broccoli is packed with vitamins A and C and contains B vitamins, calcium, and iron, too. Kids who don't want to eat cooked broccoli often like it raw with a dip.

Soil: Broccoli needs a soil rich in nitrogen. Dig 3 to 4 inches of composted manure into the soil 2 weeks before planting.

Temperature: Broccoli likes cool, moist conditions. It grows best when temperatures average between 40° and 65°F. Mature plants can tolerate light frost, but seedlings may be damaged. Protect young plants from extreme temperature swings in early spring with cloches or row covers.

Time to harvest: 55 to 78 days.

How to plant: The easiest way to grow broccoli is to buy transplants from a local nursery, although it's not difficult to grow from seed. Sow seeds for a spring crop indoors 7 to 9 weeks before the last expected spring frost; they should germinate in 4 to 5 days. After germination, place pots or flats in a sunny area and maintain the temperature at 60° to 65°F. Keep the growing medium moist but not wet. The best size for transplanting is when seedlings are 6 inches tall and have two to four leaves. When planting seedlings in the garden, set them an inch or two deeper than they were growing in their cell packs or flats. Space the plants 1 to 2 feet apart in rows 2 to 3 feet apart. Firm the soil around them, and water well.

For fall crops, start seedlings indoors or sow seeds directly in the ground in midsummer. In mild-winter climates, plant in late fall for a spring harvest.

Care: Keep the soil moist (dry soil will make the stems tough), and water deeply to soak the soil during dry weather. Make sure the plants' roots stay cool by applying 4 to 6 inches of mulch. Keep the broccoli area weeded.

How to harvest: Cut broccoli heads before the tiny flowers begin to turn yellow. Don't just cut off the main head and throw away the plant. Cut the main head just below the point where the stems separate. Cut the stem close to the base of the head to stimulate the growth of smaller side shoots, which you can harvest. Any heads bearing yellow flowers are past their peak.

Tips for success: The secret of growing broccoli is to keep it growing steadily, which happens with nutrient-rich soil, plenty of water, and cool temperatures. Feed broccoli once a month with fish emulsion (follow the label directions) or side-dress with bloodmeal or fish/seaweed fertilizer, and water deeply.

Brussels Sprouts

Brussels sprouts look like tiny cabbages growing along a thick, tall stalk. They grow best in cool weather. Depending on where you live, it is often better to plant them in summer for a fall harvest. Because many nurseries have seedlings available only in spring, you may have to grow your own plants from seed.

Soil: Rich, well-drained soil with lots of organic matter to hold moisture. They prefer heavier clay soil over light, sandy soil. Amend the soil with phosphorus and potassium sources such as phosphate rock and greensand or kelp meal.

Temperature: Brussels sprouts need cool weather; they grow best when temperatures average 60° to 65°F.

Time to harvest: 110 to 130 days.

How to plant: If you buy transplants in spring, get them into the garden as early as you can, even before the last frost. Space the plants 2 feet apart, and plant deep enough so the lowest leaves are just above the soil. Firm the soil around the base of each plant and water well. Or plant seeds directly in the garden in midsummer (later in warmer climates). Plant seeds $1/2$ inch deep and 2 inches apart in moist soil. When the plants are about 6 inches tall, thin them to 2 feet apart.

Care: Feed once or twice a month with a fish/seaweed fertilizer (follow the label directions). Brussels sprouts plants have shallow roots. If it's windy where you live, stake the plants to keep the wind from blowing them over and uprooting them. Spread a layer of shredded leaves, grass clippings, or another organic mulch over their growing area to help conserve soil moisture and keep their roots cooler. As the sprouts develop, remove the leaves that grow below each sprout when they turn yellow, to give the sprouts more room to grow.

How to harvest: Pick the sprouts by twisting them off or cutting them off with a knife while they're small. Small sprouts are the most tender and mild flavored. The sprouts mature from the bottom of the stalk upward.

Tips for success: Brussels sprouts develop their best flavor in cold weather. Frost sweetens the flavor, so try to leave at least some of them in the garden until after the first few fall frosts.

Cabbage

Cabbage is rich in vitamin C and also contains vitamin A, B vitamins, and calcium. It's versatile in the kitchen, either raw or cooked. Slice or chop it and toss it into vegetable soup, stews, and stir-fries. Cabbage tastes sweetest and best when cooked until just tender-crisp; don't overcook it.

Soil: Cabbage grows best in rich loam soil that is moist but well drained, but it will adapt to sandy soil if there's enough moisture or to clay soil if the drainage is good.

Temperature: Cabbage needs cool weather and short days to thrive. It can tolerate temperatures as low as 20°F. Warm-climate gardeners can grow cabbage in winter.

Time to harvest: 70 to 120 days.

How to plant: Most nurseries sell cabbage seedlings in spring, and many offer them again in late summer to plant for a fall harvest. Plant them in the garden 4 weeks before your last spring frost date. Plant the seedlings slightly deeper than they grew in their cell pack or flat. Space them 6 to 12 inches apart in rows 1 to 2 feet apart.

Cabbage is easy to grow from seed, too. Plant seeds ¼ inch deep and 2 inches apart, in winter in the South or early spring in the North. Place the seedlings in a sunny location indoors, with temperatures between 60° and 70°F. Keep the growing medium evenly moist.

For a fall crop, plant seeds in midsummer, in flats or seed trays or directly in the garden. Space the seedlings 12 inches apart, and try to plant them between taller plants, such as pole beans or corn, that will provide some shade and keep the cabbage plants cooler.

Care: Cabbage needs even moisture throughout its growth. Water as needed to keep the soil moist. Mulch the plants to conserve soil moisture. If the leaves begin to yellow as plants grow, fertilize them with composted manure, blood-meal, or fish emulsion to add nitrogen. Weed around cabbage by hand to avoid damaging shallow roots.

How to harvest: Harvest any time after the heads have formed, while they feel solid. Smaller heads have the sweetest flavor. Remove the coarse outer leaves. Cracked or split heads can result from uneven watering.

Tips for success: There are early, midseason, and late varieties of cabbage. Late varieties, which you plant in midsummer, generally are good for winter storage in a cool, moist place such as a root cellar or refrigerator. Early varieties, which you plant in the garden in spring, can be tricky to grow where the weather turns hot early in summer.

Carrots

Crunchy, sweet, and loaded with vitamin A (plus B vitamins, calcium, and phosphorus), carrots are popular with otherwise picky eaters. They're easy to grow, too, in the garden or in pots. In addition to the classic long, tapered varieties such as 'Imperator', there are round carrots, small baby varieties, and medium-length carrots such as 'Danvers Half Long'.

Soil: Carrots need soil that is loose textured; free of rocks, stones, and soil clods; and not too rich in nitrogen. In rocky soil, carrots' roots grow crooked and forked. Too much nitrogen in the soil can cause hairy roots. Add some rock phosphate and kelp meal or greensand to the soil before planting to boost phosphorus and potassium levels.

Temperature: Plant carrots in cool spring weather.

Time to harvest: 50 to 95 days.

How to plant: Grow your carrots from seed. Start sowing 3 weeks before the last expected spring frost. To harvest all summer and into fall, sow more seeds every 2 to 3 weeks. Most carrots take 70 to 80 days to mature, so plant the last batch of seeds 2 to 3 months before the first expected fall frost. In USDA Zone 8 and warmer, plant carrots in fall or winter.

Scatter the tiny seeds over a prepared soil bed or, for easier weeding, plant in rows. Put a pinch of about six seeds to the inch. They will take 1 to 3 weeks to sprout (they germinate more slowly in cold soil than in warm), so mix in a few quick-growing radish seeds to mark the rows. Cover with ¼ or ½ inch of fine-textured (i.e., sifted) compost, potting mix, or sand—plus a little more in warm, dry areas—to make it easier for the delicate seedlings to emerge. Water gently to avoid washing seeds away, and keep the soil continuously moist for best germination. Thin seedlings (by pulling up or snipping off some to leave space between the rest) to 1 inch apart when the tops are 2 inches high. Be thorough, because crowded carrots will produce crooked roots. Thin again 2 weeks later, to leave the seedlings 3 to 4 inches apart.

Care: Keep the carrot area free of weeds, especially when the plants are small and may be overrun by vigorous weeds. Water as needed to keep the soil evenly moist but not soggy. Very wet soil can cause carrot roots to split. If the top of the root (called its shoulder) becomes exposed above the soil, cover it with soil to keep it from turning green.

How to harvest: Harvest carrots when they are big enough to use. Pull a few to check their size. Loosen the soil with a digging fork, then gently pull them out of the ground. If the soil is dry, water before harvesting to make pulling easier. Brush off excess soil and twist off the tops. Carrots will keep in a plastic bag in the refrigerator for up to 3 months.

Tips for success: Thinning is important for carrots, so don't neglect to do it. If the plants appear crowded as the season progresses, thin them a second time to make sure the roots have enough space. Use the thinnings as baby carrots if they're big enough.

Chard

Chard (aka Swiss chard, or leaf beet) is closely related to beets. Unlike beets, though, chard is grown for its big, mild-flavored leaves. It holds up better in hot weather than spinach and can be used in similar ways, although it's not really a substitute for spinach. Like spinach, chard grows well in cooler temperatures, too.

Soil: Well drained, fertile, and rich in organic matter. Dig compost or composted manure into the soil before planting.

Temperature: Prefers cool weather and can withstand some frost, but also tolerates warm temperatures.

Time to harvest: 50 to 65 days.

How to plant: Sow seeds directly in the garden 1 to 2 weeks before the average date of the last spring frost in your area. Plant the seeds $\frac{1}{2}$ to 1 inch deep. Seeds germinate in a week or two. Thin seedlings (or space transplants) 6 to 8 inches apart.

Care: Chard grows best when the soil around the roots stays moist (not soggy). If you live where summers are hot and dry, or your soil drains quickly, mulch the plants to keep them from flowering and forming seeds.

How to harvest: Begin harvesting as soon as the leaves are big enough to eat, usually starting about 40 days after planting seeds. Harvest leaves from the outside of the clump, breaking off the stems at the base or cutting them with a sharp knife.

Tips for success: If your soil is poor and low in nutrients, give chard a mid-season feeding of fish emulsion or other high-nitrogen fertilizer.

Chinese Cabbage

Chinese cabbage is a catchall name for several plants that take a variety of forms but share similar growing conditions and versatility in Asian dishes. They generally are ready to harvest sooner than other kinds of cabbage, and they are at their best in late fall when cold weather sweetens their flavor.

Soil: Grows best in rich, fertile soil but will also grow in average soil, although the plants may be smaller and grow more slowly. To improve soil quickly, dig 3 to 4 inches of compost or composted manure into the soil before planting.

Temperature: Grows best in temperatures of 60° to 65°F. In northern gardens, grow Chinese cabbage for a fall crop. Where winters are mild, grow it in winter and spring.

Time to harvest: 50 to 70 days.

How to plant: Purchase seedlings at a local nursery or garden center if you find them in midsummer. Or plant seeds directly in the garden from late May to late July (12 weeks before the first expected fall frost) for a fall crop. Spring planting can be tricky; if you plant too early, the plants may bolt if young seedlings are exposed to frost and cold weather. Plant for a fall harvest instead. Sow the seeds 2 inches apart, $\frac{1}{2}$ inch deep, in rows 18 to 24 inches apart.

Care: Thin seedlings when they are 4 weeks old and have four or five true leaves. Use the thinnings in salads. Thin nonheading varieties, such as bok choy, to 9 inches apart. Space heading varieties, such as Napa types, 16 inches apart.

Keep the soil evenly moist; water as needed when there's no rain. Water the soil at the base of the plants rather than sprinkling from overhead. If you applied a summer mulch around the plants, remove it in fall so the sun can warm the soil and help keep plants growing longer. In average to low fertility soil, plants benefit from a midseason application of a nitrogen fertilizer.

How to harvest: Start harvesting as soon as plants are big enough to make it worthwhile. You can pull up the entire plant and cut off the leafy part from the roots. Discard the outer leaves and use the rest.

Tips for success: In general, Chinese cabbage does best when days are short. Timing a spring planting can be perplexing, and for many gardeners planting for a fall harvest works better.

Collards

Staples of Southern cooking, collards can tolerate hotter temperatures than their relatives, kale and cabbage. But collards are cold resistant, too, and will grow in more northerly gardens.

Soil: Collards prefer well-drained, loamy soil but will grow in a variety of soils. They need lots of nutrients as they grow, so dig in plenty of compost or composted manure when you prepare the soil for planting.

Temperature: Although they grow well in hot weather, collards actually prefer cooler conditions and withstand temperatures as low as 20°F. Exposure to light frost mellows the flavor of the leaves.

Time to harvest: 80 days.

How to plant: Plant seeds directly in the garden ¼ inch deep in spring, about 4 weeks before the date of the last expected spring frost in your area. For a fall crop, scatter seeds evenly over a garden bed and cover lightly with soil 8 to 10 weeks before the first expected fall frost. Warm-climate gardeners can plant collards in late summer or early fall to harvest in winter. When the seedlings are several inches tall, thin them to stand 12 inches apart.

Care: Collards are shallow rooted, so weed around them carefully. When the young plants are 6 inches high, side-dress them with composted manure or water with a fish/seaweed fertilizer diluted according to package directions for a nitrogen boost. Repeat liquid fertilizer applications every 3 weeks through the growing season.

If your summers are hot and dry or your soil is sandy and well drained, mulch around collard plants to slow the evaporation of moisture from the soil. Water well during dry weather.

How to harvest: Harvest collards when the leaves are young and tender for milder flavor—any time after about 40 days after planting. You can pick individual leaves or cut off the entire plant at once at the stalk.

Tips for success: To extend the harvest, pick clusters of lower leaves from the stalk before they are full-sized, tough, and woody. This will stimulate the growing bud at the top of the plant to keep producing new leaves. The bare stalk may need to be staked as the season progresses.

Corn

Fresh-from-the-garden sweet corn is one of the great delights of summer. There are many kinds to choose from: yellow, white, or bicolored; extra-sweet or super-sweet; classic varieties such as 'Silver Queen' and heirlooms like 'Country Gentleman', with more of a "corny" flavor; dwarf varieties for small spaces or containers.

Soil: Loose, well-drained soil produces the best yields. If your soil is heavy and contains clay, a late-maturing variety may work best. In light, sandy soil, go for an early variety. Corn uses up a lot of nutrients as it grows, so add plenty of compost or composted manure, rock phosphate, and greensand or kelp meal to the soil before planting.

Temperature: Corn is very sensitive to frost, so don't plant it until all danger of frost is past in spring and the soil has warmed to 60°F. If the weather stays cool, lay some black plastic sheeting on the planting area to warm the soil for a few weeks before you plant.

Time to harvest: 65 to 95 days.

How to plant: Plant corn seeds directly in the garden; seedlings do not take transplanting well. Wait to plant until 2 to 3 weeks after the average date of the last spring frost in your area. Sow seeds 1 inch deep in spring; in midsummer, plant 2 inches deep.

For an extended harvest, plant at least 10 to 15 plants per person, sowing in three batches 2 weeks apart.

For good pollination (which is essential for a successful corn crop), plant corn in blocks rather than rows. A block should be at least three rows wide. Corn germinates at a rate of about 75 percent and takes 7 to 10 days. Plant three seeds together every 7 to 15 inches, and thin any extra seedlings to leave the plants 15 inches apart. To avoid disturbing any roots, cut off the unwanted plants at ground level with scissors rather than pulling them.

Care: For corn ears to develop, adequate moisture (about 1 inch per week) is essential, especially from the time tassels appear until harvest. Water stress during pollination will result in ears with lots of missing kernels, so don't skip watering. Apply water at the soil surface by using a soaker hose or drip irrigation. Avoid spraying plants from above, which can wash pollen off the flowering tops and reduce pollination and kernel formation.

When the young corn plants are 6 inches tall, side-dress them with blood meal or diluted fish-based fertilizer, and repeat the feeding when they are about knee-high. Don't remove any side shoots, or suckers, that form; they won't harm productivity, but cutting them can damage the roots.

How to harvest: When the silks on the ears turn brown (but are still moist), it's a signal that the corn kernels are ripe. To be certain, pull a leaf partway down an ear and press your fingernail into a kernel. If a milky liquid squirts out, the ear is ready to pick. If no liquid spurts out, the corn is past its peak. Twist the cob sharply downward to remove it from the stalk. Have a pot of boiling water ready on the stove for the freshest, most delicious corn you'll ever eat. And don't overcook it!

Tips for success: Stunted or partially filled ears can be caused by a number of factors: disturbance to the roots during cultivation or using a hoe to remove weeds, plants that are spaced too closely together, soil that is too acidic, insufficient moisture or nutrients, heavy rain during pollination, or damage caused by corn earworm.

Cowpea, Black-Eyed Pea, Crowder Pea, Southern Pea

Actually beans, not peas, cowpeas thrive in hot weather and are a popular crop in southern gardens. Black-eyed peas are a type of cowpea that produces seeds that sport characteristic dark "eyes." High in protein, cowpeas are perfect for soup. There are both bush and pole varieties.

Soil: Cowpeas adapt to almost any type of soil, as long as it is well drained. Soggy soil will damage the plants. Soil too rich in nitrogen will promote leafy growth instead of pod formation.

Temperature: Very sensitive to frost, cowpeas grow best where summers are long and hot.

Time to harvest: 60 days for green peas, 75 to 100 days for dried peas.

How to plant: Plant seeds directly in the garden at least 1 week after the date of the last expected spring frost in your area, when the soil has warmed to at least 65°F. Plant seeds 1 inch deep and 2 to 3 inches apart in rows 24 or more inches apart (check the seed packet for spacing for the particular variety you are planting). Apply an inoculant to cowpea seeds at planting to ensure that beneficial rhizobia are present in the soil to help the plants fix nitrogen from the air. Most seed companies sell inoculants that are effective with the legume seeds they offer. See "How to plant" for Peas on page 154 for more about using inoculants.

Care: Once established, the plants tolerate drought and heat quite well. They need no supplemental feeding as they grow and need watering only during prolonged dry spells.

How to harvest: You can pick cowpeas like green snap beans, when the seeds have reached full size but before the pods begin to deteriorate, or as dried beans. For dried cowpeas, pull up entire plants when about 90 percent of the leaves have dropped and the pods are dry. Finish drying them under cover (where rain cannot touch them). Shell the peas when they are completely dry. Store dried cowpeas in airtight containers in cool, dry conditions for up to a year.

Tips for success: Cowpeas can be susceptible to a variety of pests and diseases, so look for resistant varieties.

Cucumber

Crisp, refreshing cucumbers really live up to the description "cool as a cucumber." On a hot summer day in the garden, the flesh inside a cucumber can be 20 degrees cooler than the outside air.

There are two basic types of cucumbers: small pickling types and larger slicing types. Standard cucumber vines sprawl and take up a lot of garden space—as much as 10 feet across. There are also "bush" varieties with more compact vines suited to growing in small gardens or containers.

Soil: Well-drained loam rich in organic matter is ideal for cucumbers, as long as it's kept evenly moist. Dig plenty of compost into the growing area before planting cucumbers.

Temperature: Cucumbers need warmth and sun; they suffer and grow slowly in cool, damp weather. A late spring frost will kill the plants. Temperatures averaging 65° to 85°F suit them just fine.

Time to harvest: 55 to 70 days, but timing varies. You can pick cucumbers as soon as they are big enough to use.

How to plant: Cucumber roots are sensitive to disturbance, so it's best to plant seeds directly in the garden. Plant them after all danger of frost has passed in spring and the soil and air have warmed to at least 60°F. To get an earlier start, you can plant seeds indoors in biodegradable pots made of pressed peat or cow manure that will go into the garden soil along with the plants. Start the seeds indoors 3 to 4 weeks before you expect to move the plants outdoors, which will be about 2 weeks after the date of the last expected frost.

Traditionally, cucumbers have been planted in hills of soil mounded a few inches high. For standard varieties, make hills 4 feet apart in rows 6 feet apart; bush varieties can be planted more closely. To plant in hills, plant six or seven seeds 1 to 2 inches deep and 18 inches apart (or less for bush varieties; follow directions on the seed packet).

To save ground space, plant cucumbers on a trellis; fasten the stems to the support as they grow, using yarn or other soft ties to attach them (don't use wire, which could damage the stems).

Care: Cucumber roots are sensitive, so weed the area by hand. Mulch the soil after the seedlings are up. Water when needed to keep the soil evenly moist, and avoid letting it dry out. Moisture is especially critical when the fruits are developing.

How to harvest: Harvest pickling cucumbers every day—they grow quickly. Pick long slicing cucumbers when you need them in the kitchen, but harvest them before they begin to turn yellow. Gently twist or snip the cucumbers off the vine, being careful not to damage the vine.

Tips for success: If just one cucumber is left on the vine to fully ripen, the plant will stop producing more fruit. Keep them picked.

Eggplant

A relative of tomatoes, peppers, and potatoes, eggplant finds a place in edible landscapes as well as traditional vegetable gardens. With its star-shaped purple flowers and colorful fruits, eggplant is easy on the eyes and versatile in the kitchen.

Soil: Eggplant thrives in well-drained soil of average fertility. Enrich the soil and improve its texture by digging in an inch or more of compost. Eggplant will not grow well in heavy, soggy soil.

Temperature: Eggplant needs warm weather, so buy seedlings from a local nursery or garden center when spring weather has settled and cold snaps are no longer likely. Or plant seeds indoors 6 to 9 weeks before the average date of the last spring frost in your area. Do not move young plants to the garden until both the air and soil have warmed to at least 70°F.

Time to harvest: 115 to 150 days.

How to plant: Eggplant needs room to grow. Space plants 2 to 3 feet apart in the garden, or put each plant in a 12- to 14-inch-diameter container. If you are starting seeds indoors, soak the seeds overnight in room-temperature water to encourage them to sprout. Plant them ¼ inch deep in a loose, fine-textured growing medium such as vermiculite. Set the sown containers on a horticultural heat mat to supply bottom heat to keep the soil temperature at 80° to 90°F until the seeds sprout (which takes about 8 days).

When the seedlings are 3 inches tall, transplant them into individual pots. When outside nighttime temperatures stay above 50°F, begin gradually exposing the seedlings to the outdoors to harden them off (see page 111 in Chapter 4). As needed, transplant seedlings into larger pots while you wait for outdoor air and soil temperatures to reach 70°F, at which time it's safe to move your plants into the garden.

Care: Eggplant needs warm weather and plenty of moisture for best growth. Keep the area weeded, and spread mulch around the plants when they are established in the garden. A month after planting, water the plants with liquid fish/seaweed fertilizer diluted according to the label directions or side-dress them with compost.

How to harvest: Begin harvesting eggplant when the fruits are large enough to eat and the skin is glossy (when the skin turns dull the eggplant is past its prime). Cut the fruit from the plant with a sharp knife or pruning shears; don't pull or twist it off.

Tips for success: Eggplant is very sensitive to cold. Extended periods of temperatures below 50°F will harm them, and the plants will not produce fruit when the temperature drops below 60°F. If cool weather is predicted, cover your eggplants with row covers to protect them.

Garlic

Indispensable in the kitchen, garlic can do double duty in the garden. You can interplant it among other crops to repel insects, then harvest it later to use in your favorite recipes.

There are two kinds of garlic: softneck and hardneck. Hardneck garlic is also called seedstem garlic because in late spring it produces a flower stem that should be removed to get the best yield of bulbs. Hardneck garlic produces large cloves but is more likely to sprout when stored long term. Softneck garlic (the kind usually sold in supermarkets) has a longer shelf life and is a little easier to grow, especially in warmer climates.

Soil: Deep, rich soil in full sun. Although garlic needs good drainage, it also needs ample moisture during the growing season. Soil rich in organic matter will provide those conditions.

Temperature: Garlic needs cool temperatures during its early growth, when its leaves are developing. Later in the season, warm temperatures are beneficial when the bulbs are developing.

Time to harvest: 90 to 100 days.

How to plant: Start garlic from individual cloves. Choose large, healthy, firm cloves to plant. Plant garlic in the garden in fall, around Columbus Day in most of the country, a bit later in the Deep South. Plant cloves 1 to 2 inches deep and 4 to 6 inches apart, with the pointed end up. Cover the cloves loosely with soil and then mulch the planting area with 3 to 4 inches of shredded leaves or straw.

Care: The following spring, every 2 weeks spray the leaves with fish emulsion or seaweed fertilizer mixed according to the directions on the package. Moisture is important for good bulb formation, so water your garlic during spells of dry weather. Keep the area weeded.

How to harvest: When the leaves begin to turn brown in summer, start checking the plants often. If you pull the bulbs too early, they will be smaller. If you wait too long, the outer skin may tear and the bulbs will not keep as well in storage. Put the bulbs in a hot, dry, dark, and airy place for a few weeks to cure. Then trim the roots and trim the neck or braid together the foliage of several bulbs to hang for storage.

Tips for success: Buy garlic cloves for planting from a seed company or garden center. Supermarket garlic may be treated with an antisprouting chemical and will not grow reliably.

Kale

This nutritious member of the cabbage family has been rediscovered by gardeners and farmers' market shoppers. Compared with other cabbage relatives, kale is easy to grow. Its leaves are rich in vitamins A and C and calcium.

Soil: For the most tender leaves, plant kale in fertile soil that's rich in organic matter. Kale grown in poor, sandy soil or heavy clay soil will be tougher and less flavorful.

Temperature: Kale grows best in cool weather when temperatures average 60° to 65°F. It suffers during long periods of intense summer heat.

Time to harvest: 50 to 65 days.

How to plant: Buy seedlings at a garden center or nursery in spring or in late summer for a fall harvest. Plant seeds in the garden in early spring or mid- to late summer, $\frac{1}{2}$ inch deep. Plant transplants or thin seedlings to stand 12 inches apart. If you are planting for fall, put the plants into the garden about 6 weeks before you expect the first fall frost in your area.

Care: Kale thrives in moist—but not soggy—soil; water during dry weather. When the plants are 4 to 5 inches tall, feed them with bloodmeal or fish/seaweed fertilizer for a nitrogen boost. Otherwise, kale needs little fussing. Spreading a layer of mulch around the plants will minimize weeding.

How to harvest: Pick or cut outer leaves as needed. Use young, tender leaves in salads and older leaves for cooking. The best-quality leaves are bright green, crisp, and firm. Older, darker green leaves will be tougher and stronger flavored.

Tips for success: Light frost actually sweetens the flavor of kale, so unless you live where summers are cool, plant your kale for a fall harvest.

Lettuce

There are two types of lettuce—loose-leaf varieties and heading varieties such as the iceberg, romaine, and Boston lettuce found in supermarkets. Leaf lettuce grows as a loose clump of leaves. In head lettuce, the central leaves gather together to form compact heads. Both kinds of lettuce need similar growing conditions, but

harvest ready leaf lettuce

bolting

loose-leaf varieties such as 'Oak Leaf' and 'Salad Bowl' are the easiest to grow. If you're new to gardening, grow leaf lettuce.

Soil: The best soil for lettuce is well drained but able to retain enough moisture for plant roots, a condition that's created when the soil contains plenty of organic matter. Add compost to your lettuce bed every year. Like other leaf crops, lettuce needs soil rich in nitrogen. Adding composted manure or cotton-seed meal to the soil will boost nitrogen levels.

Temperature: Lettuce is about 90 percent water, and it thrives in cool, moist conditions. In very warm climates, you can grow it as a winter crop. Everywhere else, lettuce grows best in spring and fall. Leaf lettuce can tolerate warmer temperatures than head lettuce.

Time to harvest: 40 days for leaf lettuce, 70 days for head lettuce.

How to plant: Head lettuce is easiest to grow from plants purchased at a local nursery or garden center. Leaf lettuce also grows quickly from transplants but is simple to grow from seeds sown in the garden. To plant seeds, scatter them evenly over the surface of moist soil and rake lightly to cover them. Or plant the seeds $\frac{1}{4}$ inch deep and as thinly as you can. After planting, water if needed to keep the soil moist (but not soggy). When the seedlings have four leaves, thin the plants to 12 inches apart. If you want to harvest young lettuce leaves for microgreens, space plants 4 inches apart.

Care: To promote fast growth, water the plants with a fish/seaweed fertilizer solution (diluted according to the label directions) a couple of times as the plants grow. Lettuce tends to bolt in hot weather. Just before this happens, the plants grow taller and develop a bitter white sap. To prevent this change, pinch off the top center of the plant.

How to harvest: Pick lettuce in the morning when the leaves are most crisp. Pick individual leaves from the outside of the clump. Or, if you prefer, cut the entire plant with a sharp knife just above the ground.

Tips for success: Watch out for slugs, which find tender lettuce leaves irresistible. If you find ragged holes in your lettuce leaves, deter slugs by trapping them with rolled-up newspapers, inverted flowerpots, or boards or by sprinkling a border of diatomaceous earth (horticultural grade, not the type used in swimming pool filters) around the plants.

Melons

Melons are not the easiest crops to grow, but they're worth the effort. Vine-ripened melons have sweetness unmatched by commercially produced fruits that are harvested for shipping before they reach peak ripeness. Watermelons, muskmelons (aka cantaloupes), and winter melons (including honeydews and crenshaws) all grow in the United States.

Soil: Melons need soil that is loose textured and well drained but also able to retain enough moisture for plant roots. Amend the soil with compost before planting melons.

Temperature: Melons need warm soil and the sunniest spot in the garden to thrive. They won't grow well in soil cooler than 60°F. If the seedlings get chilled, the vines may not produce fruit later on. Melons cannot tolerate any frost.

Time to harvest: 75 to 90 days, depending on the type of melon.

How to plant: If you live in a cool climate where the frost-free growing season is shorter than 100 days, start with homegrown seedlings or transplants from a local nursery or garden center to have enough growing time. Plant seeds indoors in individual 3- to 4-inch peat pots. Start them a week before the date of your last expected spring frost. Give indoor seedlings a bright, sunny windowsill and constantly warm conditions. Plant three seeds ½ inch deep in each pot and set them on a horticultural heat mat to keep the soil at 75°F. If you live in a warm climate, plant seeds directly in the garden, ½ inch deep. When the plants are 2 inches tall, thin them by snipping off two of them to leave the strongest one in each peat pot, or to leave two or three plants in each hill in the garden. Try to transplant seedlings to the garden before they have more than three leaves. Young melon seedlings adapt to transplanting better than larger plants.

Most melons seem to grow best in raised mounds, or hills, about 1 foot high and 2 to 3 feet wide. When you plant or transplant them in the garden, make mounds of soil 4 to 6 feet apart (bush varieties with shorter vines can be 2 feet apart). You want to end up with two or three plants in each hill.

Care: Melons grow best when they receive plenty of nutrients. Feed them with fish emulsion or a fish/seaweed fertilizer, diluted according to the label directions, when you plant them in the garden, when the small fruits appear, and about 2 weeks later as the fruits are developing. Melons need plenty of water, especially when the plants are blooming and small fruits are developing. Thoroughly soak the soil during dry weather. Cut back on watering when the melons are ripening for sweeter flavor.

How to harvest: You can often tell when cantaloupes and muskmelons are ripe by their delicious aroma. When a watermelon is ready to pick, the spot where it's been resting on the ground will turn creamy to golden yellow. The stem of a ripe melon should break easily—often just lifting the melon off the ground will sever the stem.

Tips for success: After midsummer, remove flowers and the smallest fruits from the vines. The little fruits may not have enough time to ripen before cold weather sets in, and the plants will then be able to concentrate their energy on ripening the bigger melons.

Mesclun

These popular mixtures of baby salad greens are easy to grow at home. You can find mesclun seed mixes from online or mail-order seed companies and in local garden centers. There are many kinds to choose from—some mild flavored, some spicy; all-lettuce mixtures; Asian greens; and more.

Soil: Mesclun is picked young and is best when it grows fast. For that, you need fertile, fine-textured soil that contains plenty of organic matter and nutrients. When you prepare the soil, dig in compost and/or other amendments and break up any clumps. Then rake out the soil to make a smooth, level surface.

Temperature: Mesclun thrives in the cool temperatures of spring and fall. Hot summer weather causes some plants to bolt and others to develop a stronger, in some cases hotter or more pungent, flavor.

Time to harvest: Begins 3 weeks after planting.

How to plant: Grow mesclun from seed. You can plant seeds indoors in bio-degradable pots to move out to the garden after a few weeks, but it's easiest to plant seeds right in the garden. Before you plant, make sure the soil is moist but not soggy. Water before planting if the soil is dry. Because they are mixes of different plants, mesclun seeds vary in size, but they can be tiny (such as arugula seeds, for example) and hard to handle. Follow the directions on the packet of seeds you have purchased for how deep to plant the seeds. Pour some seeds into your hand and broadcast them by moving your hand over the planting area and allowing the seeds to trickle out over the ground.

Press the seeds into the soil or cover them with soil to the recommended depth, then gently water with a fine mist from a hose or a watering can with a rose attachment. Make sure the soil stays evenly moist until the seeds sprout and begin to grow.

Care: To keep the plants growing, give them a nitrogen boost every couple of weeks with fish emulsion or a fish/seaweed fertilizer diluted according to the label directions.

How to harvest: When the leaves are 3 to 4 inches tall, harvest can begin. You can use scissors to cut individual leaves from the outside of the leaf clump or cut off the whole plant just above the ground with a sharp knife or garden shears. Leave the roots in place and many of the plants will produce a new clump of leaves. You may be able to get a third picking before the plants' energy is spent.

Tips for success: Even moisture and a steady supply of nitrogen are key to growing tender, flavorful mesclun.

Onions

Onions come in a host of sizes and shapes, from small pickling onions to large Spanish types, and a variety of colors. You can pull most kinds when young to use as scallions (although the perennial bunching onion produces excellent scallions) or let them mature. Small, pungent varieties will keep through winter if you store them in a cool, dry place. Larger, sweeter onions (such as Vidalia or Spanish types) will not keep well in long-term storage.

Before you choose which onions to grow, check the daylength requirements. Onions are either "short-day" or "long-day" types. Short-day onions grow best in the South, where summer days are only about 12 hours long. Long-day onions are better suited to northern gardens with a summertime daylength of 13 to 16 hours.

Soil: Onions will thrive in any soil that is well drained, near neutral in pH, and rich in organic matter. Heavy clay soils make it difficult for onions to form big bulbs.

Temperature: Onions generally prefer cool weather, especially during the early stages of growth when they're producing leaves. Later in the growing season, when the bulbs are developing, warmer temperatures are better.

Time to harvest: 50 to 70 days for scallions, 100 to 160 days for mature bulbs.

How to plant: You can grow onions from seeds, sets (immature bulbs grown the previous year), or seedlings. Seeds give you the biggest choice of onion varieties, but they can take 5 months to mature and are susceptible to disease. Sets give you the smallest choice of varieties, but they are the easiest to plant and the earliest to produce a harvest. If you're a first-time onion grower, go with sets. When you buy them locally, look for bulbs about ½ inch in diameter. Smaller ones may not grow well, and larger ones may go to seed before they produce harvestable bulbs. Seedlings are available in local garden centers or from mail-order seed and nursery companies. Seedlings will produce bulbs faster than plants you start from seeds, but they can be affected by diseases.

Plant onion sets 2 inches deep and 4 to 6 inches apart, with the pointed stem end facing up.

Care: As the plants grow, keep them weeded and hoe or cultivate around them weekly to keep the soil loose. As soon as the plants are 2 to 3 inches tall, spread a layer of mulch between the rows to conserve moisture and deter weeds. Onions need a steady supply of moisture or the bulbs may crack or become too strong flavored. Clip off any seed stalks that appear.

How to harvest: Harvest onions for scallions before the plants are 10 inches tall. If you want to store your onions for winter use, let the plants grow until the tops fall over by themselves. After the tops have died down, leave the bulbs in the ground for a week or two, when their skin will begin to toughen (making for better storage quality). When the leaves are brown and shriveled, dig up the bulbs with a garden fork or spade. Spread the bulbs outdoors in a sunny, airy place for 3 to 7 days to dry and cure. Then move them indoors to a warm, dry, shady spot to finish drying for 3 to 4 more weeks.

Tips for success: In general, the stronger an onion's flavor, the better it will keep in winter storage.

Peas

These are one of the great treats of the spring garden, and once you grow your own peas you too will eagerly await shelling the first harvest of green (also called garden) peas or popping the first sugar snap pea right into your mouth when it comes off the vine. Peas are among the earliest vegetables ready for picking each year.

Traditionally, peas grew on long vines. Many still do, and they need to be supported on trellises, netting, or tepees. There are also bush varieties that grow on shorter-vined plants that are self-supporting. In addition to traditional garden peas that are shelled to eat, there are also sugar, or snow, peas, whose flat pods are eaten whole, and sugar snap peas, whose pods and seeds are delicious at all stages of maturity.

Soil: In the North, where the soil warms slowly in spring, sandy loam soil is best for peas because it warms up more quickly than heavier soils. Wherever you live, peas will thrive in well-drained, fertile soil. Peas, like other legumes, draw their own nitrogen from the air and fix it in nodules on their roots, so they don't need nitrogen fertilizer.

Temperature: Peas thrive in cool temperatures. The plants can survive frosts but grow poorly in temperatures above 75°F. In fact, pod production slows significantly at 70°F. Plant peas in early spring as soon as the soil warms to 40°F. Warm-climate gardeners can plant peas in fall to lie dormant over winter and sprout as early as possible for spring harvest. Gardeners in warm climates on the West Coast and along the Gulf of Mexico can grow peas as a winter crop.

Time to harvest: 56 to 75 days.

How to plant: In most of the country, plant peas directly in the garden 4 to 6 weeks before the date of the last expected spring frost, when the soil temperature is at least 40°F. If you have not grown peas or beans in that location before, treat the seeds with a bacterial inoculant powder to help them grow better. The rhizobia bacteria promote the formation of root nodules on the peas, which contain beneficial bacteria that convert nitrogen in the air into a form the plants can use to fuel their growth. To use inoculant, you wet the seeds, roll them in the powder, then plant them.

Plant pea seeds 2 inches deep in light, sandy soil or 1 inch deep in heavier clay soil. Space the seeds of bush (or dwarf) peas 1 inch apart in rows 2 feet apart. Let bush varieties of peas climb over 1- to 2-foot twiggy branches stuck into the ground along the row; these simple supports make picking easier and keep the pods out of the dirt. When the plants come up, thin them so they are 2 to 3 inches apart. Plant vining peas in double rows 6 to 8 inches apart on opposite sides of 5- to 6-foot-tall supports. Make the two rows of peas 3 feet apart.

Care: Spread a layer of mulch around the pea plants to conserve soil moisture and to help keep the soil cool. Water if the soil dries out during spells of dry weather. It's especially important that the soil not dry out when peas are germinating or blooming or the pods are developing. Peas planted in fertile soil should not need any supplemental fertilizing during the growing season.

How to harvest: Pick garden peas for shelling at their peak of ripeness, when the peas have filled out the pods but the pods are still fresh and green, before they begin to yellow or shrivel. Peas are usually ready to pick about 3 weeks after the flowers appear. Pick daily or every other day. If you wait too long, the sugar in the peas begins to turn to starch. If your garden peas are past their prime, you can dry the peas and use them in soup. To dry peas, shell them and spread them out to dry in a single layer in a warm, dry, airy place. It takes about 3 weeks for the moisture to evaporate from them. Pick sugar snap peas when the pods are full size and the peas inside are large. Pick snow peas when the pods are still flat and the peas inside have not yet begun to swell. To avoid damaging the delicate vines, cut the pods from them instead of pulling them off.

Tips for success: As soon as peas are picked, their sugar begins to turn to starch. For the very best flavor, cook them as soon as you can after picking.

Peppers

Whether you like them sweet or hot, the choice of peppers to grow gets bigger every year. Sweet bell peppers may be green when you pick them or can ripen to red, orange, yellow, purple, or chocolate brown. Hot peppers range in flavor from mildly spicy 'Anaheim' to incendiary habanero and Thai peppers.

Soil: Peppers grow best in sandy or sandy loam soil that is well drained. Enrich the soil by digging in lots of compost or composted manure before you plant your peppers. Peppers need magnesium in their soil. If a soil test shows your garden soil to be low in magnesium, you can incorporate dolomitic lime (from a garden center) or Epsom salts (which you'll find in a drugstore) to add magnesium.

Temperature: Whether sweet or hot, all peppers are very sensitive to cold and can stop growing and drop their blossoms when the temperature drops below 50°F. The ideal temperature range is 70° to 75°F. If cold weather is forecast, protect the plants with row covers.

Time to harvest: 120 to 140 days.

How to plant: The roots of pepper plants don't like to be disturbed, so unless you live in a warm climate where it's feasible to sow pepper seeds right in the garden, your best bet is to buy seedlings from a local nursery instead of planting your own seeds indoors. You might not find the exact variety you want, but you will be able to choose among an assortment of sweet and hot peppers. At the garden center, seek out healthy-looking, stocky young plants that are 4 to 6 inches tall. Ask the staff if the plants have been outdoors for a week or more or if they've recently come from a grower's greenhouse. If they're greenhouse plants. they will need to "harden off" before you plant them in the garden. (See page 111 for information on how to harden off plants.)

Young peppers are very susceptible to transplant shock, which can interrupt growth for weeks. To avoid shocking the plants, be sure the soil temperature is at least 60°F before planting them in the garden. Wait until 2 to 3 weeks after the last spring frost. Do the transplanting on a cloudy day or in the early evening to reduce the danger of sun scorch; if this is not possible, provide temporary shade for the new plants. Space plants 15 to 18 apart in the garden, or give each plant its own 12- to 14-inch-diameter container. Large-fruited varieties, such as bell peppers, benefit from support; put stakes or small cages in place at planting time.

Care: Water the young plants as soon as you plant them, and be sure to water when necessary to keep the soil evenly moist. Don't let your peppers dry out; they absolutely need continual, even moisture all during the growing season. Moisture is critical when the flowers bloom and the fruits are forming. But don't go overboard and drown the plants—you don't want the soil to become waterlogged or to have puddles form. If you live where summers are hot and the sun is strong, your pepper plants may get sunburn; to prevent it, try to plant them where they will get some shade during the hottest part of the day. Pull weeds by hand to avoid injuring peppers' delicate roots. Mulching the plants helps limit weed growth and conserves soil moisture.

How to harvest: Pick sweet peppers whenever you think they're big enough to use, whether they're green or fully ripe. Pick hot peppers anytime to use fresh. When fully ripe, pick them to dry or pickle. When harvesting any type of pepper, cut the stem rather than pulling the fruit from the plant so you don't break the plant or disturb its roots.

Tips for success: Peppers cannot tolerate any frost. If there's an early frost warning for your area, harvest all your peppers no matter whether they're green or mature.

Potatoes

Native to the Andes mountains of South America, potatoes thrive in the cool northern half of the United States and the southern half of Canada. Gardeners in other areas can enjoy successful crops by planting potatoes in very early spring or, in warm regions, in fall or winter for spring harvest.

Soil: Potatoes need space, sunshine, and fertile, well-drained soil. Acid soil (pH 5.0 to 6.8) provides good growing conditions and reduces the chance of a common disease called scab.

Temperature: As long as the soil is dry enough to work, you can plant potatoes 4 weeks before the last expected spring frost date. The soil should be at least 40°F. Potatoes grow best when daytime temperatures are 60° to 69°F, although they are tolerant of frosts and even light freezes. Temperatures below 25°F may kill young leaves, but new sprouts should appear within 2 weeks.

Time to harvest: 90 to 120 days.

How to plant: Although you can grow some potato varieties from seed, it's far easier to plant certified disease-free "seed potatoes" purchased from garden centers or Internet and catalog suppliers. (Potatoes from the grocery are often chemically treated to prevent the eyes from sprouting; even if your supermarket potatoes sprout in storage, do not use them to start a crop in the garden.) Plant seed potatoes whole, or cut them into good-size pieces, each of which should contain two or three eyes—the puckered places where sprouts develop. For the sake of productivity, avoid planting whole seed potatoes or cut pieces that are smaller than golf ball size. Cure the pieces by spreading them out in a bright, airy place for 24 hours, or until they are slightly dry and the cut surfaces have hardened. Space potatoes 10 to 14 inches apart. If you're going to harvest early (and therefore have smaller potatoes), you can plant them as close as 8 inches apart. Cover the seed potatoes with 4 to 5 inches of soil.

Care: As the vines grow, push soil, leaves, straw, or compost up around them to keep the developing tubers covered. This is called "hilling." When exposed to sunlight, tubers turn green and develop a mildly toxic substance called solanine. Once the plants bloom, stop hilling up the soil and apply a thick mulch to conserve moisture and keep down weeds. Water deeply during dry spells; potatoes like consistently moist soil and are prone to cracking if the moisture fluctuates a lot. If grown in good soil, potatoes need no fertilizer during the growing season. Mulching with straw helps keep the soil evenly moist and reduces pest problems. A thick straw mulch, at least 4 inches deep, seems to impede the movement of Colorado potato beetles and can help to limit the damage they cause.

How to harvest: Potatoes are ready to harvest 3 weeks after the plants' first flowers bloom. For bigger potatoes, wait to dig until the aboveground growth dies back at the end of the season. If the weather is not too warm or wet, tubers will keep in the ground for several weeks. Dig them up with a spading fork before the first frost. Potatoes that are nicked or bruised during harvesting won't keep well in storage, so eat them as soon as you can. Clean and dry the crop as quickly as possible, but avoid exposing the tubers to sunlight. Store your potato harvest in cool, dark, humid conditions.

Tips for success: Potatoes with colored flesh often lose that color when cooked in water. To keep red and purple potatoes colorful, try roasting them instead of boiling.

Radish

Most of us are familiar with the round red radishes that are found in every supermarket. There are also larger-rooted winter radishes that ripen later and can be stored longer. For your first radish experience, plant those small round red ones—they're a snap to grow.

Soil: Radishes need light, loose soil that is moist but well drained (add compost to achieve this). But the soil should not be too rich in nitrogen or you'll end up with lots of leaves and smaller, slow-growing roots. In dense or rocky soil, radishes will grow slowly, and the roots may be misshapen.

Temperature: Radishes are cool-weather vegetables. They grow so quickly that experienced gardeners like to plant them along with slower-to-sprout crops like carrots to mark the place where the slower crop is planted until it comes up.

Time to harvest: 21 to 35 days.

How to plant: Plant radish seeds right in the garden, ½ inch deep, as soon as the soil thaws and can be worked in spring. Plant every 10 days until daytime temperatures are consistently above 75°F; resume planting when temperatures begin to cool in fall. High temperatures and drought make radishes tough, strong flavored, and prone to pest problems. Sow 8 to 10 seeds per foot.

Care: When the seedlings are 1 to 2 inches high, thin them to 2 inches apart if you are growing them in rows, or 3 inches apart in a bed. If the soil is moist and loose textured, radishes need little extra care to grow. When the young plants are 3 inches high, spread a layer of mulch around them to help keep the soil cool and moist. Do not hoe or cultivate close to the plants—the roots are easily disturbed.

How to harvest: For the best flavor and crunchiest texture, pull your radishes while they are no more than 1 inch in diameter. (Pull one up 3 weeks after the plants are up to check root size.)

Tips for success: Early planting is the key to good radishes. Long summer days can stimulate radish plants to bolt, which will lessen the quality of the roots.

Soybeans, Edamame

edamame

An excellent source of protein, soybeans have rich, buttery flavor and can be used fresh or dried. Edamame are soybeans picked and eaten while young and green, and they're enjoyed boiled or steamed and shelled as a snack or as a vegetable dish (you can substitute them for lima beans in recipes). Remove the green beans from the pods and cook them until tender.

Soil: Light, well-drained soil not too rich in nitrogen, with a pH near neutral, is best. If a soil test shows your soil is acidic, with a pH below 6.5, add ground limestone before planting soybeans.

Temperature: Plant soybeans in spring after all danger of frost is past.

Time to harvest: 75 to 104 days.

How to plant: Plant seeds 1½ inches apart and 1 inch deep in rows 15 to 30 inches apart. Treat the seeds before planting by moistening them and rolling them in a bacterial inoculant powder to improve the plants' ability to fix nitrogen in their roots. Use an inoculant formulated especially for soybeans (available from online and mail-order seed companies).

Care: Water as needed to maintain even soil moisture during germination and also when the plants are about to bloom. If the soil dries out at these times, the harvest may be drastically reduced. Water deeply at least once a week when there is no rain, being careful not to hose off any of the blossoms.

Apply several inches of mulch (after seedlings emerge) to conserve moisture, reduce weeds, and keep the soil cool during hot spells (high heat can cause blossoms to drop off).

How to harvest: Soybean plants ripen most of their pods at the same time. When the beans are plump inside the pods, you can pick individual pods by clipping them off the plants, or cut off the entire plant near its base.

If you want to dry soybeans for long-term storage, leave the plants in the garden until the pods are dry at the end of the season and 90 percent or more of the leaves have fallen. Then pull up the plants and spread them out in a dry, airy place if the weather is good. In rainy weather, bring the plants indoors and hang them upside down or spread them out in a dry, airy attic or basement to dry completely. When the beans are completely dry, shell them and store them in airtight lidded jars or in the freezer.

Tips for success: Roasted soybeans (often sold in markets as "soy nuts") are crunchy and high in fiber and protein. Start with dried beans and either soak them overnight or place a pound of dried beans in 6 cups of water and bring the water to a boil; boil for 5 minutes, then cover and let stand for 1 hour. Drain, rinse, then spread the beans on a lightly oiled baking sheet, season as desired, and bake at 300°F for about an hour or until the soybeans are lightly browned. Stir or shake every 15 minutes during roasting.

Spinach

Unlike many other vegetables, spinach will grow in partial shade (an area that receives direct sunlight for 3 to 6 hours a day, or lightly dappled sunlight all day) as well as in full sun.

Soil: Spinach will grow in a range of soil types, though its ideal soil is well-drained, sandy loam containing a good amount of organic matter. Dig in compost or composted manure in early spring before planting.

Temperature: Spinach needs short days and cool weather; in summer heat, it tends to bolt. It can withstand light frosts without damage and does best when temperatures average 60° to 65°F. Most gardeners can grow spinach in spring or fall. Where winters are mild and the temperature seldom drops below 35°F, spinach can be a winter crop.

Time to harvest: 37 to 45 days.

How to plant: You can buy spinach seedlings locally or start your own seeds as early as the soil thaws and can be worked in spring. Northern gardeners can prepare the soil in fall to be ready to plant early the following spring. Sow seeds outdoors 3 to 6 weeks before the date of the last expected spring frost in your area. Plant seeds for a fall crop 2 months before the average date of your first fall frost. Thin seedlings (or set transplants) 6 inches apart when they are 4 to 5 inches tall.

Care: Spinach has shallow, thin roots that conduct nutrients and moisture to the plant. Weeds can easily overpower spinach roots and take their moisture and nutrients, so keep the area weeded. Keep the soil moist to promote quick growth and postpone bolting; mulch can help.

How to harvest: When the outer leaves in a clump of spinach are big enough to eat, cut them individually from the plant and leave the inner leaves in place to continue growing. If you take no more than half the leaves at any given time, the plant can continue producing new ones. The other option is to cut off the entire plant right above the ground and discard the older leaves.

Tips for success: Spinach is very sensitive to daylength (the hours of daylight in a day). Long days cause spinach to produce a flowering stalk and bolt to seed; the best-tasting leaves grow before a flowerstalk forms.

Squash

There are many varieties of squash (a native American vegetable), but they all fall into two categories: summer squash and winter squash. Summer squashes such as zucchini, crookneck, and scallop or pattypan have tender skins and are harvested young; they do not store well for long periods. Winter squashes such as acorn, butternut, and Hubbard are left to mature in the garden; they have a thicker, harder rind that allows them to be stored long term. Both categories of squash are easy to grow, but they need a lot of nutrients to fuel their growth (they're known to be "heavy feeders"). Traditional squash varieties grow on long vines that sprawl over the ground and need space to grow. Newer bush varieties grow on shorter vines and are suitable for large containers.

Soil: Squash will grow in any soil that is reasonably fertile and well drained but able to retain moisture (meaning rich in organic matter).

Temperature: If your summer weather is warm and sunny, you can grow good squash. The plants are very tender and susceptible to frost, so don't plant until the soil is warm—about 60°F.

Time to harvest: 45 to 50 days for summer squash, 85 to 110 days for winter squash.

How to plant: Where the growing season is at least 120 days (3 months) long, squash seeds can go directly into the garden. Plant squash in the garden a week after the last spring frost, or when the soil has warmed to at least 60°F. The traditional way to plant squash is in hills (mounds of soil). Sow seeds ½ inch deep in a circle on the top of each hill. When the plants come up, thin them to leave the two sturdiest seedlings in each hill. In conventional rows, space the plants 3 to 4 feet apart.

Care: Squash needs moisture through the season, but it can also be attacked by diseases. To reduce the risk, water squash plants at ground level (such as with soaker hoses) rather than with overhead sprinklers or hoses that put water on the leaves. Water during spells of dry weather. Give your squash plants a boost by feeding with a fish/seaweed fertilizer diluted according to the label directions every 3 weeks as the plants grow.

How to harvest: Cut summer squash from the vines while the fruits are young and tender and the skin can be punctured with your thumbnail. If the fruits get too big, they lose flavor and become dry and woody. Don't harvest winter squash until late in fall, after some light frosts but before the first heavy frost. You should not be able to dent the rind with your fingernail. Cut squash from the vines; don't try to pull them off. Leave 3 to 4 inches of the stem attached. Handle winter squash carefully after harvest. Store them in a warm, dry location where they can cure. The exception is acorn squash, which stores better in a cool, moist place.

Tips for success: Keeping young squash plants under row covers early in the season can protect them from insidious pests such as squash bugs and cucumber beetles, both of which spread diseases, and squash vine borers. However, when the plants begin blooming, remove the row covers to let pollinators reach the blossoms.

Tomatoes

Tomatoes are the inspiration for many a beginning gardener. Beefsteaks, paste tomatoes, flavorful heirloom varieties, sweet cherries to pop into your mouth, disease-resistant varieties for problem places—there's a tomato to suit your tastes and your garden circumstances. Grow them in the ground or plant them in pots—there's nothing like the flavor of a fresh-picked, sun-ripened tomato that you grew yourself.

There are many varieties of tomatoes but two types of tomato plants: determinate and indeterminate. The stems of determinate tomato plants grow 1 to 3 feet long, and the main stem and side stems each produce about three flower clusters. When flowers form at the tips of the stems, the plant stops growing. This means determinate tomatoes produce fruit once and then stop. The bushy plants may need to be supported with stakes and wire tomato cages as they grow.

Indeterminate tomato plants have sprawling, vinelike stems that grow 6 to 20 feet long. Most of them produce about three flower clusters at every second leaf. They keep growing and producing fruit unless stopped by frost or disease, which means you can keep picking fresh tomatoes all season long. Indeterminate tomato plants need to be supported by tying them to sturdy stakes or by placing them inside tomato cages when you plant them. It also is necessary to prune the plants or they will put too much energy into growing vines rather than producing and ripening fruit. To prune tomatoes, use your fingers to snap off suckers (the sprouts that grow in the angle between the main stem and side stems) when they form.

Soil: Tomatoes love sandy loam soil that's rich in organic matter, but they'll grow in a variety of soil types as long as the drainage is good. They won't do well in heavy, soggy clay soils.

Temperature: Tomatoes are warm-weather plants. If you live in the North where the growing season is short, you can cover the soil with black plastic sheeting for a few weeks before planting to help warm the soil. Also look for early-maturing varieties. In warm southern climates where summers are hot, give your tomato plants some shade so the blossoms don't drop off during very hot weather.

Time to harvest: 90 to 140 days.

How to plant: If you're a first-timer, buy tomato seedlings from a local garden center or nursery. Most places have a reasonable selection of varieties, and you may even find heirloom tomatoes for sale. When you've gained some experience, you can plant tomato seeds indoors and grow your own transplants; that way, you'll be able to choose among a whole universe of tomato varieties.

Plant tomato seedlings 2 to 3 feet apart. Dig a hole deep enough so the young plant will sit deeper than it was growing in its nursery container. The plant will grow roots along the buried part of the stem, providing a better anchor for the plant. Fill each planting hole with water, let the water drain away, then set in the plant. Fill the hole with soil, firm it around the base of the plant, and water again. For a nutritional boost, make this second watering with fish emulsion or a fish/seaweed fertilizer diluted according to the directions on the label.

Care: Don't fertilize again until the plants begin to produce fruit or their energy will go into producing leaves. Most tomato plants need support as they grow. Place a stake behind each seedling after planting or set a sturdy cage over it. Water as needed to keep the soil evenly moist for the first few weeks until the plants establish themselves in the garden. Then spread a thick layer—2 to 4 inches deep—of mulch around the plants to conserve moisture. Mulching tomatoes with compost helps meet their nutritional needs and can prevent disease organisms from splashing onto plants from the soil below. When the first small tomatoes develop on the plants, water with fish emulsion or fish/seaweed again. A month later, feed them again.

How to harvest: When your tomatoes are richly colored, it's time to pick them. Ripe tomatoes will pull easily off the stem. If you live where summers are very hot, your tomatoes may not develop their full color outdoors. Pick them when they're pink and bring them indoors to ripen the rest of the way.

Tips for success: Tomatoes can develop blossom end rot—which looks like a scaly brown patch on the bottom of the fruit—when they receive uneven moisture. Mulching will help moderate moisture levels. Tomatoes are prone to various diseases and blights, which you can recognize by wilting and yellowing leaves. Planting disease-resistant cultivars can help. But if your tomatoes are struck, grow them in a different location or in pots next year. Disease organisms can remain in the soil for 3 years.

Turnips

Grow turnips for their round, flattened, or cylindrical roots or for their nutrition-packed leaves, which contain vitamins A, B$_2$, C, and E plus minerals. One classic way to serve turnips is cooked and mashed like potatoes.

Soil: Rich, loose soil will allow the roots to develop easily. Enrich the soil by digging in compost and rock phosphate before planting turnips.

Temperature: Turnips like cool weather, so plant them early to mature before summer sets in, or plant in midsummer to harvest in fall.

Time to harvest: 35 to 60 days.

How to plant: Plant seeds in the garden 3 weeks before the date of the last expected spring frost in your area, when the soil temperature is at least 40°F. Plant a fall crop about 2 months before the average date of your first fall frost. Moisten the soil where you will plant the seeds. Pour some seeds from the seed packet into your hand and move your hand over the planting area, letting the seeds trickle between your fingers and scattering them as evenly over the ground as you can. Cover the seeds with ¼ inch of soil if you are planting in spring, or ½ inch of soil in midsummer. When the seedlings emerge, thin them so the remaining plants are 3 to 4 inches apart. Use the young tender leaves from the thinned plants in salads.

Care: Spread mulch around the plants to keep the soil cool and conserve moisture. Water if the weather is dry. In good soil, you won't need to fertilize your turnips as they grow.

How to harvest: If you plan to harvest both leaves and roots from a single planting of turnips, pick only 2 or 3 leaves from each plant to avoid robbing the root of nutrients. Dig or pull turnips when the roots are still small, about 2 inches in diameter. Older, bigger turnips won't be as sweet and succulent. Small roots may be easily pulled by hand, but use a digging fork to loosen the soil along the row when harvesting larger turnips meant for winter storage.

Tips for success: Hot weather can ruin the flavor of turnips, making the leaves tough and the roots woody and bitter. If you experience an early heat wave, pull all your turnips and use them small.

10 FAVORITE HERBS FOR YOUR ORGANIC GARDEN

Every gardener should grow at least a few herbs, even if only in pots on a sunny porch. Herbs contribute to our cuisine and our well-being, and they serve as useful and decorative additions to all kinds of gardens. The term "herb" has different meanings to botanists and gardeners. In botanical terms, an herb is basically any seed-bearing plant that isn't woody; it's where the word *herbaceous* comes from, as in herbaceous perennial. For gardeners, what distinguishes an herb from other plants is its usefulness. In this sense, an herb is defined as a plant or plant part valued for its medicinal, savory, or aromatic qualities.

There are nearly as many ways to incorporate herbs into your garden as there are herbs to choose from. A traditional herb garden is delightful, but herbs add interest to flower gardens, too, and they are often grown as companion plants in vegetable gardens. While it is a myth that herbs grow best in poor soil, most are easy to grow in conditions similar to those favored by vegetables—typically full sun and well-drained soil that has been amended with plenty of organic matter. Only a few herbs are prima donnas that demand coddling. And some that are not hardy in northern winters must be brought indoors through the cold months of the year.

Basil

An essential herb for many cooks, basil lends its uniquely spicy, rich, minty-peppery flavor to classic Italian tomato sauce and pesto, to Thai dishes, and to the cuisines of Mediterranean countries. Dried basil can get you through winter, but there's nothing like the piquant flavor of the fresh herb. There are many basil varieties to choose from, and each has its own distinctive qualities.

Soil: Moist but well-drained, fertile soil rich in organic matter. Basil does not fare well in dry soil. Dig compost or composted manure into the soil before you plant.

Temperature: Basil is a warm-weather plant that is very sensitive to cold. Don't plant it out in the garden until after the date of the last expected spring frost in your area. Basil seeds germinate at soil temperatures of 75° to 85°F. The plants suffer when temperatures dip below 50°F.

How to plant: Practically every nursery and garden center sells basil seedlings, and you will probably be able to choose among several varieties (and colors—there are some tasty, and ornamental, purple basil varieties, such as 'Purple Ruffles' and 'Dark Opal') that have their own distinctive flavors.

Give basil a location in full sun. Plant nursery plants in the garden at the same depth they were growing in their nursery containers. Space them 12 inches apart for smaller-leaved varieties such as 'Spicy Globe' and 18 inches apart for larger-leaved kinds such as 'Genovese'.

talk the talk
Plant Types

ANNUAL: A plant that completes its life cycle in one growing season and then dies.

BIENNIAL: A plant that completes its life cycle in 2 years, growing stems and leaves in the first year and producing flowers and seeds in the second year.

COLE CROP: A vegetable in the cabbage family (Cruciferae or Brassicaceae). Cole crops include cabbage, broccoli, cauliflower, Chinese cabbage, collards, kale, and mustard.

DECIDUOUS: The term for a plant that sheds all of its leaves at the end of a growing season.

EVERGREEN: A plant that keeps its leaves through winter.

HERBACEOUS: A plant that dies back to the ground each year; not woody.

LEGUME: A plant in the botanical family Leguminosae (or Fabaceae) that can draw nitrogen directly from the air and store it in underground nodules on its roots. Legume plants form pods, which are edible in beans and peas. Other familiar legumes include clover, lupines, and wisteria.

PERENNIAL: A plant that flowers and sets seed for two or more seasons.

TENDER: A plant from a tropical or subtropical region that won't survive winter outside in North America except in subtropical regions such as Florida and Southern California.

WOODY PLANT: A perennial plant such as a shrub or tree that doesn't die down to the ground each year.

If starting basil indoors, sow seeds ⅛ inch deep in pots or flats filled with a light-textured potting mix such as one made of equal parts perlite and vermiculite. Moisten the potting mix before you plant the seeds. Press the seeds lightly into the potting mix to cover them. Keep the potting mix moist but not soggy. Transplant the seedlings into the garden when they are a few inches high, but not until at least a week after your average last frost date. If you live in a warm climate, you can plant seeds directly in the garden when you are sure the last spring frost has passed and the soil temperature is at least 50°F.

Care: When your garden soil is nice and warm, spread mulch around the plants to conserve moisture. Basil does not like to dry out. Water as needed to keep the soil moist. To encourage bushier growth (and more leaves to harvest), pinch off the tips of the stems often—once a week or so. Pinch back to just above the next set of leaves on the stem. Also pinch off flower heads as they form so the plants put their energy into producing leaves.

How to harvest: Cut or break off sprigs of basil whenever you need them. If you need to pick a lot of basil, perhaps to make a batch of pesto sauce, you can cut entire stems or even harvest an entire plant at once, cutting the main stem close to the ground.

Tips for success: Plant seeds for a second crop of basil in midsummer when the soil and air are nice and warm to keep a steady supply of this useful herb on hand for pairing with tomatoes. At the same time, sow a few seeds in outdoor pots to have containers of basil to bring indoors when the weather turns cool in fall.

Chives

Unlike basil and dill, which are annuals, chives are perennial and come back every year. They're ridiculously easy to grow, and their mild onion flavor is a welcome addition to many dishes.

Soil: Any average garden soil; chives are not fussy.

Temperature: Hardy in USDA Zones 3 to 9, chives need a cold dormant period in winter, when the leaves die back to the ground. New leaves begin to grow in early spring and remain harvestable all summer and well into fall.

How to plant: It's possible to start chives from seed but a whole lot easier to just buy a plant or two. If you've got friends or neighbors who grow chives, they might be willing to give you some bulbs to get your own clump started. Chives grow from little bulbs that form a clump that gets bigger every year, and gardeners who grow them may be looking to divide their own clump to reinvigorate it. Chives grow well in full sun to light shade.

Care: Chives are tough and need practically no care. They produce round purple-pink flower heads in spring on slender stalks. After they bloom, you may want to remove the flower stems from the plant—they're solid, not hollow like the leaves, and you probably won't want to eat them. Chives don't need fertilizing or watering except in very poor soil or extreme drought conditions.

How to harvest: Leaves are ready to harvest in 75 to 85 days from planting seeds. Harvest a few leaves from transplants as soon as they are big enough to use. Snip off stems with scissors whenever you need them. Chopped leaves are easy to freeze and use all winter long. The edible flowers make colorful, tasty additions to salads; cut off the flower head at its base to harvest for the kitchen.

Tips for success: To keep chives from self-sowing new plants in addition to expanding their root clumps, cut off the flowering stems at their base before the flowers dry out and drop their seeds onto the ground.

Cilantro/Coriander

Cilantro and coriander are the same plant. The name *cilantro* generally refers to the plant's leaves, and *coriander* is more often used to mean the seeds that are produced after the flowers bloom (if the flowers are left on the plant). Cilantro is an essential flavoring in the cuisines of many countries, including Mexico, Central and South America, India, and Thailand. Coriander seed flavors dishes in India, Morocco, European countries, and parts of Asia.

Soil: Average soil that's light and well drained but not too rich in nitrogen (too much nitrogen weakens the flavor).

Temperature: Cilantro thrives in warm temperatures.

How to plant: Plant cilantro in a sunny to partially shady location. Cilantro is easy to grow from seed, and the plants have long roots that make them difficult to transplant. Plant seeds in the garden when all danger of frost is past. Plant them $\frac{1}{2}$ inch deep; they need darkness to germinate. When the seedlings are a few inches tall, thin them to stand 4 inches apart. If you like to cook with cilantro, sow more seeds every 2 weeks through summer to keep a steady supply of fresh leaves at the ready.

Care: Keep the plants weeded. Water plants during spells of dry weather.

How to harvest: Cilantro leaves are ready to harvest in 50 to 55 days. It takes 90 to 105 days for coriander seeds to develop. Pick young sprigs of cilantro whenever you need them in the kitchen. Small, immature leaves have the best flavor. To harvest the seeds, cut whole plants when the leaves and flowers turn brown and the smell of the seeds starts to change from musky to citrusy. Place the plants upside down in a paper bag and hang the bag indoors in a dry, airy location. As the seeds dry, they should fall to the bottom of the bag.

Tips for success: If you grow cilantro from seed, be sure to plant the seeds deeply enough or they may germinate poorly.

Dill

Both the leaves and seeds of dill are used in cooking. When dill plants are in bloom, their heads of small flowers attract beneficial insects; many gardeners like to plant them along the edges of the garden.

Soil: Reasonably fertile, moist, but well-drained soil is ideal for dill.

Temperature: Plant dill in early spring, as soon as the soil thaws and can be dug, while the weather is cool. When the plants bloom in summer, the leaves lose quality, so for a continuous supply of fresh leaves, sow new seeds every 2 to 3 weeks.

How to plant: Choose a location for your dill where it can remain year after year. Although the plants are annuals, if you allow some plants to bloom and produce seeds, the seeds will drop to the ground when they mature and produce new plants next year (a process called self-sowing). Moisten the soil and scatter dill seeds over the soil surface as evenly as you can, and gently press them in. Don't cover the seeds; they need light to germinate. When the seedlings come up, thin them to 6 to 12 inches apart.

Care: Dill needs moist soil; water the plants during dry weather.

How to harvest: Clip off fresh leaves, close to the plant's stem, as needed throughout the season. Dill leaves (called dillweed) are best used fresh and do not last long in the refrigerator. You can dry the leaves, but their flavor will be milder than when fresh. To harvest seeds, cut the flowering stems when the flowers mature and the seeds are a light brown color (generally 2 to 3 weeks after the flowers bloom). Cut the stems long enough that you can tie them in bundles to dry. Hang the bundled stems upside down in a dark, airy place to dry. You can spread newspaper beneath them to catch falling seeds or place the stems with the flower heads down in paper bags to catch the seeds. Any seeds that don't drop off by themselves can be removed by hand when thoroughly dry.

Tips for success: If you like dill, plant several successive batches of seeds (or plants) a few weeks apart in spring and early summer to extend the harvest of fresh leaves.

Mint

There are many mints—peppermint and spearmint are the best known and most widely grown, but there are also orange mint, pineapple mint, Corsican mint, apple mint, and many more. Mints have a multitude of uses, from teas to jellies to candies to seasoning lamb, peas, fruit salads, and beans—mints are versatile.

Soil: Moist but well-drained, fertile soil is ideal, although many mints seem able to grow practically anywhere. Mint thrives in partial shade.

Temperature: Plant mint whenever plants become available locally. Most mints are hardy in USDA Zones 4 or 5 to 9.

How to plant: Mint is easy to grow . . . too easy, for many of us. Mint spreads, and the best way to control it is to plant it in a pot. If you want to plant mint in the garden, allow *lots* of space for it and be prepared to curb its enthusiastic growth before it overtakes less vigorous plants. Buy small plants from a local nursery or a reputable online or mail-order source. Mints are not reliable from seed—they may not reproduce their parent exactly. Plant your mint plants at the same depth in the garden as they were growing in their nursery container. Mints spread, so space plants 12 to 18 inches apart.

Care: Mints don't need any fussing. Although you grow them for their leaves, nitrogen fertilizers can do them more harm than good and make plants prone to rust disease. Mints need moisture to thrive; water during spells of dry weather. Regularly cutting the plants to harvest leaves will promote fresh new leaves and bushier growth. At the end of the season, after you make the final harvest, cut the plants back to ground level.

How to harvest: Cut sprigs and stems as needed. Young leaves are the most tender and flavorful. Mint is at its best when you use it fresh, but you can also dry or freeze the leaves for storage.

Tips for success: The key to success with mint is to keep it contained. Except for Corsican mint, most mints will take over the garden . . . and beyond . . . if you let them. If you want to grow mint in your garden, make barriers to control the roots. Sink sheet metal 10 inches deep in the ground around the mint plants to keep the roots from spreading. Better yet, grow your mint in pots.

Oregano

What would spaghetti sauce be without oregano? This aromatic perennial herb is easy to grow in the garden or in pots. It's widely available in garden centers and nurseries, but it's important to make sure you get the right kind. Common oregano (*Origanum vulgare*) is an upright plant that has larger leaves but little flavor. Instead, buy Greek oregano (*O. heracleoticum* or *O. hirtum*), which has smaller, more intensely flavored leaves. This plant grows as a low mound of deliciously aromatic deep green leaves and bears small white flowers in summer.

Soil: Well-drained soil is essential; if your soil tends toward heavier clay, try growing oregano in a raised bed into which you have incorporated some grit or very fine gravel to loosen the texture. If a soil test shows the pH to be acidic (below 7.0), dig in some horticultural lime (ground limestone) before planting.

Temperature: Oregano is native to the Mediterranean region and thrives in hot, sunny weather. Plant it in the garden when plants become available locally.

How to plant: You can start oregano from seed, although seed-grown plants can be variable, but it's easiest to buy young plants and transplant them to your garden.

Care: Other than weeding, oregano needs little care. Water the plants during extended spells of dry weather.

How to harvest: Pinch off individual leaves whenever you need them, or cut the stems just as the flowers start to form. Oregano dries easily for long-term storage. Bundle the stems together and hang them in a dark, airy location until thoroughly dried. Then remove the leaves from the stems and store them in airtight lidded jars.

Tips for success: Greek oregano will generally survive winter as far north as USDA Zone 5 and grow again in spring. If you live in a colder climate, you probably will need to plant new oregano each year.

Parsley

Parsley has a multitude of uses in the kitchen. It appears on many a restaurant plate garnishing a steak or fish fillet, but you should eat that little sprig—parsley is rich in vitamin C, containing three times as much by weight as oranges. There are two types—curly parsley and flat-leaf, or Italian, parsley. The frilly, curly kind is more decorative, but many cooks favor the flavor of the flat-leaf type.

Soil: Moist but well-drained soil of average to good fertility.

Temperature: Parsley can go into the garden in spring when the soil temperature warms to about 50°F.

How to plant: Parsley seeds are notoriously slow to germinate, but if you want to try them at home, it's best to plant them indoors in pots. Soak the seeds in warm water overnight, or for at least several hours, before you plant them. And start early—they can take 4 to 6 weeks to sprout. Keep the potting mix moist. Transplant to the garden when the plants are a few inches high. Moisten the soil before you plant. Space the plants about 8 inches apart.

Care: Keep your parsley well weeded. Water during dry weather (watering at ground level is better than watering from overhead, since parsley is susceptible to crown rot). To keep the plants vigorous, regularly cut outside stems back to the ground. Promptly remove any flowerstalks that form.

How to harvest: Pick stems whenever you need parsley in the kitchen. At the end of the season, you can harvest sprigs and freeze them in self-sealing plastic freezer bags to use over winter. Parsley can be dried, too, but it loses much of its flavor.

Tips for success: Parsley is a biennial, meaning that in warm climates it will survive winter in the garden and grow again a second year. However, during that second season, the plant will bloom and produce seeds. The leaves of flowering parsley are still perfectly edible, although their flavor becomes more pungent. Many gardeners prefer to plant new parsley every year.

Rosemary

Rosemary is an evergreen shrub native to the Mediterranean region. Warm-climate gardeners can keep it in the garden year after year. North of USDA Zone 7, you'll need to start with new plants each spring or try growing rosemary in a pot to bring indoors over winter. The dark green, needle-like leaves have a refreshing, piney scent and a pungent flavor that beautifully complements pork and lamb. If you're lucky, your plant will bloom, in winter or spring, with small sky blue flowers.

Soil: Well-drained soil with a pH near neutral is best. If a soil test shows your soil to be acidic (with a pH below 7.0), add some lime or crushed eggshells or wood ashes to the soil. If your soil is of very poor quality, add some all-purpose organic fertilizer before planting.

Temperature: Rosemary can survive winters outdoors in USDA Zone 8 and warmer, and sometimes in Zone 7 in a protected location. With protection and perfectly drained soil, a few varieties selected for their hardiness are capable of making it through winter in southern Zone 6, but their survival rates tend to vary from year to year depending on the severity of the winters.

How to plant: Germination rates for rosemary seeds are low, and plants grow slowly—it can take 3 years for a seed-grown plant to reach harvestable size. So buy plants for your garden. Plant them as deep in your garden as they were growing in their nursery container. Give rosemary a location in full sun. If you live in the North, you may have to treat rosemary as an annual. Rosemary can be tricky to grow in a pot. On one hand, excellent drainage is essential for the plant's roots—they can rot in moist soil. Be sure to use a potting mix that drains well; a blend made for cacti and succulents would be a good choice. On the other hand, rosemary is not a cactus—it does need regular watering. But the water must drain away promptly.

Care: Water rosemary during dry weather, but don't soak the soil. If you bring a potted rosemary plant indoors over winter, mist the branches daily.

How to harvest: Cut sprigs of leaves a few inches long from the tips of the stems whenever you need them. You can also cut branches to dry the leaves for long-term storage. Hang the stems in a dark, airy place until the leaves are completely dry, then pull the leaves from the stems and store them in an airtight jar. To keep the plant healthy, don't harvest more than 20 percent of its leaves at a time.

Tips for success: Growing rosemary involves a balancing act to provide the right conditions: a combination of well-drained soil or potting mix and regular watering without keeping the roots too wet.

Sage

Sage is a hardy, woody-stemmed perennial plant called a subshrub (a low-growing plant with woody stems). Its stems and rough-textured leaves are covered with soft down, giving the leaves a silver green color. Sage plants grow 18 to 30 inches tall, and mature plants bloom with upright clusters of tiny purple flowers in late spring or early summer. Sage is native to the northern Mediterranean coast and is hardy in much of the United States.

Sage's aromatic flavor has a citrusy note in fresh leaves that disappears when the leaves are dried. Fresh or dried, it's a classic ingredient in poultry stuffing and sausage and a good seasoning for chicken and shell beans such as Great Northern.

Soil: Sage thrives in well-drained soil of average fertility with a slightly alkaline pH. If a soil test shows your soil to be acidic (with a pH below 7.0), add some lime or crushed eggshells or wood ashes to it before planting your sage. Give sage a location in full sun to partial shade.

Temperature: Sage is hardy in USDA Zones 4 to 9. It doesn't do well in the extreme North or South.

How to plant: Plant young sage plants in the garden in spring when all danger of frost is past, planting them as deep as they were growing in their nursery container. Space the plants 12 inches apart. Water after planting and for the first few weeks to keep the soil moist, but not wet, until the plants settle in and grow new roots in the soil. You can also plant seeds indoors 6 to 8 weeks before the date of the last expected spring frost in your area. Plant them in pots or flats of moist potting mix. They germinate in 1 to 3 weeks with temperatures of 60° to 70°F. Keep the potting mix moist, but not soggy, until it's time to move the plants to the garden.

Care: Once established, sage needs little watering except during prolonged spells of dry weather. Divide plants that are at least 2 years old.

How to harvest: Clip off leaves and stems whenever you need them during the growing season. Sage leaves can be dried for long-term storage. Cut whole stems and hang them to dry in a dark, airy place. Or remove leaves from stems and spread them on a screen to dry in a shady, airy location. When the leaves are dry, store them in airtight containers.

Tips for success: Prune sage plants in spring to keep them growing vigorously, to guarantee a supply of fresh, young leaves, and to maintain the plants' shape.

Thyme

Thymes come in a host of varieties and fragrances, and the plants are beautiful additions to the front of an herb garden. The perennial, woody plants form low, sprawling mats of tiny leaves, with little white, pink, or magenta flowers. Plants grow from a few inches to a foot high. Thymes are deliciously fragrant and flavorful. The most widely grown and easiest to grow is the aromatic common thyme (*Thymus vulgaris*), but there are also citrusy lemon thyme and thymes whose scents have notes of balsam, coconut, nutmeg, orange, or oregano. Versatile thyme can add flavor to chicken, beef, lamb, veal, and fish as well as vegetables, soups, and eggs.

Soil: Thyme needs light-textured, dry, well-drained soil with a near-neutral pH (generally from pH 6.5 to 7.5). Soggy, heavy soil will spell doom for thyme, no matter the pH.

Temperature: Thyme is hardy in USDA Zones 5 to 9.

How to plant: It's easiest to buy plants for your garden. Plant them as deep as they were growing in their nursery container, and space them 6 to 8 inches apart. Give thyme a sunny to partially shady spot in the garden. If you feel adventurous, plant seeds outdoors in the garden 2 to 3 weeks before the date of your last expected spring frost. Or start seeds indoors in light, well-drained potting mix in late winter to early spring. It can take 2 to 4 weeks for seeds to sprout. Cover the tiny seeds lightly. Mist the pots daily, until the seeds germinate, so that the potting mix never dries out. When the plants come up, water at the base of each plant when the potting mix feels dry. Feed them after 2 weeks with fish emulsion diluted according to the label directions. When the young plants are 4 inches high, you can move them out to the garden after hardening them off. (See page 111 for information on how to harden off plants).

Care: As long as your garden soil is well drained, thyme won't need much care. (In poorly drained soil it becomes vulnerable to fungus diseases.) Weed the plants when necessary. During spells of dry weather, water your thyme at the base of the plant—overhead watering weakens the flavor. It's better to have the plants a bit drier than too wet. If you live in the North, mulch thyme plants in late fall to protect them over winter.

How to harvest: Pick or cut stems of thyme whenever you need them during the growing season. Strip the leaves from the wiry stems to use them. To dry leaves for storage, cut stems—or cut off the entire plant 2 inches above the ground in midsummer. Bundle bunches of stems together and hang them in a dark, dry, airy place. When the leaves are completely dry, strip them off the stems and store them in airtight jars.

Tips for success: Bees love thyme blossoms, so by planting thyme you can do your part to support these endangered insects that are essential to the production of so many of our food plants.

20 EASY ANNUALS FOR YOUR ORGANIC GARDEN

Annuals are garden favorites because of their continuous season-long bloom. Colors run the spectrum from cool to hot, subtle to shocking, and plants are as varied in form, texture, and size as they are in color. In the strictest sense, an annual is a plant that completes its life cycle in 1 year—it germinates, grows, blooms, sets seed, and dies in a single growing season. Among the plants gardeners grow as annuals, however, are several that are actually tender perennials, including wax begonias, impatiens, and zonal geraniums. We treat them as annuals because they're not winter hardy in most climates and are killed by cold temperatures and must be replaced each season.

The majority of annuals prefer loamy soil that's moist but well drained, with plenty of organic matter. If you've prepared the soil well before planting,

talk the talk
Botanical Nomenclature

BOTANICAL NOMENCLATURE: The internationally accepted system of naming plants according to their characteristics and their relationships to other plants, developed by Carolus Linnaeus in the 1700s. Plants are classified into families, genera, species, and varieties or cultivars.

CULTIVAR: Short for "cultivated variety." Any plant that is bred for specific characteristics, such as color, fragrance, disease resistance, or other desirable qualities.

GENUS: A group of one or more species with closely similar flowers, fruits, and other characteristics.

LATIN BINOMIAL: In the system of botanical nomenclature, each plant has a two-part name that often (but not always) is derived from Latin or Greek. The first part of the name is the plant's genus; the second is its species. Following the genus and species in many plants' identifying information is a variety or cultivar name.

PLANT FAMILIES: Botanists group species and genera of plants that share many common characteristics into families. Botanical names of plant families end in the Latin suffix "aceae," although some names in common usage do not follow that rule. Examples include Rosaceae (the rose family) and Fabaceae (also called Leguminosae; the pea/bean family).

SPECIES: A group of individual plants that share common attributes and are able to breed together.

VARIETY: A botanical subdivision of a plant species that differs from other members of the species in minor but consistent ways.

ongoing maintenance for annuals is pretty basic. Keep the soil evenly moist throughout the growing season, supplying about an inch of water per week. (Annuals that thrive in drier conditions are noted in the profiles that follow.) Water early in the day to give plants a chance to dry out before evening. This helps prevent leaf spot and other fungal and bacterial problems.

Mulching to conserve moisture and to limit competition from weeds will help keep beds of annuals looking good with less work on your part. Likewise, regular applications of organic fertilizer such as liquid seaweed diluted according to the label instructions will contribute to annuals' ongoing good looks.

Many annual hybrids have been selected for compact growth, so you may not need to pinch or stake them. However, some older cultivars and those grown for cut flower production may need support. Tall plants, such as 'Rocket' snapdragons, may need staking, especially in areas with strong winds or frequent thunderstorms. Many annuals benefit from thinning or disbudding. This increases flower size and stem strength. Removing spent flowers, or deadheading, keeps annuals in perpetual bloom. Remove yellowing or damaged foliage during the growing season to keep down disease problems. If plants get too dense, remove a few of the inner stems to increase air circulation and light penetration.

Remove plants from beds and pots at the end of their season. For some, this will be upon first frost; for others, a bit beyond. Whenever the plants die or look brown and crispy, pull them and add them to your compost pile.

Wax Begonia
(*Begonia semperflorens*)

Easy-to-grow wax begonia is a tender perennial grown as an annual that blooms continuously all summer and into fall. The neat, compact plants have glossy green, reddish, or bronze leaves and separate male and female flowers. Wax begonias are great plants for shady gardens, and deer don't bother with them.

Height and spread: 6 to 12 inches high and up to 12 inches wide.

Bloom time: All summer until fall frost.

Flower color: Red, pink, or white.

Where to plant: Partial to full shade, but they bloom best in partial to light shade. Begonias can tolerate full sun in cooler climates. Bronze-leaved varieties tolerate more sun, and green-leaved plants can take more shade. Begonias can tolerate some drought but are at their best in moderately moist but well-drained soil of average to good fertility.

How to grow: Wax begonias are readily available wherever plants are sold, and buying plants is the easiest way to grow them. You will find small seedlings sold in flats (most economical) as well as larger plants that cost more but create a more immediate presence in the garden.

You can grow begonias from seed, but the seeds are very tiny and hard to sow, and you have to plant them indoors months before the average last frost date for your area. If you do want to try your hand at growing from seed, scatter them as evenly as you can over the surface of a moist, fine-textured potting mix and press them in gently. Keep the soil evenly moist. Set plants out in the garden after the last frost.

Fertilize wax begonias with a fish/seaweed product, diluted according to the label directions, every 2 to 3 weeks to keep them blooming.

Use in the garden: Edging, front of the garden, containers and window boxes.

Tips for success: You can take cuttings from plants in mid- to late summer and root them in pots for winter houseplants. Next spring, you can move the plants out to the garden.

Calibrachoa, Million Bells
(*Calibrachoa ×hybrida*)

Calibrachoa looks like a miniature version of its petunia relatives and is sometimes referred to as trailing petunia. Whatever you call it, calibrachoa is indispensable in summer containers. The flowers are about an inch across, but plants produce loads of them. They come in an appealing array of colors and bloom all summer long and on into fall.

Height and spread: 3 to 6 inches high, trailing stems grow 6 to 12 inches long. Plants grow about 12 to 18 inches across.

Bloom time: All summer into fall. In southern gardens, million bells can also be planted in fall.

Flower color: Shades of red, pink, rose, orange, yellow, purple, and white.

Where to plant: Full sun; plants produce fewer flowers in shady conditions. Average, well-drained soil. Grows best in evenly moist—but not wet—soil. Don't let the soil become very dry.

How to grow: Most garden centers and nurseries carry potted plants in a good selection of colors. Set plants in the garden at the same depth they were growing in their nursery container. Dig a hole just deep enough to accommodate the rootball. Seeds of calibrachoa are not available to home gardeners, since the plants are patented and may only be grown commercially. Space plants 12 to 18 inches apart in the garden or closer together in containers.

Use in the garden: Plant calibrachoa at the edge of a pot to spill over, in hanging baskets, or in the front of the garden.

Tips for success: Feeding the plants regularly is important to keeping them blooming prolifically.

Catharanthus, Madagascar Periwinkle

(Catharanthus roseus)

Also known as vinca (not to be confused with the cream-edged green-leaved vine so widely planted in pots), catharanthus loves heat. The bushy plants have glossy green leaves that beautifully complement the flowers. In USDA Zones 10 and 11 the plants are perennial, but everywhere else they're grown as summer annuals.

Height and spread: 6 to 12 inches high and 8 to 12 inches wide.

Bloom time: All summer until fall frost.

Flower color: Rose pink, light pink, red, lavender, and white, often with a contrasting color eye.

Where to plant: Give catharanthus a spot in full sun to light shade. Well-drained soil is essential. Average fertility is fine.

How to grow: Madagascar periwinkle is hard to grow from seed, so buy plants from a local garden center or nursery. The plants need warm temperatures, so don't look for them (or plant them) until reliably warm weather arrives. Catharanthus needs good drainage and may grow poorly in very humid conditions. Don't water them with an automatic overhead sprinkling system that runs overnight. It's better to water by hand or with soaker hoses or drip irrigation, directing the water to the base of each plant.

Use in the garden: Perfect for pots or the front to middle of the garden.

Tips for success: A great asset of catharanthus is its ability to tolerate dry conditions. Also, the plants are self-cleaning, meaning that the old flowers drop off and don't require you to deadhead (remove) them. Similar color palette and flower form make Madagascar periwinkle a good stand-in for impatiens in hot, dry sites and where downy mildew precludes planting impatiens.

Celosia, Cockscomb

(*Celosia argentea*)

The velvety flower heads of celosia, aka cockscomb, come in a range of warm colors and a variety of flower forms, some of them looking like the demented creations of a mad scientist. Celosia flowers may be fan shaped; curled and twisted to resemble coral or a brain or a rooster's comb; feathery and plumy; or piled vertically into loose spires. Those fanciful blossoms grow on upright, branching plants. Celosia flowers make great cut flowers, and they dry well, too.

Height and spread: 6 inches to 3 feet tall and 8 to 18 inches wide.

Bloom time: All summer.

Flower color: Red, scarlet, rose, magenta, pink, orange, salmon, yellow, and cream.

Where to plant: Full sun. Plants appreciate afternoon sun in warm-climate gardens. Any reasonable garden soil will suit them. Celosia can grow in dry, infertile soil, but if you want the biggest possible flower heads, prepare the soil by adding a high-phosphorus fertilizer such as rock phosphate.

How to grow: Buy nursery plants in flats or pots and plant them at the same depth they were growing in their nursery containers. You can also plant seeds indoors in flats or containers of loose-textured potting mix kept evenly moist. Plant seeds about a month before the date of the last expected spring frost in your area. Or plant seeds right in the garden after the last frost, when the soil has warmed. Space plants, or thin seedlings, 8 to 18 inches apart. Give celosia a spot in full sun. Feed the plants monthly with an all-purpose organic fertilizer according to the package directions. Water the plants regularly, especially if you want big flowers. Tall varieties may need to be fastened to stakes to support the flower heads.

Use in the garden: Grow celosia in pots or garden beds. Dwarf varieties can go in the front of the garden, taller types in the middle or back of the bed. If you like the flower forms, grow celosia in a cutting garden and bring the flowers indoors to enjoy up close.

Tips for success: Deadhead (remove old flowers) as soon as flowers fade to keep the plants producing new ones. Cut back to the base of each flower's stem.

Cosmos

(*Cosmos bipinnatus, C. sulphureus*)

The lovely wide-petaled daisy flowers of cosmos are 2 to 4 inches across and bloom on upright plants with feathery, delicate-textured leaves. Cosmos is easy to grow, and the plants may self-sow (drop their seeds onto the ground) to produce new plants next spring.

Height and spread: 2 to 5 feet, depending on the variety you grow, and about 1 foot wide.

Bloom time: Midsummer until fall frost.

Flower color: Rosy pink, crimson, white, scarlet, gold, orange, or yellow.

Where to plant: Full sun is best, but plants will do all right in partial shade. Plant in well-drained soil of average fertility; established plants can tolerate some drought, but soggy soil will ruin them.

How to grow: Cosmos is easy to grow from seeds. Plant them directly in the garden when the danger of frost is past in spring. Moisten the soil before planting, and water as necessary to keep the ground evenly moist until the plants are up. Thin the seedlings to 12 to 14 inches apart. Cosmos needs to be deadheaded to keep on blooming. To deadhead the first blooms of the pink, crimson, and white flowers of *Cosmos bipinnatus*, cut off the spent blooms just below the flower and new buds should form below the place where you cut. After these flowers have bloomed, cut off their stems right above the next leaves on the stem. Orange, red, and yellow flowers of *C. sulphureus* also can be cut back to the next set of leaves. Tall varieties may need to be tied to stakes for support.

Use in the garden: Plant tall varieties in masses in the back of the garden. Shorter types are lovely in the middle ground of the garden or in pots. They make terrific cut flowers, too.

Tips for success: Many nurseries and garden centers sell cosmos plants. If you buy them, be aware that the plants don't like having their roots disturbed by transplanting, so buy the smallest, youngest (and healthiest) plants you can find—bigger is not necessarily better in this case.

Geranium
(*Pelargonium* ×*hortorum*)

Our familiar bedding geraniums are not botanically geraniums at all (those in the genus *Geranium* are hardy perennials) but actually belong to the genus *Pelargonium*. Geraniums rank among the most reliable, easy-to-grow, and popular plants for summer beds, borders, and pots. Actually tender perennials, geraniums are grown as annuals or houseplants except in USDA Zones 10 and 11, where they can grow outdoors all year. The plants are sometimes called zonal geraniums because the leaves of some cultivars are marked with dark or colored bands, or zones. Other varieties have plain green leaves. The plants are upright and branching, with thick stems and fleshy leaves with scalloped or pointed edges. The flower heads are rounded clusters of individual small flowers atop tall, straight stems.

Height and spread: 1 to 2 feet high and 8 to 12 inches wide.

Bloom time: All summer until frost.

Flower color: Shades of red, scarlet, orange, salmon, pink, rose, lavender, and white.

Where to plant: Full sun or, in warm climates where the sun is intense, with some shade in the afternoon. Well-drained soil of average fertility and moisture (neither too rich nor too poor, neither too wet nor too dry) suits them fine. Soil too rich in nitrogen will encourage leafy growth rather than flowers. In a container, give geraniums a light, well-drained potting mix.

How to grow: Garden centers and nurseries are full of pots of blooming geraniums in spring and early summer, so choose your colors. You can grow geraniums from seeds, but you'd have to start them indoors in midwinter, so why bother? It's probably not worth the effort if you're new to gardening. If your geraniums seem to want to grow one single stem, pinch off the tip of the stem to encourage the plant to produce branches and grow bushier. Plant geraniums in pots or the garden at the same depth as, or a bit deeper than, they were growing in their nursery pots. As the flowers fade and turn brown, cut them off at the base of the flower stem to keep the plant looking fresh and producing new buds. Water geraniums when the soil or potting mix feels dry about an inch below the surface. Feed geraniums with a fish/seaweed fertilizer diluted according to the label directions every few weeks.

Use in the garden: Geraniums are classics for pots—a tub of blooming red geraniums is a Memorial Day must in many communities. You can plant geraniums in pots of all sizes, by themselves or mixed with other colorful annuals, or mass them in a garden bed.

Tips for success: Deadheading (removing old flowers along with their stems) is critical for geraniums, so factor that activity into your decision if you're considering planting a bed full of them. They're easy to grow but do take some maintenance to keep them looking their best.

Helichrysum, Licorice Plant
(*Helichrysum* spp.)

This genus of plants used to include the strawflower, whose papery-petaled blossoms in bright, warm colors are among the best of all flowers for dried arrangements. Botanists now place the strawflower in the genus *Bracteantha*. And the name *Helichrysum* now belongs to a group of sprawling, trailing foliage plants (*H. petiolare*) called licorice plant for the aroma released by the fuzzy, rounded to heart-shaped leaves when you stroke them. Licorice plant is attractive, versatile, and easy to grow if you don't overpamper it. In the warmest parts of the country (USDA Zones 10 and 11), helichrysum is perennial.

Height and spread: 6 to 9 inches high and to 3 feet across. The long stems sprawl or trail from a hanging basket or pot.

Foliage color: Leaves are silvery green, lime green, or marked with a darker green central area in one cultivar. The plants may bloom with yellow button flowers, but they're grown primarily for their beautiful foliage.

Where to plant: Give helichrysum full sun to partial shade. Well-drained soil of average fertility is best.

How to grow: It's easiest to buy licorice plants for your pots. Plant them at the same depth they were growing in their nursery container. Position the plants at the edge of a pot or hanging basket where the long stems can spill over.

Good drainage and not too much water are the big keys to growing licorice plant. Let the soil or potting mix dry out somewhat between waterings; constantly moist soil can lead to root rot.

Use in the garden: Licorice plant is a lovely addition to pots and window boxes. The silver-leaved forms are especially beautiful combined with pink, purple, and blue flowers, and they'll soften brighter, bolder reds, oranges, and golds.

Tips for success: Combine in containers with other drought-tolerant plants and water judiciously. Helichrysum won't last in moist, heavy soil. The plants can tolerate drought but will turn brown and rot in wet soil.

Impatiens
(*Impatiens walleriana, I. hawkeri*)

Bedding impatiens (*Impatiens walleriana*), the most popular of all bedding plants, has been continuously improved by breeders for decades. Long a reliable performer, impatiens has some pros and cons for 21st-century gardeners. In the plus column, impatiens is easy to grow and a classic plant for shady beds and borders. But deer love it, which is a problem in many gardens. In 2012, bedding impatiens was hit by downy mildew disease in much of the eastern United States. Whether or not you live in an affected area, if you plant impatiens, you'll need to monitor it carefully as described below. Or find a substitute plant. New Guinea impatiens (*I. hawkeri*) has not been affected by downy mildew and can be a good alternative if you have the right conditions.

Height and spread: Bedding impatiens: 4 to 12 inches high, depending on the cultivar. New Guinea impatiens: 12 to 24 inches tall with a similar spread.

Bloom time: All summer until frost.

Flower color: Bedding impatiens: shades of pink from pastels to hot pink and lavender pink, red, orange, salmon, white. New Guinea impatiens: red, scarlet, coral, salmon, intense shades of pink, lilac, red violet, and white. The leaves of New Guineas may be dark green, bronze, or streaked with yellow or pink along the center.

Where to plant: Any well-drained but moist garden soil. Bedding impatiens will grow in partial to full shade or, with enough moisture, in a fully sunny location. New Guinea impatiens is best in full sun to partial shade.

How to grow: Plant impatiens after all danger of frost is past and the weather has warmed in spring. Nurseries and garden centers usually have good selections of impatiens, so it's probably not worth the effort of starting your own seeds if you're a new gardener. You will find plants in plastic cell packs and flats (which typically contain eight cell packs, or a total of 48 plants), carry packs (plastic carriers with a handle that hold six plants in 2-inch compartments), and pots of various sizes. Moisten the soil before planting. Dig a hole for each plant big enough to hold the root system and deep enough so the plant will sit at the same level it was growing in its nursery container. If you are planting just a few pots of impatiens, dig a hole for each plant, fill it with water, let the water drain out, then set in the plant. Fill in with soil, then firm the soil around the base of the plant and water again. If you are planting from a flat, it's easier and quicker to water the plants after you've gotten them all into the ground. If your soil is well dug, crumbly, and porous, you can make planting holes for the seedlings just using your fingers. Drop each plant into its hole, firm the soil around the stem, and move on to the next one. Space impatiens 6 to 12 inches apart.

Impatiens doesn't need lots of fussing, but it does need even moisture. If your plants get dry, they will show you by wilting. You may be able to revive them with a good drink, but the plants will have been stressed and may be more vulnerable to pest and disease attacks. It's better to water as needed to keep the soil or potting mix evenly moist. For the best bloom, add some all-purpose organic fertilizer to the soil before planting. As the plants grow, every 2 to 3 weeks feed them with fish emulsion or a fish/seaweed fertilizer diluted according to the directions on the label. The plants will drop their old flowers by themselves (a process called self-cleaning), so you don't have to deadhead them to remove faded blooms.

Use in the garden: Impatiens can be planted in masses in beds and borders or under trees or shrubs, or planted along walkways or the edges of garden beds. They're also excellent candidates for pots and window boxes.

Tips for success: In areas where bedding impatiens has been hit by downy mildew, you may not find plants for sale, and it would be unwise to plant them if you do. The disease spores will be in the garden soil, where they can remain viable for several years, and may also be carried on the wind, so planting more impatiens will prolong the disease's damage. Plant something else instead: New Guinea impatiens, begonias, torenia, lobelia, and coleus are some substitutes to consider.

Marigold
(*Tagetes* spp.)

Free-blooming, easy-to-grow marigolds are a great source of bright yellow and orange color for sunny gardens and pots. They're a good choice for a child's first garden, too.

Height and spread: The tallest marigolds with the biggest flowers are African, or American, marigolds (*Tagetes erecta*), which produce globe-shaped flowers up to 4 inches in diameter at the tops of their stems. Plants can grow to 4 feet high (though most are 12 to 18 inches) and 2 feet across. Like other marigolds, they have fernlike leaves made up of narrow, oblong leaflets. French marigolds (*T. patula*) are smaller, 6 to 18 inches high, with correspondingly smaller flowers. Signet marigolds (*T. tenuifolia*) are smallest of all, growing 6 to 12 inches high. Their flowers are more delicate-looking, with fewer petals, and the leaves are finer-textured than those of French or African marigolds.

Bloom time: All summer until frost, if old flowers are removed regularly.

Flower color: Mostly shades of orange, gold, and yellow. Some French marigolds are a blend of orange and mahogany red. So-called white marigolds are actually a creamy pale yellow color, not pure, icy white.

Where to plant: Marigolds need a bright, sunny location. Well-drained soil is important for success, and average fertility and moisture suit them fine. Soil that is too rich will produce lots of leafy growth but weaker flower stems that are prone to bending and breaking. Marigolds can tolerate dry soil but will suffer during prolonged drought. Marigolds grow best in hot weather, so don't plant them outdoors until all danger of frost is past in spring.

How to grow: Garden centers and nurseries offer marigolds in cell packs, flats, or pots. Plant them in holes just deep enough to hold the roots, and firm the soil around each plant after planting. They're easy to grow from seed, too. Sow seeds indoors, 6 to 8 weeks before the date of your last expected spring frost, in light-textured potting mix kept evenly moist until the seedlings come up. If you live in USDA Zone 9 or warmer, you can plant seeds directly in the garden. Whether planting indoors or out, barely cover the seeds with moist potting mix or soil. In the garden, space African marigold plants 1 to 2 feet apart, French or signet marigolds 6 to 12 inches apart. Water after planting to settle the plants into the garden or container.

If your soil is poor, feed marigolds once a month with fish or fish/seaweed fertilizer diluted according to the label directions. Water when the soil is dry; they don't like constant moisture. To keep your marigolds blooming, you need to deadhead them. Remove old flowers by cutting off the stems just above the nearest set of leaves. This can be time consuming, especially for French and signet marigolds, but it has to be done or the plants will produce seeds and—their mission accomplished—stop blooming.

Use in the garden: Plant marigolds in garden beds and borders, pots, or window boxes. French and signet marigolds make nice edging plants.

Tips for success: Be sure to remove old flowers from your marigolds every week or two to keep them flowering. Marigolds have a reputation for repelling harmful nematodes from the garden, but not all marigolds possess this ability. If you want to plant marigolds to repel pest nematodes, grow French marigolds, especially the cultivars 'Nemagold', 'Queen Sophia', 'Petite Blanc', or 'Tangerine'.

Morning Glory
(*Ipomoea* spp.)

Morning glory vines, with their big, wide, funnel-shaped flowers, are ideal for decorating a fence, a lamppost, or the post holding up your mailbox. Or you can grow them on a trellis or tripod for a vertical accent in the garden. Morning glories will often self-sow (drop their seeds on the ground) and come back again next year by themselves. The vines have heart-shaped leaves that can be 4 or more inches across; some have leaves divided into several lobes (segments). Among the most beautiful—and popular—morning glory cultivars is the aptly named 'Heavenly Blue', whose true blue flowers seem to reflect the summer sky above.

morning glory

Height and spread: 8 to 10 feet long.

Bloom time: All summer until frost.

Flower color: Purple, pink, blue, violet, crimson, and white; some varieties are streaked or flushed with another color.

Where to plant: Morning glories need full sun and grow best in soil that is light and well drained—even sandy—and rich in organic matter. They thrive in warm temperatures and do not grow well in cool weather or wet soil.

How to grow: It's easy to grow morning glories from seed. The only trick is that the seeds have hard outer seed coats, so it helps to carefully nick the seed with a sharp knife or file (known as scarification) or to soak the seeds in water overnight or for several hours before you plant them to soften the seed coats. Plant the seeds directly in the garden when all danger of frost is past in spring. Moisten the soil before you plant, and sow the seeds ½ inch deep. When the seedlings come up, thin them to 6 to 8 inches apart. The plants appreciate evenly moist soil, so water them when the weather is dry. Keep the area weeded. In subsequent years, you may need to weed out morning glory plants that come up where you don't want them.

Use in the garden: Grow morning glories on a lattice or netting to create a flowery screen in the back of the garden. Or let the vines twine up a tall tripod or trellis to create a vertical accent. Morning glories can also camouflage a chain-link fence or decorate a railing, lamppost, mailbox, or arbor. Provide morning glories with their own sturdy support, and make sure they cling to it as they climb skyward. These vigorous vines will readily clamber up other plants growing near them in the garden and are quite capable of overwhelming their more subdued neighbors.

Tips for success: Cultivated morning glories have a wild relative, commonly called bindweed, that looks very similar, though the leaves and pale pink to white flowers are smaller. But bindweed, as the name implies, can be a real thug in the garden, twining its vigorous stems around other nearby plants you want to grow and strangling them. If you see morning glory–like vines growing in places where you did not plant them last year, pull them up while they're still small. Do the same with morning glory seedlings that come up where you don't want them. It can be annoying to have to weed out morning glory seedlings, but many gardeners believe it's worth it to have the beautiful flowers.

Nicotiana, Flowering Tobacco

(*Nicotiana ×sanderae*)

These bushy plants bear star-shaped flowers with tubular throats. The leaves are spatula shaped and a bit sticky to the touch. If you enjoy an evening stroll in the garden after work, nicotiana may be for you: The flowers are often at their best—and even lightly fragrant—late in the day.

Height and spread: 1 to 2 feet high and about 12 inches wide.

Bloom time: All summer.

Flower color: Red, shades of pink, white, pale lime green.

Where to plant: Nicotiana grows in full sun to partial shade in soil of average fertility that's moist but well drained.

How to grow: You can purchase transplants from a nursery or garden center or grow plants from seeds. To grow from seed, plant the seeds indoors in containers of a moistened, light-textured potting mix 6 to 8 weeks before the date of the last expected spring frost in your area. Don't cover the seeds, just press them lightly into the soil; they need light to germinate. Whether you plant seeds or transplants from the nursery, keep the soil evenly moist but not soggy. Space the plants (or thin the seedlings) to 9 to 12 inches apart. Regular moisture is important for nicotiana, so water as needed during dry weather. Feed the plants with fish emulsion or a fish/seaweed fertilizer every 2 to 3 weeks, diluted according to the label directions. Nicotiana blooms abundantly, but it's important to deadhead it regularly, removing spent flowers by clipping off each old flower right below its base; new flower buds should form on the stem.

Use in the garden: Plant nicotiana in the middle ground of a garden bed or border or along a path you like to stroll on summer evenings to enjoy its subtle, pleasant fragrance.

Tips for success: Nicotiana grows best when temperatures are moderate and humidity is low—it doesn't like hot, steamy conditions or frost. On very hot days, the flowers may not open. If your plants decline in midsummer, try sowing fresh seeds to start a new round of plants.

Pansy
(*Viola ×wittrockiana*)

Wide-petaled pansies with their impish faces (formed by dark markings around the center of the flower) are the first annuals to show up in garden centers in spring and are hard to beat for early color in much of the country. They're also available in fall—a great time to plant them. In warm-climate gardens, pansies are ubiquitous in winter pots and garden beds.

Height and spread: 6 to 10 inches tall and 6 inches across.

Bloom time: Whenever the weather is cool and plants are available in your area—spring into early summer, autumn, or winter into early spring.

Flower color: Pansies embrace most of the color spectrum, blooming in shades of blue, purple, pink, red, orange, yellow, white, and deep blue black. Some cultivars have the distinctive dark "face" markings, and others do not.

Where to plant: Full sun to partial shade, in soil that is well drained but fertile—rich in organic matter and nutrients.

How to grow: Nurseries and garden centers generally carry a reasonable selection of pansy plants when it's appropriate to plant them locally. It's easiest to buy plants for your garden or pots. When the weather grows too hot and the plants decline, pull them out and replace them with warm-weather plants. For a bigger choice of varieties, you can plant seeds. Sow them indoors in pots or flats or moist potting mix 12 weeks before the average date of the last expected spring frost in your area. Transplant seedlings to the garden about 2 weeks before you expect the last frost. In warm climates, plant pansy seeds in the garden in fall for winter flowers. Pansies need even moisture, so water them when the soil starts to feel dry. If your soil is of average or poor fertility, feed pansies every 2 or 3 weeks with fish emulsion or a fish/seaweed fertilizer diluted according to the directions on the label. Deadhead pansies to keep them blooming; cut off stems of faded, wilted flowers at their base. Keep your pansies weeded.

Use in the garden: Plant pansies in pots or window boxes or in the front of a garden bed or border. They make attractive companions for spring bulbs.

Tips for success: Except in the South, where pansies grow better in winter, planting pansies in fall is a great idea. The plants will bloom until the weather turns quite cold and will die back over winter, but they will regrow the next spring to bring early color to your garden.

Petunia

(*Petunia* ×*hybrida*)

The 2- to 4-inch-wide, funnel-shaped flowers of petunias have long been garden favorites. Plant breeders have expanded the range of colors and plant forms, so today's petunias can play an increasing number of roles in the flower garden. There are many, many petunia varieties on the market. Some are upright, bushy plants, and others, such as the Supertunia and Wave series of petunia cultivars, have long, trailing stems. One delightful old-fashioned petunia, which is hard to find in garden centers these days but is available from specialty seed suppliers, is *Petunia integrifolia*, a contributor to the gene pool of the contemporary trailing petunias. This species has trailing stems and flowers of a cool shade of purple pink. The plants bloom well all season long.

Height and spread: 8 to 12 inches.

Bloom time: Late spring into fall.

Flower color: Shades of red, rose, pink, purple, white, and soft yellow, some edged or striped with white or another color. One dramatic variety contrasts dark purple black with bright yellow. Some varieties have double flowers (with twice the usual number of petals) with ruffled edges.

Where to plant: Plant petunias in full sun to partial shade; they do well with some afternoon shade. Any well-drained soil of average fertility should be fine for them. Petunias can tolerate some drought but will suffer in heavy, constantly wet soil.

How to grow: Nurseries and garden centers stock lots of petunias, though the newest cultivars usually dominate the plant tables. The easiest way to put petunias in your garden or pots is to buy plants. For the greatest selection, you can grow them from seeds. Although petunias can tolerate cool weather and thus show up fairly early in local garden centers, it's safest to wait until after the last spring frost to plant them in the garden. Dig a hole deep enough to hold the roots. Fill the hole with water, let the water drain away, set in the plant, firm the soil around it, then water again.

To plant seeds, sow them indoors in pots or flats of moist, light-textured potting mix 10 to 12 weeks before you want to plant them outdoors. Scatter the tiny seeds as evenly as you can over the surface of the soil in the flat, or sprinkle a few in each small pot or compartment of a cell pack. Don't cover the seeds with soil; petunias need light to sprout. Keep the potting mix evenly moist until they do. When the little seedlings have grown several sets of leaves, you can transplant them to pots if you started them in flats. If you are growing them in a germination medium that does not contain any soil, water them with a fish/seaweed fertilizer diluted to half the strength recommended on the label. When the plants reach 3 to 4 inches tall, pinch out the centers to promote bushy growth and more flowers. In the garden, space plants 10 to 12 inches apart.

Petunias can tolerate some drought, but they will rot if kept constantly wet. Don't water them until the soil has dried somewhat. They tend to look messy after rain but generally perk up when the sun comes out. Picking off the dead flowers keeps the plants looking neater. Petunias grow best when you feed them regularly. Fertilize monthly with an organic fertilizer containing a high proportion of phosphorus (P), or add rock phosphate to the soil before planting and again at the end of the growing season for next year. It's also helpful to give them a dose of fish/seaweed fertilizer diluted according to the label directions once every week or two. Regular feedings will help keep your petunias thriving. But the plants, especially Wave and Supertunia types that have longer stems, may grow straggly and disheveled in midsummer, with flowers just at the tips. Cut the stems way back and continue a regular schedule of watering and fertilizing to keep plants growing vigorously, and the plants should regrow and bloom again in fall.

Use in the garden: Grow petunias in the front of mixed beds and borders or in a bed all by themselves. They're also good performers in containers and window boxes. The trailing types will spill over the edge of a pot or hanging basket, or sprawl over the ground as a groundcover in places where they won't get stepped on.

Tips for success: If your petunias get straggly but you don't want to lose all their flowers until fall, try cutting back some of the stems each week over a period of several weeks. If you're lucky, the first stems you cut back will start to rebloom about the time you're cutting back the last of the old stems.

Portulaca, Rose Moss

(*Portulaca grandiflora*)

Called rose moss because of its big (for the size of the plant), bright flowers and low mats of needlelike leaves, portulaca is an old-fashioned flower that's hard to beat in sunny, dry gardens. The skinny leaves are fleshy and succulent and hold moisture to get the plant through dry weather. The flowers are lovely—1 to 2 inches wide and ruffled, with a silky texture. Some are double, with twice the usual number of petals. The flowers close in late afternoon (and on rainy days) and reopen in the morning.

Height and spread: Less than 6 inches high; spreading 6 to 12 inches.

Bloom time: All summer into fall.

Flower color: Warm shades of yellow, orange, salmon, pink, magenta, red, and white.

Where to plant: Portulaca needs full sun and very well-drained soil. A hot, dry, sunny spot is ideal. The plants tolerate poor, dry soil with aplomb. Moist or wet soil will be their undoing.

How to grow: Portulaca shows up in garden centers, usually in flats, but it's easy to grow from seed, too. When the soil warms up in spring, plant the tiny seeds directly in the garden. Scatter them over the surface of moist soil. Portulaca is pretty much carefree. It seldom needs water, and fertilizing it can reduce the amount of flowers the plants produce. Weed around them if you need to, but otherwise you can probably leave the plants alone.

Use in the garden: Portulaca makes a delightful edging for a sunny, dry garden. You can tuck it into spaces between paving stones or into soil-filled crevices in a dry-stone wall. Or grow it in pots or window boxes.

Tips for success: Portulaca often self-sows (drops seeds onto the ground) to produce new plants next year. When the new seedlings come up in spring, dig up and relocate any that appear where you don't want them. Over a period of years, you may find more and more of the volunteer seedlings are a magenta pink, which seems to be a dominant color.

Rudbeckia, Black-Eyed Susan, Gloriosa Daisy, Coneflower

(*Rudbeckia hirta*)

The dark-centered, golden yellow daisy flowers of annual rudbeckia bring a hint of warm summer sunshine into the garden. The cultivar 'Gloriosa' has red markings in the yellow petals, and 'Gloriosa Daisy Mixed' blooms in yellow, gold, bronze, and brownish red. The cultivar 'Irish Eyes' has bright yellow petals and a green center. Annual coneflowers grow on bushy, upright plants with hairy leaves and stems.

Height and spread: 2 to 3 feet high and to 2 feet wide.

Bloom time: Midsummer into fall.

Flower color: Golden orangey yellow, bright yellow, bronze, and orange.

Where to plant: Full sun, in average to rich soil that is well drained. Plants perform best in dry summer weather.

How to grow: Garden centers and nurseries carry annual rudbeckias, but many don't get in plants until midsummer when they are fully grown and blooming. You could save a spot for them in your garden and put in plants from the nursery, or perhaps plant them to follow spring-blooming annuals such as pansies. To get a head start, plant seeds indoors in spring to move out to the garden after the last spring frost. Deadhead often to remove old flowers, cutting each flower stem back to the nearest set of leaves on the stem below it. Water the plants during extended spells of dry weather, and use soaker hoses or drip irrigation to deliver water at ground level. Overhead watering can encourage disease. The hairs on leaves and stems trap moisture, which can lead to fungus diseases in humid, rainy climates.

Use in the garden: Black-eyed Susan is a good addition to a cottage garden or other informal flowerbed or border. Plant them in a mass for long-lasting visual impact. The flowers are a good choice for cutting for summer bouquets.

Tips for success: Black-eyed Susan and gloriosa daisy may self-sow (drop their seeds onto the ground) if you don't remove the dead flowers. Their seeds survive winter and germinate in spring when the soil warms up. If the seedlings come up in the right place, the work is already done! But more than likely, you'll have to transplant some of these "volunteers" to a better spot where they'll be appreciated.

Salvia, Sage
(*Salvia splendens, S. farinacea*)

Perennial garden sage is a staple of the kitchen garden, but it has many ornamental relatives grown for their flowers. Many flowering sages are perennials, but some are annuals; others are perennial in warm climates but grown as annuals in cooler climates where they cannot survive over winter. Scarlet sage (*Salvia splendens*) sports spikes (vertical clusters) of tubular to elongated bell-shaped, brilliant scarlet red flowers along thin, vertical stems all summer. There are also varieties with coral, purple, pink, or white flowers. The plants are bushy, with rich green leaves. Mealycup sage (*S. farinacea*) is perennial in southern climates and grown as an annual elsewhere. Its dense spikes of tiny flowers are blue (as in the cultivars 'Victoria' and 'Blue Bedder') or white.

Height and spread: 10 inches to 3 feet high and 8 or 9 to 18 inches wide.

Bloom time: All summer until frost

Flower color: Brilliant red, coral, salmon, white, purple, blue.

Where to plant: Full sun to partial shade (some afternoon shade is beneficial in warm-climate gardens) in well-drained soil of average fertility. Salvias need even moisture and some humidity—they tend not to grow well in dry climates.

How to grow: Plants are readily available from nurseries and garden centers in cell packs and pots of varying sizes. Transplant them to your garden after the last spring frost at the same depth they were growing in their nursery container. Space plants 10 inches to 2 feet apart. The plants become bushier as they grow larger. Or sow seeds indoors in early spring, 6 to 10 weeks before the date of the last expected frost in your area. Plant seeds in moist, light-textured potting mix; press the seeds in lightly but don't cover them because salvia seeds need light to germinate. When the plants are blooming, deadhead them (cutting back the flower spike to the next set of leaves below it on the stem) when the flowers fade. Fertilize the plants every few weeks with fish emulsion or a fish/seaweed fertilizer diluted according to the directions on the label.

Use in the garden: Grow salvias in garden beds and borders or in containers. The flowers are good for cutting, too.

Tips for success: Deadheading the flowers as soon as they fade will keep the plants blooming all summer long. If you wait until the old flowers turn brown, blooming will slow down.

Snapdragon
(*Antirrhinum majus*)

Snapdragons have delighted generations of children who love to pinch the flowers' sides to make the dragon's mouth open and close. Depending on where you live, you can plant snapdragons in spring or fall. The plants may survive over winter in northern gardens, although they may develop rust disease. The flowers bloom along vertical stems (called spikes) in early summer. Tall-growing varieties provide vertical punctuation or background in garden beds and borders or mixed container plantings.

Height and spread: 9 inches to 3 feet high and 6 to 12 inches wide.

Bloom time: All summer into fall, if deadheaded.

Flower color: Red, pink, rose, orange, yellow, lavender, and white.

Where to plant: Grow snapdragons in full sun, in well-drained, evenly moist soil of average to good fertility.

How to grow: You can find snapdragons at local nurseries and garden centers. Shorter varieties are often sold in cell packs and flats, and taller varieties appear in pots of varying sizes. You can even buy fully grown blooming plants. In USDA Zone 7 and north, plant your snapdragons in spring. South of Zone 7, plant them in fall to bloom in spring. You can grow snaps from seed, but it's easier to purchase plants. If you do plant seeds, start them indoors 8 to 12 weeks before the date of the last expected spring frost in your area. Don't cover the seeds with soil. They need light to germinate, so just press them lightly into moist potting mix. Keep the mix evenly moist until the seedlings are up. In the garden, space plants (or thin seedlings) 6 to 8 inches apart for small varieties, or at least 12 inches apart for taller-growing types. Give the plants plenty of space to allow for air circulation that can reduce the risk of rust disease. Snapdragons grow best when their soil is evenly moist, so water them during spells of dry weather. Feed snapdragons growing in pots or in gardens of average fertility every few weeks with fish emulsion or a fish/seaweed fertilizer diluted according to the label directions. When the flowers on a flowering stem have faded, cut off the stem at its base. In tall-growing varieties, such as 'Rocket', when the main initial blooming stem is cut back, smaller side shoots will usually develop and bloom.

Use in the garden: Snapdragons are lovely in a cottage garden, in beds and borders, or in pots. Tall-growing kinds make excellent cut flowers, so plant them in your cutting garden. Shorter varieties such as 'Floral Carpet' are delightful in the front of the garden.

Tips for success: Snapdragons grow best in cool weather, so you can put plants out in the garden as soon as the soil can be dug in spring. The plants can tolerate some light frost, but protect them if freezing temperatures threaten.

Sunflower
(*Helianthus annuus*)

Sunflowers are summertime classics, and they're easy to grow from seeds. They come in a wide range of sizes, from $1\frac{1}{2}$-foot dwarfs to the giant sunflower, which can grow 10 or more feet tall and produce huge flowers a foot across. Some plants produce one large flower; others branch and produce several flower heads. Most sunflowers have a large, dark center made up of small disk flowers ringed by yellow petals (actually ray flowers).

Height and spread: 18 inches to 10 or more feet tall and 1 to 2 feet wide.

Bloom time: Mid- to late summer.

Flower color: The classic sunflower is golden yellow, but there are also cultivars that bloom in shades of yellow, cream, orange, maroon, and red brown.

Where to plant: Full sun to partial shade, in any well-drained soil of average fertility.

How to grow: Plant seeds directly in the garden when all danger of frost is past in spring. If possible, plant sunflowers on the north side of the garden where they won't cast shade on shorter plants growing nearby. Plant seeds 1 inch deep and 6 inches apart. Sunflower seeds sprout readily, so you will probably need to thin the seedlings by removing excess plants. Thin dwarf and medium-size cultivars to 12 inches apart and large types to 18 to 24 inches apart. Water well after planting. Sunflowers are drought resistant, but they grow better if you water them regularly as the flowers are developing and maturing. Spread a layer of mulch around them to keep down weeds. Sunflowers are generally trouble free, though deer may eat them if they're accessible. If you grow giant sunflowers for their seeds, encase the flowers in mesh bags or cheesecloth to protect them from birds.

Use in the garden: Sunflowers are delightful, cheerful plants. Their thick stems and large leaves give them a coarse appearance that makes them a challenge to combine with other flowers. A cottage garden or other informal setting will suit them best. Plant tall varieties in the back of the garden. Giant sunflowers can be grown in the vegetable garden to serve as supports for pole beans. Or plant them in a row to make a privacy screen or windbreak.

Tips for success: If you grow sunflowers for their edible seeds, harvest the seeds as soon as they start to turn brown, or when the back side of the seed head turns yellow. The heads will probably droop when seeds are mature. Cut the seed heads with 2 feet of stem attached and hang them upside down in a dry, well-ventilated place until they're completely dry. Extract the seeds by rubbing two seed heads together or by using a wire brush to dislodge them. Spread out the seeds on a rack or sheets of newspaper until fully dry. Then store them in plastic bags to use for feeding birds. Or spread them on baking sheets and place in a 200°F oven for 3 hours or until they are crisp. Then shell and eat them.

Sweet Alyssum
(*Lobularia maritima*)

One of the earliest annuals to bloom in spring, diminutive sweet alyssum is a perfect companion for pansies. You may also find plants for sale in fall—another good time to plant them along with pansies. Clusters of tiny, honey-scented white flowers on sprawling plants just 4 to 9 inches high make sweet alyssum a charming edging plant for flower gardens. The flowers support beneficial insects, such as braconid wasps, that help to control insect pests such as aphids.

Height and spread: 4 to 9 inches high and 6 inches wide.

Bloom time: Spring into autumn, though blooming may slow down in hot summer weather.

Flower color: White is the original color, but there are also cultivars that bloom in shades of lavender, darker purple, pink, rose, and apricot.

Where to plant: Full sun to partial or light shade, in any well-drained soil of average fertility.

How to grow: Sweet alyssum loves cold weather and can go into the garden as soon as you find plants for sale in local nurseries. The plants often drop their seeds on the ground and self-sow to come back next year. The seeds need light to germinate. Sweet alyssum is easy to care for. Water it during spells of dry weather, and pull weeds that come up among the plants.

Use in the garden: Stage it as edging in beds and borders or plant it at the edge of pots and window boxes to tumble over the side. Tuck sweet alyssum into crevices in dry-stone walls or rock gardens. Or plant it as a carpet under roses, spring bulbs, or pansies.

Tips for success: If bloom slows in hot weather, shearing back the plants and fertilizing them with a fish/seaweed fertilizer diluted according to the label directions can rejuvenate them and promote renewed flowering.

Zinnia, Common Zinnia
(*Zinnia elegans*)

Bright-colored zinnias have been cottage-garden favorites for generations. What conjures up the relaxed feeling of summer better than a bouquet of zinnias on a picnic table? The many-petaled flowers are easy to grow and come in a range of sizes. The bushy plants have sturdy stems covered with bristly hairs and coarse-looking, oblong leaves of dull green. A separate species, the narrow-leaved zinnia (*Zinnia angustifolia*), bears smaller flowers with fewer petals in a

lilliput zinnia

more limited color range of colors. But it keeps on producing them all summer and into fall.

Height and spread: Common zinnia: 6 inches to 3 feet tall and up to about 14 inches wide, depending on the cultivar. Narrow-leaved zinnia: 12 to 15 inches high and up to 12 inches wide.

Bloom time: Mid- to late summer; narrow-leaved zinnia blooms all summer long.

Flower color: Common zinnia: shades of red, rose, pink, peach, orange, pale green, and white. Narrow-leaved zinnia: yellow, gold, or orange.

Where to plant: Full sun, but plants will tolerate light shade in warm climates. Well-drained soil of average fertility is best, although zinnias will also grow in soil richer in nutrients.

How to grow: Many garden centers sell pots of zinnias already in bloom; you can pop them right into the garden for instant color. Zinnias grow well from seeds, too. Plant them indoors in containers of moist potting mix 2 to 3 weeks before the last expected spring frost in your area. But unless you live in a cold climate where the growing season is short, it's easiest to plant seeds right into the garden, after the last frost, when the soil is warm. Barely cover the seeds, and keep the soil or potting mix evenly moist until the seedlings are up. Space the plants (or thin the seedlings) 6 to 14 inches apart for common zinnias or 6 to 12 inches apart for narrow-leaved zinnias. Plants can tolerate some drought, so water them only when the soil is very dry. The big drawback to zinnias is their susceptibility to powdery mildew, a fungus disease that is most prevalent in humid weather. If that describes typical summer conditions where you live, spacing the plants farther apart to allow for good air circulation can help prevent mildew. If you notice spotting or a powdery white coating on leaves, remove the affected leaves right away. If you use an automatic sprinkler system, be sure it has a rain sensor so plants do not get watered in rainy weather. Water early in the day, but not overnight, so that foliage dries well before nightfall. Spraying the foliage with an antidesiccant spray may also help prevent mildew. Deadhead the plants to keep them blooming.

Use in the garden: Grow zinnias in a cottage garden or an informal flower-bed or border. Use narrow-leaved zinnias and dwarfs in the front of the garden and taller types farther back.

Tips for success: When zinnia flowers get old, they turn brown and moldy. Remove them from the plants before they reach that stage to keep the garden looking neat and to lessen the chance of disease. Remember, moisture and humidity are zinnia's enemies. Good air circulation and prompt removal of affected leaves and flowers can prolong the life of the plant.

20+ POPULAR GARDEN PERENNIALS

Perennials are all-purpose plants—you can grow them wherever you garden and in any part of your garden. There's a perennial to fit almost any spot in a landscape, and with a little planning, it's possible to have them in bloom throughout the frost-free months. In addition to the endless variety of sizes, shapes, colors, and plant habits, there are perennials for nearly any growing conditions your garden has to offer.

5 for Long-Lasting Color

Grow perennial flowers that bloom for weeks or months, and you (and local pollinators) can enjoy more of nature's most vivid colors with less effort. Here are five perennials recommended for their long-lasting good looks in the landscape by some of *Organic Gardening* magazine's experienced gardeners.

1. **Anise hyssop (*Agastache foeniculum*). 'Golden Jubilee' is an attractive, drought-tolerant native plant with bright chartreuse foliage. It keeps blooming well into fall, attracting all sorts of pollinators and beneficial insects.**
2. **Nepeta, catmint (*Nepeta × faassenii*). If you cut catmint back hard in early summer, it will regrow and bloom for the rest of the season.**
3. **'Autumn Joy' sedum (*Sedum* 'Autumn Joy'). Widely used for a reason—it looks great from spring through fall and even into winter. Plant it in a mass for a striking, trouble-free groundcover.**
4. **Hardy geraniums (*Geranium* spp.). Most species never need deadheading, unless you're especially persnickety, and the foliage looks great and keeps its neat shape all season.**
5. **Echinops, globe thistle (*Echinops* spp.). The round flower heads look beautiful even when they're dry.**

Most perennials prefer loamy soil with even moisture and full sun. Gardeners who have these conditions have the widest selection of plants from which to choose. However, if you have a shaded site, there are dozens of perennials for you, too.

Perennials add beauty, permanence, and seasonal rhythm to any landscape. Their yearly growth and flowering cycles are fun to follow—it's always exciting to see the first peonies pushing out of the ground in spring or the asters blooming bravely into late fall. Look at your gardening spaces and think about where you could add perennials. There are a number of ways to use perennials effectively in almost any yard.

The 20-plus perennials described here are those you are most likely to find for sale as container-grown plants at garden centers and nurseries in spring. For the most part, they are easy to grow, long lasting, and require moderate amounts of maintenance. While many perennials are easily started from seeds—and some of those listed here will increase by self-sowing—it can take a few seasons for some of them to grow large enough to contribute visually to your garden. Starting with purchased plants (or divisions from a fellow gardener) lets you enjoy the colors and textures of perennials much sooner and, as you gain gardening experience, gives you opportunities to divide mature plants to rejuvenate them and increase their presence in your garden.

Achillea, Yarrow
(*Achillea* spp.)

The flattopped flower heads of yarrows are beautiful, dependable additions to summer flower gardens. The flowers bloom atop straight, tall stems that seldom need to be staked. The mounds of leaves below are finely textured and fernlike, green or grayish green in color, and aromatic when bruised or rubbed with your fingers. Yarrows grow 18 inches to 4 feet tall, depending on the cultivar, and most are suited to growing in USDA Zones 3 to 9.

Bloom time: Early to midsummer; regular deadheading (removal of old, brown flowers) can prolong blooming through much of the summer for some cultivars.

Flower color: Bright golden yellow, soft yellow, white, pink, red, orange, and cream.

Where to plant: Full sun, in well-drained soil of average fertility. The plants tolerate poor, dry soils and are generally tough and adaptable. In more fertile soils, they may lean over when blooming and may need staking. Yarrows do well in hot, dry climates but can suffer in humid weather.

How to grow: Plant yarrow in spring or fall, whenever plants are available in local nurseries. Or you can order from an online or mail-order nursery. Set plants in the garden at the same depth they were growing in their nursery containers. For plants shipped by mail, follow the planting directions sent with the plants. Water at planting and as needed to keep the soil moist—not wet—for a few weeks after planting while the plants establish themselves in your garden and send new roots out into the soil. When the plants settle in, they will grow best in drier soil. Yarrows with gray green leaves may suffer leaf diseases in humid climates.

Divide yarrow plants every 2 to 3 years to keep the plants vigorous. Before winter, cut back the plants to a few inches above the ground.

Use in the garden: The flat flower heads of yarrows contrast beautifully with spiky, vertical flowers such as salvia and veronica or those of daylilies or Shasta daisies. Yarrow flowers also are good for cutting and drying.

Tips for success: Varieties with silvery or gray green foliage do not tolerate humidity well and may be short-lived in gardens where summer weather is often humid.

Aster
(*Symphyotrichum* spp.)

Asters are a great source of color for late-season gardens. Plants are easy to grow and produce clusters of daisylike flowers on branching, upright plants. They grow 1 to 4 or more feet high, depending on the species. If deer are problematic in your garden, they may munch on your asters. Many asters grow well in USDA Zones 4 to 9.

aster

Bloom time: Late summer and early autumn.

Flower color: Shades of purple, pink, blue, and red, plus white.

Where to plant: Full sun, in well-drained soil of average fertility.

How to grow: Plant asters in spring or fall, when plants are available in nurseries and garden centers. If you already have asters in your garden, you can divide the plants in spring and replant the divisions. Don't crowd the plants. Although asters need well-drained soil, they also like moisture. Water them during dry weather, applying water to the soil at the base of the plants rather than sprinkling from overhead. If the soil is too dry, asters will be shorter than normal, may lose their lower leaves, and won't bloom as well. If it's too wet, they may be short-lived. To promote bushier plants, pinch off the tips of the stems in early summer. If your asters grow tall and floppy, you will need to fasten them to stakes for support.

Use in the garden: Plant asters in the middle of an informal garden. Their billowy forms and cool-colored flowers provide a lovely contrast to the warm yellows, golds, bronzes, oranges, and reds of chrysanthemums and to yellow goldenrod. Asters are perfect for meadow gardens, and they also mix well with ornamental grasses.

Tips for success: If asters are crowded together with poor air circulation, they can be attacked by powdery mildew disease. Give them space.

Astilbe, False Spiraea
(*Astilbe* spp.)

Shade garden favorites, astilbes form mounds of attractive, toothed leaves divided into leaflets—the foliage resembles ferns. In summer, fluffy plumes of tiny flowers rise above the leaves on thin, wiry stems. The plants may be 1 to 4 feet tall, depending on the species and cultivar. Once considered to be reliably deer resistant, astilbe now finds a place on the deer menu in some gardens. The plants can withstand winter cold in USDA Zones 4 to 8.

Bloom time: Early to late summer, depending on cultivar.

Flower color: Shades of red, rose, pink, lavender pink, and white.

Where to plant: Astilbe grows well in partial shade. Where the summer sun is strong, astilbe foliage may sunburn and the flower colors may look bleached and paler than normal. In northern gardens, they can take full sun. Their preferred soil is moist but still well drained, rich in organic matter, and with a mildly acidic pH. Dig compost or other organic matter into the soil before you plant astilbe.

How to grow: Plant astilbe in spring when plants show up in local nurseries and garden centers. Sprinkle some all-purpose organic fertilizer around each plant in spring to promote good growth. If your soil tends to be dry, water astilbe during dry weather. If slugs and snails pose problems, you can pick them off by hand at night (wear gloves!) or trap the pests in a shallow container of beer placed so the rim is even with the soil surface. Cut back the plants to a few inches above the ground in late fall. For best growth, divide astilbe plants every year or two.

Use in the garden: Create drifts of astilbes in semishady borders, in moist woodlands, and along streams. Smaller types are ideal for the front of shady borders and in rock gardens.

Tips for success: If deer are present in your garden, spray your astilbes with an organic deer repellent to protect them.

Chrysanthemum, Garden Mum
(*Chrysanthemum ×grandiflorum*)

The most beloved of all fall-blooming flowers, chrysanthemums seem to be everywhere soon after Labor Day. There are loads of mums, but the kind that's so ubiquitous in nurseries, garden centers, big box stores, and supermarkets is the cushion mum (the ones sold as cut flowers are daisy mums). To create their rounded, symmetrical shape and abundant bloom, commercial growers pinch back the stems throughout the plant's development. It's a painstaking process. When you grow mums in your garden, they'll be looser and lankier plants, although still colorful. They will probably bloom earlier, too. Garden mums may be 1 to about 3 feet high. They can be grown in USDA Zones 4 to 10.

Bloom time: Late summer into fall; chrysanthemums will bloom before the end of summer in many home gardens.

Flower color: Shades of red, orange, russet, yellow, bronze, lavender, purple, and white.

Where to plant: Mums need full sun; in even partial shade, they'll be lackluster. Give them average to rich soil that is well drained but able to hold moisture long enough for plant roots to absorb it.

How to grow: You can order mums from online and mail-order nurseries, and these plants should have a good chance of succeeding in the garden. You can also buy plants in bud in late summer or early fall—they seem to be everywhere. Blooming plants sold as hardy mums may or may not actually overwinter in your garden. In any case, most mums are hybrids that cannot be guaranteed to look like their parents if you try to grow them from seed. Water chrysanthemums during hot, dry weather. Feed the plants in spring and again in midsummer with an all-purpose organic fertilizer. Spray the plants with a hose once a week to help prevent aphids and mites from establishing themselves on the foliage and stems. If you want to grow the bushiest possible plants, pinch off the tips of all the stems to the nearest set of leaves when the plant is 5 inches tall and again before mid-July in northern gardens or mid-August in the South. Mum plants typically bloom for 3 to 4 weeks. When the flowers bloom, cut them off when they fade to make room for fresh, new blossoms. If you live in a cold northern climate, you can mulch the chrysanthemums in late fall when the ground freezes to protect them over winter.

Use in the garden: Practically synonymous with autumn, mums are a staple of fall garden beds, borders, and containers.

Tips for success: Chrysanthemums need ample moisture, but their roots should not sit in wet soil. Give them well-drained soil but water when the soil dries out, and spread a layer of mulch around the plants to conserve moisture around their roots.

Coreopsis, Tickseed
(Coreopsis grandiflora, C. verticillata)

Coreopsis brings its yellow daisy flowers to the garden for many weeks in summer. If you're willing to remove the old, spent flowers, the plants will keep on producing them all summer long. *Coreopsis grandiflora* cultivars grow 2 to 3 feet high and 12 inches wide, with flowers on tall stems above a clump of narrow green leaves. Threadleaf coreopsis (*C. verticillata*) grows 2 to 3 feet high and 2 feet wide, with feathery, thin leaves. Hardiness varies with the species, but most are suited to USDA Zones 3 to 8 or 9.

Bloom time: Late spring to fall.

Flower color: Bright golden yellow, soft pastel yellow, pink, orange, and red.

Where to plant: Coreopsis need full sun to put on their best show. They'll grow in any well-drained garden soil of average fertility. They don't do well in heavy, wet soils but can tolerate some drought.

How to grow: Plant coreopsis plants in spring when they become available locally. Plant them at the same depth they were growing in their nursery containers, spacing plants about 12 inches apart. If you ordered plants by mail, follow the directions for planting supplied by the company. The most important thing you can do for coreopsis is to deadhead (remove the old flowers) regularly—even every day, if you can—cutting each old flowering stem back to its base. It can be time consuming if you have a lot of plants, but it will definitely keep the plants blooming. Threadleaf coreopsis, such as the cultivars 'Zagreb' and 'Moonbeam', produce lots of flowers on very thin stems—they're hard to deadhead if you don't have unlimited time and patience. You can instead shear back the plants by about half their height in late summer (you can use hedge shears) and the plants should rebloom in fall. Threadleaf coreopsis will spread if it's happy and expand its growing area. Dig up plants that spread beyond where you want them to be.

Use in the garden: Coreopsis shines in the middle ground of a flower garden.

Tips for success: Coreopsis are lovely additions to the garden, but they tend to be short-lived, especially red and pink cultivars, and may disappear from the garden after a couple of years. The golden yellow cultivars seem to be the sturdiest and most resilient.

Echinacea, Purple Coneflower
(*Echinacea purpurea*)

Native to the Midwestern prairies, purple coneflower now grows in gardens across much of the country. The flowers are purple pink daisies with a prominent bronze orange center. There are also cultivars that bloom in white and in warm colors such as orange and yellow. Plants grow 2 to 4 feet high and about 2 feet wide, with coarse-textured narrow, oblong leaves. They're generally suited to USDA Zones 3 to 8 or 9. The plants may attract beneficial soldier beetles in late summer; if you spot them on the plants, leave them alone to do their pest-hunting work.

Bloom time: All summer into fall.

Flower color: Shades of purple pink, white, orange, yellow, red.

Where to plant: Full sun, in well-drained soil of average fertility. Echinacea can tolerate poor soils better than rich ones. They won't last long in heavy, wet soil.

How to grow: Plant echinacea in spring or fall. Keep the soil evenly moist after planting for a few weeks until the plants establish themselves in the garden and send out new roots. Thereafter, water them only during times of extended drought—they can tolerate dry conditions except in extreme circumstances. The plants will bloom all summer without deadheading, but removing old blossoms improves the plants' appearance in the garden. If you leave the remains of flowers (actually seed heads) standing in late summer and fall, the seeds will likely attract visits from migrating birds. The downside (if you don't want more coneflowers) is that any uneaten seeds will fall to the ground and produce new seedlings next spring—your coneflowers will spread. Echinacea may be attacked by Japanese beetles or powdery mildew disease. Pick off the shiny bronze beetles if they appear. Allowing enough space between plants for good air circulation can help prevent mildew. If the disease strikes (the leaves develop a whitish coating), it will disfigure the leaves but probably won't kill the plant.

Use in the garden: Purple coneflower is ideal for a naturalistic meadow or prairie garden or for an informal flower garden. Echinacea also finds a place in gardens of healing herbs.

Tips for success: Echinacea will be tall and floppy in rich, fertile soil, so don't fertilize it.

Ferns

Although they don't bloom, ferns are classic perennials for shady gardens. They're easy to care for, often they will grow in full shade where many other plants won't, and deer don't eat them in most gardens. There are ferns for wet sites and dry places, for sunny spots or for every degree of shade, for cold climates and warm zones. Ferns come in a range of heights and a host of textures.

Foliage color: Most are some shade of green, but there are also standouts such as the Japanese painted fern, whose fronds are ribbed in maroon and overlaid with silver.

Where to plant: Most ferns need moist soil that's rich in organic matter, though some grow better in drier places. One way to find out which ferns generally grow

ferns

well in your area is to contact your county's Cooperative Extension office (which you can find with an online search or in a listing of county government offices in a phone book). Some ferns have particular pH requirements, so it's wise to test your soil before buying ferns so you can plant compatible species. Prepare the soil for planting ferns by digging in compost.

How to grow: Garden centers and nurseries carry some ferns, and that's a good place to get started. But you'll find a better selection from online and mail-order nurseries. One big concern with buying ferns is to purchase nursery-propagated plants rather than ferns that have been collected from the wild. Never buy wild-collected ferns. If you do, you will be helping to endanger an ecosystem wherever the plants were taken. Ferns sold at bargain prices are a red flag that can indicate wild-collected plants. Don't hesitate to ask the company where their plants came from before you buy.

Plant ferns in fall (the best time in many gardens) or early spring. If you buy ferns locally, plant them at the same depth they were growing in their nursery container. When you remove the fern from its pot, if you find a dense, tight mass of roots, use a sharp knife to make three or four shallow cuts lengthwise up into the rootball from the bottom. The cuts will break up the root mass and make it easier for new roots to grow beyond it into the soil. If you buy plants from an online or mail-order source, you may receive bare-root plants not growing in a pot of soil. Follow the planting directions you receive with the plants. Ferns that have creeping rhizomes (horizontal underground stems) should be planted just $\frac{1}{2}$ to 1 inch under the soil surface. Ferns that grow from a single crown should be planted with the crown (the point where roots meet fronds) a few inches above the soil surface. Established ferns don't need a lot of care. You can remove browned or damaged fronds, and in spring you will need to get rid of last year's old fronds. Spread a layer of organic mulch around and among your ferns to keep down weeds. The mulch will decompose and add organic matter to the soil, and you won't have to fertilize the ferns.

Use in the garden: Plant ferns to fill in empty spots in shady gardens or under shrubs and trees. Ferns can also fill in when spring bulbs die back after blooming. You can use ferns to edge a path through a shady garden, or plant them alongside a patio or deck. They're good complements to bright-colored annual and perennial flowers. Some can spread and serve as groundcover in an area that does not get foot traffic. Of course they're an essential component of a woodland garden.

Tips for success: Don't plant ferns too deep or the plants will die. Follow the planting directions accompanying mail-order plants or on the tags of garden-center ferns.

Geranium, Cranesbill, Hardy Geranium
(*Geranium* spp.)

Hardy geraniums are very different from the *Pelargonium* hybrids that spill out of hanging baskets and pots and brighten summer annual gardens. The hardy geraniums are charming, lovely plants for sunny to partially shady gardens. Cranesbills have five-petaled, slightly cup-shaped flowers that grow on sprawling, floppy plants from to 18 inches high. The attractive green leaves may be scalloped or divided into segments called lobes. Cranesbills grow in USDA Zones 4 to 10, but the growing range varies among species.

Bloom time: Mid- to late spring into summer; some species produce a good flush of bloom in spring and then bloom sporadically through much of summer.

Flower color: Shades of pink from light pink to bright magenta, purple, blue, and white.

Where to plant: Cranesbills are ideally suited to partially shady locations that might be found at the edge of the woods. In warmer climates, give them some shade. They thrive in soil that is well drained but able to hold moisture long enough for roots to absorb what they need. Average fertility is best.

How to grow: Plant hardy geraniums in spring or fall, setting them as deep as they were growing in their nursery containers. If you ordered plants by mail, follow the planting directions that accompanied them. Keep the soil evenly moist for a few weeks after planting until the plants establish themselves in the garden. After that, they can tolerate dryness but not prolonged drought conditions. In warm climates, the plants do better with more moisture, so water when the soil is dry. If the plants look ratty in midsummer, you can cut back the stems to promote bushy new growth.

Use in the garden: Most hardy geraniums work best in the front of an informal bed or border. The smallest ones can be used as groundcovers in places where they won't be stepped on.

Tips for success: Cranesbills generally bloom longer in cooler climates. Don't plant them in rich, fertile soil or the sprawling plants will be even floppier.

Helleborus, Hellebore, Lenten Rose
(*Helleborus* hybrids)

Hellebores are by far the earliest perennials to bloom in many gardens. They open their flowers in late winter—they'll bloom in snow—for early spring. Even better, deer don't touch them. Many of the hybrid hellebores found in today's gardens were bred from the old-fashioned Lenten rose (*Helleborus orientalis*), but they are now classified by botanists into their own species: *H. × hybridus*. Their cup-shaped or flat-petaled flowers that either droop or face outward bloom in a host of intriguing colors. They last an astonishingly long time—2 months or more. The plants grow as clumps of stems 18 to 24 inches high and 24 to 30 inches wide. The evergreen leaves are dark green and divided into segments that fan out from a central point like spokes of a wheel. Even after the flowers finally fade, the plants have great presence in the garden. Most of these hellebores are suited to USDA Zones 4 to 9, although some are best in Zones 6 to 9; check the hardiness rating for the hybrid you want to buy.

Bloom time: Late winter to early spring.

Flower color: Shades of pink, maroon, purple, and chartreuse, creamy white, and dramatic black (actually a very dark purple, but it truly does look black).

Where to plant: Plant hellebores in partial to full shade—they can thrive in the shade of a tree. Soil that is well drained is important—hellebores cannot tolerate heavy, soggy soils. They do handle dry conditions quite well. Once they've become established in the garden, you'll need only to water them occasionally. Soil containing lots of organic matter is ideal for hellebores; dig plenty of compost into the soil when you plant. The plants need loose soil to sink their long roots deep into the ground. Local nurseries and garden centers usually carry some hellebores, and you can also buy plants from online and mail-order sources. Since most modern hellebores are hybrids, you'll have to buy plants, not seeds. Space them 24 to 30 inches apart. Water as needed to keep the soil from drying out for the first few weeks after planting while the plants are sending new roots out into the soil. The plants are evergreen, and once a year you can remove the old leaves just before the flowers open, although it's not absolutely necessary. Don't remove the old leaves too soon—they protect the developing flower buds. Water hellebores only during extended periods of drought.

Use in the garden: Hellebores are hard to beat for early color and year-round interest in flowerbeds and borders. Or plant masses of them under trees.

Tips for success: Planting hellebores in well-drained soil that's rich in organic matter is the most important key to success.

Hemerocallis, Daylily
(*Hemerocallis* hybrids)

The orange flowers of the tawny daylily (*Hemerocallis fulva*) are a common sight along American roadways in summer. You can buy the plants for your garden, but there are so many more colors and forms available among daylily hybrids. Some are even delightfully fragrant. The flowers are trumpet shaped, but in some cultivars the petals are narrow and spidery or wavy. The flowers bloom atop straight, stiff stems above a low clump of strap-shaped leaves. Daylilies come in a range of sizes, from 12- to 24-inch-high 'Stella de Oro' and its relatives (which keep blooming all summer long if you remove the old flowers) to towering cultivars such as 56-inch-high 'Moon Ladder'. They grow in USDA Zones 3 to 9.

Bloom time: Summer. There are early, midseason, and late-blooming daylilies. By planting cultivars with different bloom times, you can enjoy daylily flowers in your garden for much of the summer.

Flower color: Many warm shades of yellow, orange, apricot, and red, also purple, some with a contrasting central "eye."

Where to plant: Full sun to partial shade; pastel-colored flowers retain better color in partial shade. Daylilies will grow in any average to fertile garden soil that is well drained but able to hold moisture long enough for roots to absorb what they need.

How to grow: Plant daylilies bought from a local nursery or garden center at the same depth they were growing in their nursery pot. If you bought your daylilies by mail or online, follow the planting directions sent along with them. The plants do need some maintenance during the growing season, but they're generally easy to grow. Water at planting and as needed to keep the soil moist—not wet—for a few weeks while the plants establish themselves in the garden. Thereafter, they should be able to tolerate some dryness.

Daylilies bear their flowers in clusters, opening one flower at a time in succession. Pinch off each flower at its base after it blooms (they last only a single day). When all the flowers on a stem have bloomed, cut off the stem at its base. When the plants finish blooming, you will probably need to begin removing dead leaves to keep the plants looking neat. Dying leaves are typical for daylilies. You can reach into the plants and pull out the brown, dry leaves with your hands. Small pests called thrips may attack daylilies and cause the flower buds to turn brown. Control them with insecticidal soap.

Use in the garden: Daylilies are lovely additions to flowerbeds and borders. You can plant a mass of them in a bed of their own or on a bank. Small varieties work well in containers.

Tips for success: One huge caveat with daylilies is that deer love to eat them. If deer are present in your area, try planting just a few daylilies to see if they'll be eaten. If they are, and you still want daylilies, you may have to enclose your garden—or your property—with deer fencing 10 feet high. Or spray the plants with a deer repellent every 2 weeks. If deer pressure is intense, you may need to spray every week.

Hosta, Plantain Lily
(*Hosta* spp. and cultivars)

Hostas are classics for shady gardens. The plants bloom, sending up tall stems of trumpet-shaped flowers of white or pale purple (some of which are fragrant) above the leaves in mid- to late summer. But we grow hostas primarily for their beautifully patterned leaves. They come in practically every shade of green. The leaves range in size from a few inches to a foot or more long and may be narrow and pointed to broad and rounded. They can be smooth or puckered. Whatever their shape, the leaves grow in mounds. The plants range in size from 6-inch dwarfs to 4-foot giants. Hostas generally are suited to USDA Zones 3 to 8.

Bloom time: Mid- to late summer, although the foliage is the main attraction.

Foliage color: Leaves come in many shades of green, from deep forest green to dusky blue green to luminous chartreuse or even gold, and they may be a solid color or edged, streaked, flamed, or otherwise patterned with white, yellow, or a contrasting shade of green.

Where to plant: Hostas are shade plants, growing best in partial to full shade. Some can stand full sun in northern gardens if the soil is moist and fertile. Hostas generally prefer soil that is well drained but moist and rich in organic matter. Add compost to their area every year.

How to grow: Purchase plants locally or from an online or mail-order source. If you buy locally, plant them at the same depth they were growing in their nursery container. If you have small plants shipped to you, follow the handling and planting directions from the supplier. Hostas thrive in evenly moist soil; water them during dry weather as they grow. In winter when they are dormant, they can be drier. Hostas are deer favorites; if you must share your garden with deer, you will have to surround it with a 10-foot fence or spray your hostas with deer repellent often, perhaps every week or two. Slugs are also fond of juicy hosta leaves. Make traps to lure them to destruction to keep them from chewing holes in your hostas. Plantain lilies form clumps that expand gradually over the years. If your plants become crowded, divide them in spring or early fall. Dig them up, split the root clump into pieces, and replant the pieces to grow new plants. At the end of the growing season, cut back the stems of your hostas to a few inches above the ground. If you are planning to divide your plants, cutting back the stems before you do so will make them easier to handle.

Use in the garden: Grow in groups or use showy cultivars as specimens. Hostas cover dying bulb foliage, so they make excellent companions for spring-blooming bulbs. Plant where they will brighten shady areas beneath trees. They combine well with ferns, hellebores, heucheras, and other shade plants.

Tips for success: Hostas can take some sun, especially in northern gardens. But don't plant them where they will be exposed to hot sun in the afternoon—it will burn the leaves.

Iris
(*Iris* spp. and cultivars)

Graceful, elegant irises are an important part of the late-spring flower garden, often blooming along with peonies. Named for the Greek goddess of the rainbow, irises come in a spectrum of colors. The plants vary in height from 4-inch dwarfs to 5-foot-tall bearded cultivars, but all of them have smooth-edged, sword-shaped leaves. Bearded irises (*Iris* × *germanica* cultivars) have large, ruffled flowers, but they need a lot of maintenance. Easy-to-grow Siberian irises (*I. sibirica*) have narrower, pointed petals and bloom in just a few colors but are easier to combine with other flowers in a garden. Most species and cultivars grow in USDA Zones 3 to 9.

Bloom time: Late spring.

Flower color: Bearded irises: many shades of yellow, pink, purple, lavender, blue, red, orange, peach, maroon, brownish red, dark purple black, and white. Siberian irises: shades of violet and white.

Where to plant: Irises flower best in full sun, although they appreciate some afternoon shade in hot climates. Soil that is well drained but fertile and rich in organic matter is ideal.

How to grow: You can plant irises in spring or fall, but fall is often the better time, especially in warmer climates. For Siberian irises, purchase plants from a local nursery or garden center or an online or mail-order nursery company. Plant them in the garden at the same depth they were growing in their nursery container. If you order by mail, follow the planting directions you receive with the plants. Bearded irises grow from rhizomes (horizontal underground stems that in this case look something like oblong bulbs). Planting depth is critical. Bearded irises are susceptible to a number of rots, pests, and diseases. It's important to not completely bury the rhizomes but to leave the tops of them exposed, except in hot climates. Dig a planting hole just deep enough to leave the top half of each rhizome uncovered; set the rhizomes horizontally. Position the plant so its fan of leaves points in the direction you want the plant to grow. Firm the soil around the roots. Water irises after planting to settle the roots into the soil. Fertilize irises in spring and early fall with an all-purpose organic fertilizer or one meant for flowering plants.

Water Siberian irises during spells of dry weather. Water bearded irises regularly while they're blooming to keep the soil from drying out; about 6 weeks after flowering, the rhizomes go dormant and become quite tolerant of drought. Siberian irises need little maintenance. You can remove the seed capsules after flowers finish blooming by cutting back the flowering stems by about two-thirds of their length. But the seedpods aren't visually intrusive, so you can leave them in place if you like. Bearded irises need to have the old, mushy flowers removed regularly to keep the plants looking neat. Don't cut off the entire flower stem—buds lower on the stem will open after the higher flowers have bloomed. Cut off the stem at its base when the last flower has wilted. Bearded irises suffer from a variety of leaf diseases, so trim off any damaged leaves or parts of leaves when you spot damage. If a lot of leaves are affected, cut back all the leaves to about 5 inches above the ground. After you cut off diseased leaves, dip your shears or clippers in a solution of one part bleach to nine parts water. Dispose of the leaves in your trash; don't toss them on the compost pile or leave them in the garden. Divide bearded iris rhizomes every 3 or 4 years in late summer or fall after plants have finished blooming. Cut back the leaves to a few inches. Dig up the root clump and split the rhizomes apart, each with a fan of leaves attached. Discard the woody central part of the root clump and replant the newly divided rhizomes with their top side uncovered. Water well after division is complete.

Use in the garden: Smaller bearded irises are perfect in rock gardens and along paths and beds. For mid- to late-spring bloom, plant taller ones in a perennial border or a separate bed to provide optimal conditions. Siberian irises are good choices for borders and wet sites, such as along a stream or the edge of a pond, although they prefer slightly drier conditions in winter.

Tips for success: If you are a new gardener, start with Siberian irises rather than the bearded types. Bearded irises are flashy and gorgeous, but they do take work. Siberians are much easier to grow.

Leucanthemum, Shasta Daisy

(*Leucanthemum ×superbum*)

In summer, Shasta daisy bears classic yellow-centered white daisy flowers on straight stems lined with narrow, toothed-edged green leaves. The plants form clumps of stems 2 to 3 feet high and 2 feet wide, and they will expand in good growing conditions. Shasta daisies are suited to gardens in USDA Zones 5 to 9. The cultivar 'Alaska' can survive in Zone 4.

Bloom time: Early to midsummer.

Flower color: White with yellow center.

Where to plant: Full sun, in soil that is average to fertile and well drained but able to retain some moisture.

How to grow: Plant Shasta daisies in spring, when plants are available in local nurseries and garden centers, or when online and mail-order nurseries will ship them to your area. Plant at the same depth plants were growing in their nursery container. Follow planting instructions sent along with mail-order plants. Water at planting and for a few weeks thereafter while the plants are establishing themselves in the garden. Through the season, water them during spells of dry weather. Tall plants may need to be supported with stakes. Remove old flowers as they fade, cutting back the stems to just above the next buds below the old flower. This kind of deadheading will encourage the plants to keep blooming—maybe all summer. In late summer when the plants are finished blooming, new leaves will grow at the base of the plant. When that happens, you can cut off all the old stems and new stems may grow and produce new flowers (they'll be smaller than the first round of bloom). The abundant blooming may wear out the plants; Shasta daisies can be short-lived. Fertilize established plants in spring with an all-purpose organic fertilizer or one meant for flowers. In midsummer, feed them with a fish/seaweed fertilizer diluted according to the directions on the label. Before winter, cut back any tall stems to a few inches above the ground.

Use in the garden: Plant Shasta daisies in the middle or back of a flowerbed or border, depending on the height of the variety you are growing. Shasta daisies make terrific cut flowers, so grow them in a cutting garden if you have one.

Tips for success: Shasta daisies can die out during their winter dormant period if their soil is waterlogged. Avoid planting them in spots where water tends to puddle. Adding plenty of compost to the soil before you plant them can help ensure decent drainage in most soils throughout the year.

Monarda, Bee Balm
(*Monarda didyma*)

This charming member of the mint family bears shaggy-looking, 2- to 3-inch flowers in mostly warm shades atop tall, straight, square stems in summer. The deep green leaves are fragrant, releasing an aromatic, citrusy scent on hot days or when brushed against. The plants grow 2 to 4 feet tall and form clumps to about 2 feet wide. Bee balm is suited to USDA Zones 4 to 9. The plants can attract bees, butterflies, and other pollinating insects, as well as hummingbirds.

Bloom time: Early to midsummer.

Flower color: Shades of red, pink, and purple, as well as white.

Where to plant: Full sun, in soil that is well drained but moist and rich in organic matter. Very wet or very dry soils can be problematic for bee balm.

How to grow: Plant bee balm in spring, setting plants from a local nursery or garden center at the same depth they were growing in their nursery container. If you order plants from an online or mail-order source, follow the planting directions you receive with them. Space plants about 2 feet apart. Do not crowd them; bee balm needs good air circulation. Water at planting time and as needed to keep the soil moist for the first few weeks while the plants establish themselves in the garden and send out new roots. Deadhead to extend the blooming season, cutting the flower stem back to the next lowest set of leaves with flower buds. Bee balm spreads to form clumps and can become invasive in good conditions. To keep it in bounds, divide the plants every couple of years. To do this, cut back the plants in spring or fall to a few inches above the ground. Dig up the clump of plants and split it into the size you want, then replant that portion of the clump. Or simply pull up unwanted new plants and toss them in the compost.

Use in the garden: Bee balm is lovely in a cottage or wildflower garden. The leaves and flowers are edible (when grown organically) and can be added to salads. You can also dry the leaves and use them to make tea.

Tips for success: One problem with bee balm is that the plants are susceptible to mildew, especially after they finish blooming. Giving plants plenty of space will help, as will ensuring they have soil that is well drained but not dry. If mildew does strike and disfigure the leaves with a grayish white coating, cut back the stems to the new leaves that are growing at the base of the plants. Discard the mildewed stems with the trash; don't put them on the compost pile.

Nepeta, Catmint
(*Nepeta ×faassenii*)

Aromatic and easy to grow, catmint (not to be confused with the catnip so beloved by kitties, which is *Nepeta cataria*) produces its loose spires of small blossoms over many weeks in summer. The plants grow 1 to 3 feet high and $1\frac{1}{2}$ to 3 feet across, with grayish green, scalloped leaves on sprawling (or upright, in some cultivars) stems. Catmint grows in USDA Zones 3 or 4 to 8 or 9. Good news: Deer don't eat it.

Bloom time: Early to late summer. Cutting off the old flowers or cutting back the plants by half or two-thirds after they bloom often will stimulate another round of bloom.

Flower color: Lavender blue; the flowers are neither truly blue nor truly purple.

Where to plant: Full sun is best; plants tolerate partial shade but will not bloom as profusely. Give nepeta well-drained soil of average fertility. It can adapt to relatively dry soils.

How to grow: Plant in spring or fall, whenever plants are available locally, or when online and mail-order suppliers will ship to your area. Plant them at the same depth plants were growing in their nursery containers, or follow the planting directions you receive with mail-order plants. Water well at planting time and as needed to keep the soil evenly moist—not wet—for a few weeks while the plants are settling into the garden. Once established, nepeta can tolerate dry conditions. The leaves may begin to yellow in late summer, especially if your garden experiences heavy rains. If this happens, cut them back by half to two-thirds to improve their appearance and stimulate fresh new growth.

Use in the garden: Catmint is a lovely companion for roses and for other pink flowers in an informal bed or border or a cottage garden. The sprawling varieties can be planted along a sidewalk or garden path to soften the edges.

Tips for success: Catmint thrives in hot weather and can take dry conditions, but it doesn't do so well in steamy, humid locations. Like other members of the mint family, catmint can spread vigorously in congenial conditions. Dig up any plants that get out of hand.

Paeonia, Peony
(*Paeonia* cultivars)

Peonies have been flower garden favorites for hundreds of years. The big, beautiful, fragrant flowers are the queens of the early-summer perennial garden, and the bushy plants with their handsome, segmented green leaves are attractive all season and make a great backdrop for later-blooming flowers. Better yet, peonies are easy to grow and not eaten by deer. Grow peonies in USDA Zones 3 to 8.

Bloom time: Late spring to early summer.

Flower color: Many shades of pink, rose, and red, as well as white and cream.

Where to plant: Full sun, in fertile, well-drained soil. Long-lived peonies can remain in place for years, so it pays to prepare the soil before planting by digging in compost.

How to grow: The best time to plant peonies is in fall—September or October in northern gardens or October to November in the South. If you buy plants in bloom at a local nursery in spring, be careful not to plant them any deeper than they were growing in their nursery pot. Plant peonies with the "eyes"—the tips of the pointed, pinkish new stems—just 1 to 2 inches below the soil surface in northern gardens, or close to the soil surface in warm climates. Remove the old flowers when they finish blooming or they will turn into ugly blobs of brown mush. Cut the flower stem back to a leaf lower on the stem. Peonies can suffer leaf diseases. If you notice browning or spotty leaves, cut them off as soon as you see them. If leaves drop, pick them up. Dispose of all damaged leaves in the trash—do not compost them. At the end of the growing season, cut back the plants to a few inches from the ground.

Use in the garden: Peonies are classics for flowerbeds and borders or cottage gardens. They make wonderful cut flowers, too.

Tips for success: If your peonies fail to bloom, it may well be because they are planted too deep. Check to make sure the crowns (where roots meet stems) are no deeper than 2 inches below the soil surface. If you notice ants on your peony buds or blossoms, don't worry. They are gathering nectar and won't hurt the flowers. Shake off any ants before bringing cut flowers indoors.

Phlox, Garden Phlox
(*Phlox paniculata*)

A lovely addition to flower gardens, garden phlox, or summer phlox, bears large, pyramid-shaped clusters of flowers, which may be delightfully fragrant, in summer. Plants grow 2 to 4 feet high and about 2 feet wide, with narrowly oblong green leaves. Garden phlox is suited to USDA Zones 4 to 8 or 9.

Bloom time: Summer to early fall.

Flower color: White and many shades of red, pink, orange, lavender, and purple, some with a central "eye" in a contrasting color.

Where to plant: Full sun, or partial shade in southern gardens, in well-drained but moist, fertile soil rich in organic matter.

How to grow: Plant phlox in spring or fall, when plants are available locally. Dig some compost into the soil before you plant. Set nursery plants at the same depth they were growing in their nursery container. Allow plenty of space between the plants for good air circulation. Water at planting and as needed to keep the soil evenly moist for a few weeks while the plants are settling into the garden and then throughout the growing season. Try to water at ground level rather than sprinkling plants from overhead. Garden phlox need plenty of nutrients to support their growth. Scatter some organic all-purpose fertilizer around the base of each plant when you plant it. In subsequent years, fertilize the plants in early spring. If summer weather is humid where you live, it can be helpful to remove up to one-third of the stems in each clump of phlox plants to ensure that air can circulate freely around and through the plants. Phlox plants often drop seeds onto the ground to self-sow and produce new plants. Because the phlox you plant in your garden are most likely hybrid varieties, the seedlings that come up around them won't look like the parent plants. They will probably be a magenta color, and they will eventually crowd out the plants you want if you don't remove these errant seedlings. Garden phlox is prone to powdery mildew disease. If your plants become badly infected, cut back the stems to a few inches above the ground. Dispose of the diseased plant parts in the trash, not your compost pile. Keep watering the area when necessary, and fertilize again to promote new growth from the roots. Better yet, plant mildew-resistant cultivars such as 'David', 'Natascha', 'Robert Poore', and 'Shortwood'. In fall, cut back the plants to a few inches from the ground.

Use in the garden: Phlox is lovely in the middle ground of a flowerbed or border. It's a good choice for a cutting garden or a cottage garden of old-fashioned flowers.

Tips for success: To prevent phlox from self-sowing, remove the old flower clusters when they fade or when the seeds that follow are still green, before the seeds have a chance to ripen and drop to the ground.

Rudbeckia, Orange Coneflower, Black-Eyed Susan
(*Rudbeckia fulgida*)

The dark-centered, orangey yellow daisy flowers of coneflower are a familiar sight in late summer. Tough and easy to grow, orange coneflower thrives in many informal garden beds and borders. Plants grow $1\frac{1}{2}$ to $2\frac{1}{2}$ feet tall and to $2\frac{1}{2}$ feet wide, with sturdy, branching stems and coarse-looking dark green leaves. The name black-eyed Susan correctly belongs to the annual species, *Rudbeckia hirta*, but gardeners often apply it to the perennial species, too. The perennial species grows in USDA Zones 3 to 9.

Bloom time: Midsummer into fall.

Flower color: Bright orangey yellow.

Where to plant: Full sun is best, though plants can tolerate partial shade. Well-drained soil of average fertility suits this coneflower.

How to grow: Plant rudbeckia in spring or fall when plants are available locally. Set nursery plants at the same depth they were growing in their nursery container. If you order plants by mail or online, follow the planting directions sent along with them. Water after planting and as needed to keep the soil from drying out for a few weeks while the plants settle into your garden. Thereafter, orange coneflower is resilient and needs little maintenance. The plants will bloom on and on even if you don't remove the spent flowers. In fact, birds like to pull the seeds from the cone-shaped centers as they mature. Rudbeckias spread by means of rhizomes (horizontal underground stems), and they can also self-sow, dropping mature seeds onto the ground to produce new plants. In any case, you will likely find yourself with a colony of coneflowers that may crowd out less pushy plants. Dig or pull plants that come up where you don't want them. After a few years, if the center of the clump of plants produces fewer flowers, dig up the plants and divide the root mass into pieces by cutting down into it with a sharp spade. Throw out the piece from the center of the clump and replant the younger, outer sections.

Use in the garden: Grow orange coneflower in beds and borders, in a meadow garden, or in masses in a sunny bed of their own. They also make good cut flowers.

Tips for success: Rudbeckia appears in many lists of deer-resistant plants, but deer have developed a taste for it in an increasing number of gardens. If deer are a problem in your area, plant just one or two coneflowers as an experiment, to see if the deer sample them, before you plant a large swath.

Salvia, Sage
(*Salvia ×sylvestris*)

The ornamental relatives of culinary sage are a tremendous asset in flower gardens. The most widely grown perennial cultivars bear slender, upright clusters (called spikes) of tiny blue or violet flowers that will keep on coming all summer long if you regularly cut off the old, faded ones. The flowering spikes are borne above a bushy mound of leaves, for a total height of $1\frac{1}{2}$ to 3 feet. Plants are about

1½ feet wide. Some salvias are only perennial in warm-climate gardens, but cultivars of this hybrid species do best in USDA Zones 5 to 9. They're deer resistant, too.

Bloom time: Late spring through summer, if deadheaded.

Flower color: Blue, violet, deep purple.

Where to plant: For best bloom, plant salvia in full sun (plants may be floppy in shady locations). Well-drained soil of average fertility is ideal; in rich, fertile soil, the plants won't be as sturdy.

How to grow: Plant salvia in spring or fall, when plants are available in local nurseries and garden centers, or when mail-order suppliers will ship to your area. Set plants at the same depth they were growing in their nursery pots. If you received plants by mail, follow the planting directions sent with them. Water at planting time and as needed to keep the soil from drying out for the first few weeks while the plants establish themselves in the garden. Thereafter, salvia will need to be watered during extended dry spells but can tolerate some dryness. Critical to getting the best performance from perennial salvias is to remove the old flower spikes as they fade. Cut back the flowering stem to the next pair of leaves on the stem, and new flowers will grow from the cut places.

Use in the garden: Perennial salvias are splendid performers in the middle ground of a bed or border. The vertical lines of their flower spikes provide a visual counterpoint to the forms of rounded flowers such as peonies, poppies, coreopsis, and yarrows. Their blue color beautifully complements yellow and pink flowers.

Tips for success: Don't just deadhead old salvia blossoms once. Repeat the process throughout the growing season as flowers fade, and the plants will keep producing new blossom stalks.

Sedum, Stonecrop
(*Sedum* cultivars)

For late-season color, sedums are hard to beat. The fleshy, succulent plants produce tiny flowers in dense clusters that resemble small heads of light green broccoli early in the season. When those minute buds open in late summer, the "broccoli" develops and deepens in color. As the blossoms fade, they gradually turn brown but still add interest to the garden in fall. Sedums are easy to grow and long-lived. The ones most beloved of perennial gardeners grow about 2 feet high and 18 inches wide, with scalloped leaves on upright, stiff stems. Many of them grow in USDA Zones 4 to 10.

Bloom time: Late summer into autumn.

Flower color: Depends on the cultivar. Pink, hot pink, pinkish white, or salmon deepening to coppery bronze.

Where to plant: Best in full sun but will take partial shade. Any well-drained soil of average fertility is fine. Once established, sedums will hold up in poor, dry soils and hot, dry weather.

How to grow: Plant sedums in spring or fall when you can find them at local nurseries and garden centers or order them by mail. Set nursery plants at the same depth they were growing in their container. For plants you receive by mail, follow the planting instructions sent along with them. Water well at planting. Sedums do best when kept on the dry side, and they can tolerate some drought. Once established in the garden, sedums need little care. If deer are ravenous in your area and begin to nibble your sedums, spray the plants with an organic deer repellent every couple of weeks. Sedums used to be reliably deer resistant but are no longer so in many gardens. There's no need to deadhead sedums; their dried flower heads add interest to the garden in winter. Cut back the stems to a few inches above the ground in late fall or in early spring before new growth begins.

Use in the garden: Sedums provide a sculptural presence in the garden all season, serving as a backdrop or companion to earlier bloomers. They come into their own in late summer, when they can anchor the middle ground of a bed or border.

Tips for success: Sedums contain sap that can irritate the skin of sensitive people. To avoid any potential problem, wear gloves when cutting back the plants or handling their cut stems.

10 MORE GARDEN-WORTHY PERENNIALS TO CONSIDER

Use this table to find basic growing information for 10 more promising garden perennials. The first column describes the plant: time of bloom (which varies somewhat by location), flower color, noteworthy form or foliage characteristics,, and height. In warmer climates plants usually bloom in the early part of the season listed; in cooler climates they'll typically bloom later.

PLANT AND DESCRIPTION	NEEDS	CARE TIPS
Campanula spp. and cultivars, harebell, bellflower		
Blooms late spring to midsummer; bell-shaped flowers in blue, violet, white. 8–30 inches tall.	Zones 3–9. Full sun to light shade. Moist but well-drained soil rich in organic matter.	Mulch during winter in Zones 3–6. Divide plants in spring every few years.
Dianthus spp., garden pink		
Blooms early to midsummer. Pink or white, fragrant flowers above low mound of narrow leaves. 6–18 inches tall.	Zones 3–9. Full sun to light shade, afternoon shade in warm climates. Well-drained soil with neutral to mildly alkaline pH.	Susceptible to fungus and rust diseases; needs good air circulation. Divide every few years for best growth.
Dicentra eximia, fringed bleeding heart		
Blooms late spring through summer. Pink to red, narrowly heart-shaped flowers, fernlike leaves. 12–18 inches tall.	Zones 3–8. Partial to full shade, needs more shade in warm climates. Moist but well-drained soil, neither dry nor soggy.	In cooler climates, mulch over winter.
Gaillardia ×grandiflora, blanketflower		
Blooms in summer. Orange, red, yellow daisy flowers, often bicolored. 18–30 inches tall.	Zones 4–9. Full sun. Well-drained soil, average to poor fertility. Does not tolerate wet soil.	May only last 2 or 3 years. Do not fertilize.
Helenium autumnale, sneezeweed		
Blooms late summer to fall. Yellow daisy flowers with orange, red, or brown markings. 3–5 feet tall.	Zones 4–8. Full sun to partial shade, moist soil but not heavy and soggy.	Plants may need staking. Divide older plants for strong growth.

The second column describes the best site for the plant: USDA Hardiness Zones where it grows well, how much sun or shade it prefers, what kind of soil, and how much moisture it needs. Soil pH is noted if a plant has special requirements.

The third column gives care tips, such as whether the plant needs regular deadheading or frequent division.

PLANT AND DESCRIPTION	NEEDS	CARE TIPS
Lupinus cultivars, lupine		
Blooms late spring to midsummer. Red, yellow, blue, white and bicolored pea-like flowers in tall vertical clusters. 3–5 feet tall.	Zones 4–8. Full sun to partial shade (some shade needed in Zones 7–8). Well-drained, evenly moist, mildly acidic soil rich in organic matter.	Tend to grow best where summers are cool.
Papaver orientale, Oriental poppy		
Blooms late spring to early summer. Large, cup-shaped flowers in shades of red, pink, orange, white. 2–3 feet tall.	Zones 2–7. Full sun to partial shade. Well-drained soil rich in organic matter.	Plants die back after blooming but return next spring. Mulch over winter in cool climates.
Penstemon grandiflorus, Penstemon hybrids, beardtongue		
Blooms late spring to midsummer. Vertical clusters of tubular flowers in shades of purple, pink, white. 2–4 feet tall.	Zones 3–9. Full sun. Well-drained soil is a must.	Tolerates drought. Mulch over winter in cool climates.
Physostegia virginiana, obedient plant		
Late summer to early fall. Tall, straight stems bear vertical spikes of tubular flowers in lavender, pink, rose, white. 2–4 feet tall.	Zones 3–8. Full sun to partial shade (needs shade in warm climates). Any average soil; prefers moist soil.	Can spread; pull up plants that come up where you don't want them.
Veronica spicata cultivars, speedwell		
Blooms late spring to midsummer. Cone-shaped clusters of tiny blue, pink, rose, or white flowers, narrow oblong leaves. 12–18 inches tall.	Zones 3 or 4–8. Full sun to partial shade. Moist but well-drained soil.	Deadhead regularly to prolong bloom, which often lasts throughout much of summer.

EASY-TO-GROW FLOWERING BULBS

Bulbs are a diverse group of perennial plants, including true bulbs, corms, rhizomes, and tuberous roots—all structures that store nutrients to support growth and flowering. Where they are hardy, bulbs can stay in the ground year after year, performing the same functions in the garden as perennials with fibrous roots or taproots. In cold-winter regions, tender bulbs, such as dahlias, have to be dug up in fall and stored until the weather warms again in spring.

This table covers 10 popular flowering bulbs. The first column describes approximate bloom time, flower shape and colors, and plant form and height range. USDA

PLANT AND DESCRIPTION	NEEDS	CARE TIPS
Allium, ornamental onion (*Allium* spp.)		
Blooms late spring or summer. Globe-shaped clusters of small star- or bell-shaped flowers, shades of purple, pink, blue, white, yellow, above a clump of flat leaves. 6 inches–4 feet tall.	Zones 4–9; varies by species. Full sun, any average, well-drained garden soil. 2–4 inches deep.	Plant bulbs in fall or spring. When flowers fade, cut off each stem at the base. Bulbs are prone to rot and fungus in wet conditions.
Crocus (*Crocus* spp. and hybrids)		
Early spring or autumn, depending on species. Chalice-shaped flowers of purple, yellow, white, on short stems amid grassy leaves a few inches high.	Zones 4–8; varies by species. Full sun, well-drained soil of average fertility. Likes both summer heat and winter cold. 3–4 inches deep.	Can self-sow and spread to colonize an area. Often thrives below deciduous trees, blooming before trees leaf out and cast shade.
Dahlia (*Dahlia* cultivars)		
Blooms all summer until frost. Flower forms vary. Shades of red, orange, yellow, pink, purple, white, bicolors, on bushy plants with toothed, divided leaves. 1–6 feet tall.	Zones 8–11. Elsewhere dig up tuberous roots after first hard fall frost and store in cool, frost-free place over winter; replant in spring. 5 inches deep.	Remove old flowers and stems to promote continued bloom. Water during dry weather. Feed with fish/seaweed fertilizer.
Galanthus, snowdrop (*Galanthus* spp.)		
Late winter to early spring. Drooping white flowers with a green splotch on inner petals, narrow green leaves. 4–11 inches tall.	Zones 3–9. Full sun or in shade of deciduous trees, any average soil. 3 inches deep.	Among the earliest flowers to bloom; may pop up through lingering snow. Plant where they can spread to form a colony. Mulch with compost or shredded leaves in late fall.
Hyacinth (*Hyacinthus orientalis* cultivars)		
Early spring. Dense, cylindrical clusters of fragrant flowers of blue, purple, pink, white, red, on sturdy stems above a clump of narrow leaves. 8–12 inches high.	Zones 5–9. Full sun, fertile, moist, but well-drained soil rich in organic matter. 4 inches deep.	Mulch over winter in northern climates. Plants will bloom in subsequent years but flower clusters will gradually become looser and smaller.

Hardiness Zones and growing conditions are listed in the second column, along with recommended planting depth. Tips for care and cultural information are noted in the third column.

Some of these bulbs bloom in spring, others in summer. Typically, after bulbs bloom the leaves grow. (One exception is *Lycoris*, which sends up bare flower stalks in late summer, after the spring foliage has died back and disappeared.) It's important to leave bulb foliage in place to grow and nourish the bulbs for next year's flowers. Don't cut off the foliage until it yellows.

PLANT AND DESCRIPTION	NEEDS	CARE TIPS
Iris, bearded iris (*Iris* ×*germanica* cultivars)		
Early summer. Graceful flowers with 3 upright petals and 3 drooping ones, shades of red, pink, maroon, orange, yellow, blue, purple, white, on vertical stems above a fan of flat leaves. 4 inches–5 feet tall.	Zones 3–9, varying by cultivar. Full sun to partial or light shade, well-drained, fertile soil. Set plants so top of rhizome is aboveground.	Water as needed to keep soil moist when plants are actively growing. Do not feed with high-nitrogen fertilizers. Cut off stems after all flowers have bloomed.
Lilium, lily (*Lilium* spp. and cultivars)		
Summer. Trumpet-shaped flowers, some with back-curved petals, many fragrant, shades of red, pink, orange, yellow, white, on tall, branching leafy stems. 2–7 feet tall.	Zones 3–8; varies by species and cultivar. Full sun to partial shade, depending on cultivar. Light, well-drained soil rich in organic matter. Water in dry weather. Planting depth is 2–3 times height of bulb.	Don't move lilies until clumps of bulbs become too crowded. Tall stems may need staking. Deer often eat lilies.
Lycoris, magic lily, naked ladies (*Lycoris squamigera*)		
Late summer. Trumpet-shaped flowers, lilac pink, on tall, straight stems. Strap-shaped leaves grow in spring, then die back in winter. 18–24 inches tall.	Zones 6–10. Full sun, in well-drained, fertile soil rich in organic matter. Plant in fall with neck of bulb at soil surface.	Fertilize in spring, and water when needed to keep soil moist as leaves grow. When leaves die back, don't water until late summer when flowers appear.
Narcissus, daffodil (*Narcissus* spp. and cultivars)		
Early spring. Borne singly or in groups, flowers have a central cup surrounded by flat petals, shades of yellow and white, some with orange or apricot cup. Flat, narrow leaves follow flowers. 6–20 inches tall.	Zones vary; some are suited to cold climates, others to warmer regions. Full sun to partial shade; well-drained soil rich in organic matter (add compost). Can't tolerate soggy soil. 3–6 inches deep.	Mulch with compost in summer. After bloom, let leaves grow for 6–8 weeks to nourish bulbs; cut back when yellow.
Tulipa, tulip (*Tulipa* spp. and cultivars)		
Early to mid-spring. Graceful cup-shaped flowers, shades of red, orange, yellow, pink, white, purple, on straight stems above coarse-textured leaves. 6–36 inches tall.	Zones 4–8; grow as annuals in warmer zones. Full sun except in hot climates; tolerate partial shade. Well-drained, sandy soil rich in organic matter. 8 inches deep.	Attractive to deer, chipmunks, voles, mice. Not reliably perennial in many areas.

GARDEN CARE BASICS

Organic matter is the basic balancing agent in the soil, helping to
dispense both moisture and nutrients as they are needed by plants. Organic
fertilizers . . . feed the soil first, so that the earth can in turn feed
plants, animals, and people in a natural way.

**—ROBERT RODALE, "ORGANIC SOIL KEEPS THE INSECTS AWAY,"
ORGANIC GARDENING, 1971**

Watering, weeding, mulching, and feeding: After the springtime sprint of soil prep and seed planting, your garden will need ongoing care to complete the season-long marathon leading to bountiful vegetables, fruits, and flowers. The good news is that starting with healthy, organically managed soil goes a long way toward achieving your gardening goals with a modest amount of regular maintenance.

That's because organic matter in the soil helps to retain soil moisture, making it easier for plants to keep growing through dry periods. Organic matter also supports a healthy community of soil organisms that aerate the soil and break down nutrients into forms available for plants' roots to absorb. If you prepare your gardens with plenty of organic matter, your plants stand a better chance of staying healthy and productive all season long, even if you do little else for them once they're in the ground.

But caring for your garden only makes sense, after you've invested time and money in preparing and planting. In most places, that care includes supplying enough water when nature doesn't, getting rid of weeds that compete for moisture and nutrients, adding mulch (which helps minimize watering and weeding chores), and feeding your plants with fertilizer or compost. Providing all of these things will help your keep your garden going strong all season long.

As the harvest dwindles and summer changes to fall, you'll need to spend some time getting your garden ready for winter. Postharvest cleanup is well worth the effort—because when spring rolls around the following year, you'll be able to plant as soon as the soil is warm enough to work.

WISE WAYS TO WATER

Annual vegetables and flowers grow best in soil that's constantly moist without being soggy. If the top 1 to 2 inches of soil dries out, plants become stressed. That's why your plants will be healthier and more productive if you water them before the soil gets dry. A general rule of thumb for watering is to make sure your gardens get an inch of water per week, either from rainfall or from your hose, watering can, or irrigation system.

However, no one rate for watering can work for all climates and in all seasons. An inch of moisture may be just right on a pleasant day in early summer. But it may be too much on a cool day in early spring and far too little on a hot, dry day in late August. If you live in a moderate climate and get rain a few times a week, your garden will do fairly well on the "inch-per-week" method. But if the weather is hot and dry for more than 3 or 4 days, your plants will suffer.

Experienced gardeners keep track of rainfall—or the lack thereof—but also pay attention to factors such as humidity (plants lose less moisture through their leaves in humid conditions) and wind (it increases moisture loss) when considering whether it's time to haul out the hose. As you get to know your garden's conditions through the growing season and see how plants respond to different weather patterns, you'll get a feel for when to water and when to wait.

Measuring the Moisture

You can rely upon the reports from your local meteorologist to tell you if last night's rainfall provided all the water your plants will need for a few days, or you can take your own measurements and be certain that your garden is getting the moisture it needs. Either buy a rain gauge and install it in your garden or use an empty, straight-sided can or jar to catch the rain, then measure it with a ruler. An inch of rain in the can equals an inch of rain on the garden.

Here are a few tips to make watering chores more manageable and to make sure that your efforts keep your plants well hydrated while minimizing waste:

Pick your plants. When deciding what to grow, choose plants suited to the soil, climate, and site. A plant that grows best in shade, for instance, will demand lots of water in a sunny spot. As you set up your garden, try to group plants according to their water needs so you can irrigate them efficiently.

Give TLC to transplants. Every plant needs extra attention in its early days. Transplanting disrupts plants' roots and temporarily reduces their ability to absorb moisture. Check newly planted crops frequently, and don't let them wilt from lack of water.

Water early or late. Water your garden in the early morning or in the evening—cooler temperatures mean less moisture evaporates than during the heat of the day. Direct your hose or watering can at the soil around plants to get them the maximum moisture with minimum evaporation.

Take the two-knuckle test. Before you water, push your index finger two knuckles deep into your garden's soil. (You want to go down about 3 inches, so use a trowel if you have short fingers!) Feel damp? If so, don't water the garden, no matter what the plants look like. (Many appear to wilt during high heat.) Also, prioritize your water usage—seedlings, for example, have small, delicate root systems that require consistent watering. Give priority to transplants and newly planted crops, and leave established trees, shrubs, and perennials to find water in the soil with their deep roots.

Dig the drip. To use water most efficiently, use a soaker hose (which "weeps" water along its length) or, even better, a drip-irrigation system (which lets you target exactly where you want the water to go).

Skip the sprinkler. On a hot summer day, a sprinkler is a great place for kids to cool off, but these watering tools have limited use in garden situations. Most sprinklers waste water by spraying it high into the air where a good amount evaporates before it reaches the soil; water may also be wasted when it falls outside the area you intend to irrigate. Water from a sprinkler typically lands on leaves rather than on the soil where it's needed, and wet foliage puts plants at greater risk of some diseases that spread in moist conditions. A sprinkler can be useful for keeping a newly sown seedbed consistently moist—if you're starting grass seed for a lawn, for example—but it's important to target its spray area as much as possible to avoid waste. Otherwise, leave the sprinkler for the kids and deliver moisture to your plants through more targeted techniques.

A watering wand on the end of your hose makes it easier to deliver water right where it's needed—to hanging baskets or at the root zone of garden crops—without soaking the foliage unnecessarily.

watering wand

watering can with rose

The "rose," or sprinkler head, on a watering can creates a fine, rain-like spray of water that's just right for gently moistening seedbeds and young seedlings.

talk the talk
Watering

DRIP IRRIGATION: An efficient method of irrigating plants in which water drips slowly from tubes or lines placed on the soil around the base of plants to deposit water directly to the root zone of plants.

RAIN BARREL: A container for water collection, typically placed beneath a downspout to catch the water running off a roof.

ROSE: Also called a water breaker, a rose is a sprinkler-head attachment for a watering can spout or hose that divides the water flow into a gentle sprinkle that will soak into the soil without disturbing young plants.

SOAKER HOSE: A garden hose made of permeable material that lets water seep out through it or a hose that is perforated with small holes that let the water spray out. A soaker hose can be placed along a garden row at planting time and left in place all season for easy, targeted watering. If you use a soaker hose with holes, be sure to face the holes downward so the water doesn't squirt up in the air like a sprinkler.

Watering Master Class: Drip Irrigation

The benefits of drip irrigation—automated, hands-off delivery of precise amounts of water to a garden, when and where it's needed—are undeniable. Although customized systems look complicated, most manufacturers provide customer service and support that make installation of a drip system gratifyingly easy. Once a system is installed, watering is simple, with no more wrangling hoses and sprinklers.

The only skill to master in installing a drip system is the trick of connecting the main tubing to the various joints, a tool-free task that requires some hand strength. The real difficulty is earlier in the process: designing the system and determining how many of each plug, joint, and emitter will be needed. Fortunately, most companies that specialize in drip irrigation for home gardeners have specialists on staff to do that for you.

Although no two drip layouts are the same, some aspects remain constant: Water from a garden hose or other source is routed through a branching arrangement of plastic tubes to various parts of the garden, where it is applied at or near ground level via small sprinkler heads, drip emitters, or soaker lines. Water is released slowly and typically soaks in immediately; runoff is eliminated.

A programmable timer directs the frequency, time of day, and duration of each application of water. This, combined with on/off valves for each area of the garden and emitters that can be reconfigured as crops are harvested, ensures that water isn't wasted.

Systems can be customized with different types of emitters, including mini sprinkler heads with various spray patterns, special drippers for containers, and soaker drip lines. Although clogged emitters can plague drip systems, that hassle can be avoided by keeping the water filter clean and taking pains to keep dirt out of the tubing.

Saving Rain

You can help conserve water by saving rain for watering your garden. Place a barrel or similarly large container under one of the downspouts of your house so the rainwater can run right into the barrel. You might need to set the barrel on a couple of cinder blocks so the mouth of the barrel is closer to the end of the downspout and to make room to put your watering can below a spigot near the bottom of the barrel for filling. You can buy a ready-made rain barrel complete with spigot or make your own by installing a spigot near the bottom of a heavy-duty plastic trash can or a recycled plastic barrel used for shipping food such as olives.

rain barrel

Caring for Container Plants

Pay particular attention to watering and fertilizing plants growing in containers. Nearly everything they need must be provided to keep them healthy, productive, and attractive. Container plants' water needs vary considerably, depending on plant type and size, container size and material, the type of growing medium, and weather conditions. Try to group containers with similar watering requirements to make moisture management easier. Avoid letting potting mix in containers dry out completely, as it can be difficult to rewet. To keep large containers looking their best and to help them retain moisture, spread a shallow layer of mulch over the top of the growing medium, taking care to keep the mulch an inch or so away from plant stems.

Fertilize container pots by watering with diluted fish emulsion, seaweed extract, or compost tea. Or foliar feed by spraying the leaves with doubly diluted preparations of these solutions. Start by feeding once every 2 weeks; adjust the frequency depending on plant response.

MAKING THE MOST OF MULCH

The best time-saving measure a gardener can take is applying mulch, a layer of organic or inorganic material (such as shredded leaves, straw, bark, pine needles, lawn clippings, or black plastic) that is spread on the ground around plants to conserve soil moisture and discourage weeds. This goes for every garden site, from vegetable garden to flowerbed. Mulched gardens are healthier, more weed free, and more drought resistant than unmulched gardens, so you'll spend less time watering, weeding, and fighting pest problems.

There are two basic kinds of mulch: organic and inorganic. Organic mulches include formerly living material such as chopped leaves, straw, grass clippings, compost, wood chips, shredded bark, sawdust, pine needles, and even paper. Inorganic mulches include gravel, stones, black plastic, and geotextiles (landscape fabrics).

Both types discourage weeds, but organic mulches also improve the soil as they decompose. They keep the soil cool and moist—encouraging earthworms—and provide a home for garden helpers like spiders and ground beetles. Inorganic mulches don't break down and enrich the soil, but under certain circumstances they're the mulch of choice. For example, black plastic warms the soil and radiates heat during the night, keeping heat-loving vegetables such as eggplant and tomatoes cozy and vigorous.

Using Organic Mulches

There are two cardinal rules for using organic mulches to combat weeds. First, be sure to lay the mulch down on soil that is already weeded, and second, lay down a thick enough layer to discourage new weeds from coming up through it. It can take a 4- to 6-inch layer of mulch to completely discourage weeds, although a 2- to 3-inch layer is usually enough in shady spots where weeds aren't as troublesome as they are in full sun.

Wood chips and bark mulch. You can purchase bags of decorative wood chips or shredded bark from a local garden center to mulch your flower garden and shrub borders. A more inexpensive source of wood chips might be your tree-care company or the utility company. They may be willing to sell you a load of chips at a nominal price. If you catch utility crews while they are trimming trees in your neighborhood, they may give you a load of chipped material for free—but be aware that there's no quality control on such stuff, which may include shredded poison ivy, chips from diseased trees, and other unpleasant ingredients. Many community yard waste collection sites offer chipped yard debris or composted grass clippings and fall leaves to residents for free (or for a small fee). Don't count on chips or compost from a municipal collection center being free of chemical pesticides or weeds; use them accordingly in your landscape and gardens.

Shredded leaves. If you have trees on your property, shredding the fallen leaves creates a nutrient-rich mulch for free. You can use a leaf-shredding machine, but you don't need a special machine to shred leaves—a lawn mower with a bagger will collect and cut leaves into the perfect size for mulching.

You can spread a wood-chip or shredded-leaf mulch anywhere on your property, but it looks especially attractive in flowerbeds and shrub borders. Of course, it's right at home in a woodland or shade garden. Wood chips aren't a great idea for vegetable beds and annual flowerbeds, though, since you'll be digging these beds every year and the chips will get in the way. They do serve well as mulch for garden pathways, though.

Grass clippings. Sometimes called "the manure of suburbia," grass clippings are another readily available mulch, although it's a good idea to return at least some of your grass clippings directly to the lawn as a natural fertilizer. It's fine to collect grass clippings occasionally to use as mulch, and the nitrogen-rich clippings are an especially good choice for mulching vegetable gardens, where the nitrogen boost benefits many crops.

Compost. If you have enough compost, it makes a fine organic mulch that offers the added benefit of suppressing disease spores that might splash up from the soil onto plants. Compost mulch provides a gentle nutrient boost as well. Keep in mind that when any kind of mulch is dry, it's not a hospitable place for plant roots. So you may want to reserve your compost to spread as a thin layer around plants and top it with another mulch, such as chopped leaves. That way, the compost will stay moist and biologically active, providing maximum benefit for your plants.

Pine needles. Pine needles are a tidy-looking mulch. They allow water to pass through easily, and they break down slowly. Despite what you may hear, using pine-needle mulch will not make your soil significantly more acid.

Straw and hay. Another great mulch for the vegetable garden is straw, salt hay, or weed-free hay. It looks good and has most of the benefits of the other mulches: retaining soil moisture, keeping down weeds, and adding organic matter to the soil when it breaks down. But be sure the hay you use is weed and seed free, or you'll just be making trouble for your garden. And don't pull hay or straw up to the stems of vegetables or the trunks of fruit trees or you'll risk inviting slug and rodent damage.

ORGANIC MULCHING MECHANICS

Spreading organic mulch saves labor and nurtures plants by:

- Preventing most weed seeds from germinating; the few weeds that do pop through the mulch will be easy to pull.
- Keeping the soil cool and moist in summer, reducing the need to water.
- Decomposing slowly, releasing nutrients into the soil.
- Encouraging earthworm activity, improving soil tilth and nutrient content.
- Keeping dirt from splashing on flowers and vegetables.
- Preventing alternate freezing and thawing of the soil in winter, which can heave plants from the soil.

Nothing, unfortunately, is perfect. When using organic mulches, keep in mind the following facts:

- As low-nitrogen organic mulches such as wood chips and sawdust decompose, nitrogen is temporarily depleted from the soil. Fertilize first with a high-nitrogen product such as bloodmeal or fish meal to boost soil nitrogen levels.

- Organic mulch retains moisture, which can slow soil warming; in spring, pull mulch away from perennials and bulbs for faster growth.

- Wet mulch piled against the stems of flowers and vegetables can cause them to rot; keep mulch about 1 inch away from crowns and stems.

- Mulch piled up against woody stems of shrubs and trees can cause them to rot and encourages rodents, such as voles and mice, to nest in the mulch. Keep deep mulch pulled back 6 to 12 inches from trunks.

- In damp climates, organic mulches can harbor slugs and snails, which will munch on plants; don't spread mulch near slug-susceptible plants.

- Organic mulches are usually more or less acidic, depending on their content; mix some lime with the mulch beneath plants that prefer neutral or slightly alkaline soil.

If you know that a garden bed is filled with weed seeds or bits of perennial weed roots, use a double-mulching technique to prevent a weed explosion. Set plants in place, water them well, then spread newspaper and top it with organic mulch.

Using Plastic Mulch

Mulching a vegetable garden with sheets of black plastic film can do wonders. When it's spread tightly over a smooth soil surface, black plastic will transmit the sun's heat to the soil beneath, effectively creating a microclimate about 3°F warmer than an unmulched garden. Because the plastic film remains warm and dry, it protects the fruits of vining crops such as strawberries, melons, and cucumbers from rotting and keeps them clean. And of course, the mulch prevents weed growth and retains soil moisture.

Infrared transmitting (IRT) plastics cost more than standard black plastic, but they can result in even higher yields. These plastics warm the soil as well as clear plastic does but also control weeds as well as black plastic.

In raised bed gardens, lay down a sheet of plastic over the entire bed. Bury it at the edges or weight the plastic down with rocks. Then punch holes in it for the plants. A bulb planter makes quick work of hole cutting. Sow seeds or plant transplants in the holes.

Because water can't permeate plastic, the mulch retains soil moisture but it also keeps rainwater from soaking the planting bed. Thus, the ideal watering system for a plastic-covered bed is soaker hoses or drip hoses laid on the soil surface before you put down the plastic.

Don't use plastic as mulch under shrubs. Although it keeps out weeds and can be camouflaged with decorative mulch, black plastic destroys the shrubs' long-term health. Because water and air cannot penetrate the plastic, roots grow very close to the soil surface—sometimes right beneath the plastic—seeking moisture and oxygen. The shallow roots suffer from lack of oxygen and moisture and from extremes of heat and cold. Eventually, the plants decline and die. Stick to organic mulches such as shredded leaves, bark, wood chips, or compost under your trees and shrubs.

DOWNSIDES OF PLASTIC MULCH

Although black plastic mulch seems like a great boon to organic gardeners, its use is not problem free. One issue of concern with black plastic is its manufacture (it's a petroleum product) and its disposal—there are very few places it can be recycled. If you carefully lift black plastic at the end of the growing season and store it in a dry place over winter, you should be able to reuse it for several years, but eventually it will become torn and you'll have to throw it away.

An alternative is biodegradable plastic mulch (cornstarch based). These materials are designed to break down in place by the end of the growing season, and you can dig any remaining bits into the soil. However, one of the breakdown products of biodegradable plastic mulch is carbon dioxide. Black paper mulch made from recycled paper is also available, but these products are usually treated with a synthetic antimicrobial substance to prevent them from breaking down too quickly.

Unlike black plastic, landscape fabrics let air and water through to the soil beneath while keeping weeds from coming up. But landscape fabrics (geotextiles) have some of the same drawbacks as black plastic. To begin with, they are petroleum products. When exposed to light, they degrade over time, so to make them last longer, you have to cover them with a second mulch (they're ugly, so you'd want to, anyway). However, many gardeners have discovered that shrub roots grow up into the landscape fabric, creating real problems when you eventually want to remove it. And weeds that germinate in the surface mulch send roots down into the fabric, too, tearing it when you pull them out.

WINNING THE WAR ON WEEDS

Weeds compete for water and nutrients with your garden plants, they can harbor pests and diseases, and they sure can make your garden look a mess. But you don't need to spray toxic herbicides, which are harmful to people, pets, and wildlife, to keep plant invaders out of your organic garden. Use these strategies instead.

Mulch. Weed control is a key reason for using mulch. Keep your soil covered at all times to prevent light from reaching weed seeds. Spread a thick layer (2 or more inches deep) of organic mulch—straw, dried grass clippings, shredded leaves—on your garden each spring and replenish it throughout the growing season. For even better weed protection, use several sheets of newspaper, kraft paper (such as grocery bags), or corrugated cardboard under these mulches. They are nearly impenetrable by weeds.

Get a head start. Since weeds are lurking in the soil, waiting to sprout up (in some cases while the soil is still cold), they are often growing strong before you can plant. For that reason, start as much of your garden as possible from transplants rather than planting seeds. This is important for new gardeners, because often it is hard to see the difference between weeds and vegetables when they are all sprouts. But if you plant your vegetable crops in an organized way when they are 6 weeks or so old, you will find it quite easy to see what plant is misplaced and therefore a weed.

Row, row, row your plants. While there are advantages to broadcasting seeds over blocks or irregularly shaped spaces in your garden, sowing seeds in rows is helpful when it comes to separating the vegetables from the weeds. Especially if you are starting a new garden where weeds are more likely to be lurking in the soil, sowing your seeds in rows—and marking where those rows are—makes it easier to tell the weeds from the good guys when you bring out the hoe. Planting in defined rows makes it simpler to mulch in between the rows, too, for additional weed suppression.

Hand-pull. Sounds like a lot of work, we know. But pulling out a few weeds every day or at least every week keeps them from getting out of control and brings you close to your garden so you can inspect your plants for problems. Keep a bale of straw or a pile of grass clippings on hand so you'll have mulch on demand to help prevent weeds from returning after you've pulled them. Make a compost pile in a convenient spot in or close to your garden so you can easily toss vanquished weeds into it.

Weed when it's wet. In general, it's better to stay out of your garden when plants are wet, since many disease organisms spread readily in a film of moisture on foliage. But a gentle summer rain can make for first-rate weeding conditions if you don't mind getting a bit damp yourself. Weeds' roots come free more easily from moist soil, and a cloudy day can seem downright inviting compared with pulling weeds under the blazing summer sun.

Hoe. Use a hoe's sharp edge to sever weed stems from their roots just below the soil surface. Forget about the square-headed traditional garden hoe for this job—get a stirrup-shaped oscillating or a swan-neck hoe instead. To hoe your garden without cultivating a backache, hold the hoe as you would a broom.

Stop 'em before they seed. Keeping ahead of weeds can seem daunting, especially as heat and humidity begin to climb in summer and weeding becomes increasingly unappealing. Try to do a little bit each day, preferably working early in the morning before temperatures climb uncomfortably high. Prioritize your efforts by focusing on any weeds that are starting to bloom; most of these plant pests are superspeedy at going from flowers to viable seeds and superprolific, too. A single weed can produce as many as 250,000 seeds, so it's worth your while to stop as many as you can before they spread future legions of weeds over your garden's soil.

Solarize. Where you have a persistent weed problem or you need to clear a thick mat of weeds from a brand-new bed, enlist the sun's help. In late spring or early summer, pull, hoe, or rake out as many weeds as you can from the bed. Then moisten the soil and cover it with a tight layer of clear plastic, weighting or burying the edges. Leave the plastic in place for 6 weeks so the sun cooks any remaining weed seeds. This method also "cooks" many beneficial soil organisms, so it's helpful to amend a solarized bed with compost after you remove the plastic covering.

Be persistent. This is your most important long-range weapon against weeds. Mulch, then pull or hoe the weeds for a few minutes whenever you visit your garden. Do these things consistently for a few seasons and you will slowly but surely expel problem invaders for good.

Organic versus Chemical Fertilizers

Many organic materials feed both soils and plants. This is one of the most important differences between a chemical approach and an organic approach toward soil care and fertilizing. Soluble chemical fertilizers contain mineral salts that plant roots can absorb quickly. However, these salts do not provide a food source for soil microorganisms and earthworms, and they will even repel earthworms because they acidify the soil. Over time, soils treated only with synthetic chemical fertilizers lose organic matter and the all-important living organisms that help to build healthy soil. As soil structure declines and water-holding capacity diminishes, more and more of the chemical fertilizer applied will leach, or wash away, through the soil. In turn, it will take ever-increasing amounts of chemicals to stimulate plant growth. Using organic fertilizers avoids creating this kind of crisis condition in the soil.

The manufacturing process of most chemical fertilizers depends on nonrenewable resources, such as coal and natural gas. Others are made by treating rock minerals with acids to make them more soluble. Fortunately, truly organic fertilizers are increasingly available. These products are made from natural plant and animal materials or from mined rock minerals.

Organically managed soil, enriched with lots of compost, tends to provide most of the nutrients plants need. If you improve your soil from year to year with compost and other organic material, chances are you'll have healthy plants and a good harvest without having to add fertilizer.

Still, there are times when a bit of supplemental nourishment is necessary:

- If you are starting a new garden in soil that has not enjoyed years of compost applications

- If you are gardening in the South or Southwest, where organic matter in the soil tends to decompose very quickly

- For most annual vegetables, because their rapid growth may outpace their roots' ability to take up nutrients from the soil

- For crops such as tomatoes, melons, and corn that are described as "heavy feeders"

- If plants display symptoms of nutrient deficiency (see Chapter 7 for some common deficiency symptoms)

- For all plants growing in containers

If you've had your soil tested (as described in Chapter 3), you may be aware of specific nutrient deficiencies that need to be addressed. Use the recommendations from your soil test results as a guide to the amount and type(s) of fertilizers to apply to your garden before you start planting. In the absence of specific soil test results and accompanying fertilizer recommendations, consider working an organic fertilizer blend into your garden soil in spring prior to planting.

Look for products labeled "natural organic," "slow release," and "low analysis" as well as those bearing labels indicating certification from OMRI, the Organic Materials Review Institute, or NOP, the USDA's National Organic Program. Organic fertilizer materials often function as both fertilizers that feed plants and soil amendments/conditioners that feed soil organisms. As such, the amount of soluble nutrients (those three numbers on the package) typically is lower than the NPK ratio of a soluble chemical fertilizer product. Be wary of products that have an NPK ratio that adds up to more than 15; higher levels of the three plant macro-nutrients often indicates chemical sources of those ingredients.

talk the talk
Amendments and Fertilizers

BLOODMEAL: A slaughterhouse by-product, bloodmeal is dried, ground blood, used as a potent nitrogen fertilizer.

BONEMEAL: Also a slaughterhouse by-product, bonemeal is ground animal bones, used as a source of phosphorus. Bonemeal often is recommended as a fertilizer for bulbs, but adding it to planting holes risks attracting rodents and dogs, which may dig up your bulbs to get to the fertilizer.

BROADCAST: To spread fertilizer evenly across an area, by hand or with a spreading tool.

COTTONSEED MEAL: The waste left over after pressing cottonseed oil; it provides nitrogen. Pesticides sprayed on cotton crops may contaminate cottonseed meal.

FERTILIZERS: Materials that feed growing plants.

FISH MEAL: A by-product of fish processing, fish meal is made of dried and ground fish and fish parts. While primarily used as a nitrogen source, it also provides phosphorus and potassium.

FOLIAR FEED: To supply nutrients by spraying liquid fertilizer directly onto plant leaves.

GREENSAND: Mined from the sea, greensand is a mineral deposit that is a source of potassium and more than 30 micronutrients.

KELP MEAL: A dry fertilizer and growth enhancer made of dried, ground seaweed; a rich source of micronutrients.

LIQUID KELP (OR LIQUID SEAWEED): An extract of kelp meal, used as a fertilizer and plant growth enhancer; rich in micronutrients.

NPK RATIO: A ratio of three numbers that identifies the percentage of the major plant nutrients—nitrogen (N), phosphorus (P), and potassium (K)—in fertilizers.

ROCK PHOSPHATE: This phosphorus fertilizer is the mined skeletal remains of prehistoric animals. Rock phosphate provides more phosphorus than bonemeal and costs less.

SIDE-DRESS: To apply dry (as opposed to liquid) fertilizer to the soil alongside plants during the growing season.

SOIL AMENDMENTS: Materials that feed soil organisms and improve the condition of the soil; also called soil conditioners.

Dry Organic Fertilizers

Dry organic fertilizers can consist of a single material, such as rock phosphate or kelp (a type of nutrient-rich seaweed), or they may be a blend of many ingredients. Almost all organic fertilizers provide a broad array of nutrients, but blends are specially formulated to supply balanced amounts of nitrogen, phosphorus, and potassium as well as micronutrients. Commercial blends are available, or you can make your own general-purpose fertilizer by mixing individual amendments.

Applying dry fertilizers. The most common way to apply dry fertilizer is to broadcast it and then hoe or rake it into the top 4 to 6 inches of soil. You can add small amounts to planting holes or rows as you plant seeds or transplants. Unlike dry synthetic fertilizers, most organic fertilizers pose less risk of "burning" delicate seedling roots.

During the growing season, boost plant growth by side-dressing dry fertilizers along crop rows or around the drip line of trees or shrubs. It's best to hoe or rake side-dressings into the top inch of the soil.

Make Your Own Mix

Stir up a batch of your own custom blend of general-purpose organic fertilizer by combining individual amendments in the amounts shown here. Choose one ingredient from each of the three macronutrient groups below. Because these amendments may vary in the amount of nutrients they contain, this method won't produce a mixture with a precise NPK ratio. The resulting blend will have a nutrient ratio roughly between 1-2-1 and 4-6-3, with additional insoluble phosphorus and potassium. Even so, your fertilizer mix will provide a balanced supply of nutrients that will be steadily available to plants and will encourage soil microorganisms to thrive.

Nitrogen (N)	Phosphorus (P)	Potassium (K)
2 parts bloodmeal	3 parts bonemeal	1 part kelp meal
3 parts fish meal	6 parts rock phosphate or colloidal phosphate	6 parts greensand

liquid fertilizer

A fine-textured spray of liquid fertilizer can give plants a nutrient boost when it's most needed. To get the best results, schedule foliar feeding at either the beginning or end of the day, and focus spraying on the undersides of leaves.

dry fertilizer

Side-dressing during the growing season puts fertilizer in the upper layer of soil near plants so it can gradually wash into the root zone.

Liquid Organic Fertilizers

Plants can absorb liquid fertilizers through both their roots and through leaf pores. Foliar feeding can supply nutrients when they are lacking or unavailable in the soil or when roots are stressed. Use liquid fertilizers to give your plants a light nutrient boost every month or even every 2 weeks during the growing season. They are especially effective for giving fast-growing plants like vegetables an extra lift during the growing season. Some foliar fertilizers, such as liquid seaweed (kelp), are rich in micronutrients and plant growth hormones. These foliar sprays also appear to act as catalysts that increase plants' nutrient uptake.

Applying liquid fertilizers. With flowering and fruiting plants, foliar sprays are most useful during critical periods (such as after transplanting or during fruit set) or in times of drought or extreme temperatures. For leaf crops, some products may be applied biweekly.

When using liquid fertilizers, always follow the label instructions for proper dilution and application methods. For a small garden or container plants, a

Beware of Biosolids

Among the fertilizers at your local garden center, you may find biosolids, often branded using the name of the municipality from which they originated. Biosolids are fertilizer products made from treated sewage sludge. Sewage can include human waste, heavy metals, leachate from landfills, petroleum products, and synthetic substances such as volatile organic compounds (VOCs) and pesticides. Biosolid products sold to home gardeners must meet EPA standards; however, hundreds of synthetic toxic chemicals and other contaminants that may be present in sludge are not regulated by the EPA standards. Many municipalities sell or give away treated sewage sludge to consumers as compost or dried pellets, often without labeling that explains the product contains sludge. The use of the word *organic* on labels for sludge products is legal, but it is misleading, because vegetables fertilized with sludges are not considered organic according to USDA regulations.

handheld trigger-spray bottle may serve your needs; to give a liquid fertilizer boost to lots of plants, you may want a pressure sprayer that will hold a gallon or more. Set your sprayer to emit as fine a spray as possible.

The best times to spray are early morning and early evening, when the liquids will be absorbed most quickly. Choose a mild day when no rain is forecast.

Spray until the liquid drips off the leaves. Concentrate the spray on leaf undersides, where pores are more likely to be open. You can also water in liquid fertilizers around the root zones of your plants or deliver liquid fertilizers through a drip-irrigation system.

TRELLISING, TRAINING, PINCHING, AND PICKING

Depending on what's in your garden, some plants likely will need specialized attention in addition to the basic care described up to this point. Tomatoes benefit from sturdy supports to hold them upright under the weight of their ripening harvest, and vining crops such as cucumbers can be grown on trellises to conserve space and keep their fruits off the ground.

Other garden plants—herbs, annuals, perennials, ornamental vines, brambles, shrubs, and trees—each have their own needs in terms of supports, training, pinching, pruning, and deadheading. For food crops, even harvesting is a form of care, since removing ripe fruits encourages plants to continue producing.

Here's what you need to know to maintain your plants:

Deadheading. Remove faded and spent flowers to concentrate the plant's nutrients, water, and energy on producing new growth and flowers.

Dividing. Carefully dig up entire plants and as much of their roots as possible—and separate perennial plants to relieve overcrowded clumps (like daylilies. Refresh those that have died out in the middle and multiply plants so you have more to fill your gardens.

Pinching. A form of pruning for herbaceous/nonwoody plants, pinching promotes compact bushy growth. Pinch back the growing tips of herbs such as basil and mint to encourage plants to produce more leafy side shoots and to forestall the production of flowers and seeds. Perennials like chrysanthemums and asters tend to grow tall and floppy; pinch their shoots back once or twice in spring to keep them compact. By contrast, pinching out the nonproductive side shoots (suckers) that form at the junction of tomatoes' leaf stalks and stems is done to direct more of the plants' energy into flower and fruit production.

Thinning. Cut out crowded stems of perennials to increase air circulation in the center and to promote larger flowers on the remaining stems.

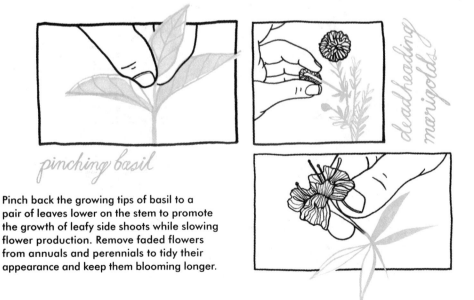

pinching basil

deadheading marigolds

Pinch back the growing tips of basil to a pair of leaves lower on the stem to promote the growth of leafy side shoots while slowing flower production. Remove faded flowers from annuals and perennials to tidy their appearance and keep them blooming longer.

Show Your Support

Plant supports fall generally into one of three categories: stakes, cages, or trellises. While some vegetable crops will produce just fine when sprawled over the ground, they require a lot of space to do so. Plants that touch the ground are more susceptible to pests and soilborne diseases. They're also susceptible to being trod upon by the gardener as you wade amid the leaves searching for harvest-size squash or melons, and ripening fruits that rest upon moist soil are prone to rotting where they touch the ground.

Stakes. Some vegetables, such as peppers and eggplant, may need staking to stand up under their load of fruits. Choose sturdy bamboo or wood that hasn't been treated with chemical preservatives. Insert stakes when plants are very young to avoid injuring their roots. Loosely tie plants to stakes with soft twine or strips of cloth every 8 to 12 inches.

Staking may be necessary for thin-stemmed perennial flowers such as coreopsis, yarrow, and garden phlox. Extremely tall plants like delphiniums often require sturdy stakes to keep flower spikes from snapping off. When staking ornamentals, choose unobtrusive supports and ties in shades of green or brown that will blend in with the stalks they're staking.

Cages. If you loop a few stakes together with string, you'll form a cage. Or you can roll a length of wire fencing into a tube—the best-known example of

this is the tomato cage. Put up cages when your plants are very small. Cages give plants more room to grow than stakes do, and you don't have to tie the plants to the cages. Anchor wire cages in place with a stake or metal pins so they won't topple over in a heavy wind.

Heavy, mounding flowers like peonies may need cagelike hoop supports (circular wire supports on legs that stick into the soil) to keep their dense blooms out of the mud. You can also stake up a clump of perennials by inserting three or four stakes around the outside of the clump and then winding twine around the stakes. Or circle a clump with twine, then tie the twine to a sturdy stake.

Trellises. Cucumbers, pole beans, and other vining crops grow well on trellises. Cucumbers and peas—even so-called bush types benefit from support—prefer a mesh or netting trellis so their tendrils can curl tightly around the support. Twining vines such as pole beans and morning glories spiral around supports as they grow. When making a trellis, use biodegradable string or netting; then just cut the string off at the end of the season and toss it in your compost pile.

Match trellises for ornamentals to the weight of the mature plant and put them in place early while plants are still young. Even climbers such as clematis vines may need a bit of training to direct them onto the trellis rather than over the ground, and "climbing" roses need to be tied to their intended support to encourage them upward.

Most garden crops can get along without stakes or strings, but many will be healthier and more productive with a little support. A single stake helps keep the stems of peppers and eggplants from bending and breaking under a heavy crop. Cages keep tomatoes upright, improving air flow and reducing disease problems. Trellising peas and beans keeps them off the ground so the pods stay clean and easy to harvest.

Harvest Hints

For vegetable gardeners, harvesting is the main event, the goal at the end of a season's labors. But harvesting tends to happen gradually rather than all at once. If you've planted quick-growing crops such as radishes or greens, it may begin as soon as 20 to 30 days from planting and before you've even set out tomatoes or sown bean seeds.

Many crops bear over a long period of time; vegetable varieties for home gardens often are bred to yield a lengthier harvest because picking a little at a time for a longer time is preferable for daily fresh use in the kitchen. Keep an eye on your garden so you don't miss a single thing when it's ready for picking.

Harvesting is the fun part of gardening, but it's worth doing right and doing at the right time to enjoy your vegetables at the peak of their perfection. Most everyone knows what a ripe tomato looks like, but harvesting clues aren't quite as clear for every crop. For example, green beans should be picked when the enlarging seeds inside the pods are just visible and okra when the pods are 3 to 5 inches long. The plant entries in Chapter 5 have tips for when to harvest specific crops; see below for a few additional helpful harvest guidelines.

Some crops need to be picked regularly to prolong the harvest. Among these are beans, peas, cucumbers, and zucchini. If even one fruit on any of these plants is allowed to become overripe, the plant will make fewer new fruits or even stop producing entirely.

Postharvest Cleanup

As the fruits of your labors start to dwindle after the first fall frost, you might be tempted to forget about your garden until next spring. But it's worth your time now to clean up the debris and protect the plants and soil so that you'll get your garden off to a healthy start next season.

GARDEN CLEANUP

- Pull or cut weeds before they produce seeds. Put seed-free weeds into your compost bin or pile to return their nutrients to the soil next season. Avoid tossing weeds with seeds or aggressive perennials like bindweed or

Make Perfect Picks

Judging when some garden crops are ready to be harvested is as much an art as a science. Good record keeping can help—by knowing when you planted, you can add on the days to harvest specified by the seed packet to get a rough idea of when production should begin. And seed packets and catalogs often include photos or descriptions of the size and color of harvest-ready vegetables for additional guidance. But many variables affect when it's time to pluck the first pod of peas from the vines or the first ear of corn from the stalk. Here are a few helpful hints to help you time your harvest:

- *Asparagus.* Harvest the third year after planting. When stalks reach 6 to 9 inches tall, cut or break them at the soil line.

- *Beans.* Beans snap in half when they're ready. Pick them every other day. Use two hands—one to support the plant while you snap off the beans with the other—to avoid breaking plants while picking.

- *Broccoli/cauliflower.* Cut 6 inches below the fully formed main head. Continue cutting side shoots as they form.

- *Cantaloupe/muskmelon.* When the skin is netted and the fruits separate easily from the vine, melons are sweet as can be.

- *Carrots.* Harvest when the roots are at least $3/4$ inch in diameter and before the ground freezes, or protect them with a thick layer of straw.

- *Corn.* Puncture a kernel with your fingernail. If a milky fluid flows out, it's time. If the liquid is toothpasty, the corn is overmature. The silk should be brown.

- *Cucumbers.* Cut from the vine when the cukes are a deep green and seeds are still soft. Smaller is better than larger.

- *Storage onions.* When about half of the leaves topple, push the rest over. Let onions cure in the soil for a week.

- *Potatoes.* Dig spuds when the plants die back.

- *Winter squash.* Harvest when your thumbnail does not readily pierce the skin. Leave a 3- to 4-inch stem to avoid storage rot.

- *Tomatoes.* Harvest at full color. An overripe tomato quickly loses its firmness. Never put them in the refrigerator.

- *Watermelon.* Pick when the tendril closest to the fruit's stem withers and the pale spot where the melon rests on the ground turns cream to yellowish.

Canada thistle into the compost unless you want to see them again (and again) in your garden.

- Pull out spent vegetable plants after they're finished producing. Add disease-free plants to your compost heap but set aside the residues of crops that were sickly or infested with pests. Bag up any problem plants and put them in the trash, or consign them to an out-of-the-way compost pile that will never be returned to your gardens.

- Collect stakes, temporary trellises, and row covers, and brush off clinging soil. To remove insect eggs, rinse the materials in a solution of one part vinegar to nine parts water. Spread them out to dry in the sun before storing for winter.

- Pick any remaining vegetables and enjoy their flavors fresh or preserve them for a taste of summer in mid-winter.

SETTLING SOIL FOR WINTER

Here are three options for replenishing your garden soil at the end of the growing season and preparing it for the winter months. Which method you choose

Winterizing Perennials

In fall, begin preparing the perennial garden for winter. Remove dead foliage and old flowers. After the first frost, cut down dead stems and remove other growth that will die to the ground. (Leave ornamental grasses and other plants that add winter interest.) After the ground freezes, protect plants from root damage due to frost heaving with a thick mulch of oak leaves or seed-free straw or hay. Evergreen boughs also are good for this purpose. Snow is the best insulator of all, but most of us can't count on continuous snow cover to protect our plants. Mulching helps keep the ground frozen during periods of warm weather, preventing the danger of alternate freezing and thawing that can heave plants' roots out of the ground.

will depend on the amount of time and the materials you have. The important thing is to prevent erosion that might be caused by wind or rain during the time when there's nothing growing in the garden. If you can also improve the soil by adding organic matter and nutrients and/or prepare it for earlier planting the following spring, your fall efforts will have been well worth the time.

1. Mulch it. In cold areas with little snow cover, mulching after the ground has frozen helps moderate soil temperatures, which is good for helpful soil organisms such as earthworms. In areas with mild, wet winters, mulch prevents heavy rains from eroding bare soil. A mulch of grass clippings mixed with chopped leaves or straw, or a topping of chunky, partially decomposed compost, will protect your garden soil from the elements, then can be dug into the soil as you prepare it for planting in the spring.

The precautions about not cultivating the soil when it is too wet or too dry apply in the fall, just as they do in spring. Both can do lasting damage to soil structure, leaving large impenetrable clods if too wet and powdery erosion-prone dust if too dry.

2. Cultivate, then mulch it. Fall digging or tilling has several advantages. It can kill pests that are in the soil or expose them to birds or other predators. Fall digging can also bury plant debris that might harbor overwintering insects. In spring, tilled soil warms faster, so you can plant sooner. On the downside, fall tilling can increase weed seed germination in spring (although a mulch should help prevent some weeds from sprouting).

3. Cultivate, then plant a cover crop. Growing a cover crop over winter will protect your soil from erosion and enrich it at the same time. Dig or till the soil in late summer or early fall, then sow grains like oats or wheat; or plant legumes, such as fava beans or red clover. Then work the plants into the soil before spring planting to boost organic matter and nutrients. See "Choose Your Cover Crop" in Chapter 3 for help in selecting a cover crop that's right for your region.

7

TROUBLESHOOTING
AND PROBLEM SOLVING

... organically grown plants will be eaten by some insects, too,
but not as many as chemically grown plants will. For organically grown
plants have built-in resistance to insect attack.

**—ROBERT RODALE, "ORGANIC SOIL KEEPS THE INSECTS AWAY,"
ORGANIC GARDENING, 1971**

Despite what you may have heard, committing to gardening organically does not mean putting up with wormy vegetables or bug-nibbled blossoms. But neither does it guarantee that your plants will be completely free of pest and disease problems. Every garden has its share of unwanted insects, disruptive diseases, and troublesome weeds. On rare occasions, one of these problems escalates beyond the level of mild annoyance and requires some action to keep it from posing a serious threat to the garden's beauty or productivity.

By managing the health of the soil, organic gardeners help to establish balance in the garden. A vibrant community of soil organisms helps plants get the nutrients they need; organic matter in the soil holds adequate amounts of moisture and air for healthy root growth; diverse plantings support populations of beneficial organisms. By providing favorable conditions for healthy growth and by avoiding the imbalances caused by excess fertilization or wholesale eradication of all insect life, organic methods give plants an advantage against pest and disease problems.

Just as stressed people are more prone to disease problems, so are stressed plants more likely to be infested by pests or infected by disease pathogens. An organic garden's best defense against pest and disease problems is its very nature—healthy soil that produces and supports healthy plants.

Achieving balance takes time, though. Soil that has been ignored, mismanaged, or abused does not change overnight into a rich, root-welcoming environment. Nor do pest insects promptly turn away at the garden's perimeter the moment you declare your intentions to tend it without synthetic fertilizers or powerful chemical pesticides. In the interim, you'll need to garden proactively to prevent problems from taking hold in your garden as well as learn what to do when troubles do arise.

Top Five
OOPS! GARDENING MISTAKES

Even experienced gardeners make mistakes that can throw the garden's balance out of whack. Here are the five mistakes most reported by readers of *Organic Gardening* magazine in 2009:

1. **Letting weeds go to seed.** This year's lapse becomes next year's frustration.
2. **Planting too close together.** Sure, the garden looks sparse in spring, but plants do grow. A lot.
3. **Overfertilizing.** Too much food leads to unhealthy growth. In plants, too.
4. **Buying plants already blooming or fruiting.** You want all their energy going to roots, not fruits, when you transplant them.
5. **All work and no relaxation makes gardening a chore.** Sit and enjoy— you've earned it.

PREVENTING AND CONTROLLING PEST PROBLEMS

Whenever you see insects in your garden, remember this: Most are no threat to plants, many are beneficial, and all of them, even the pests that eat your plants, are an integral part of the ecosystem you are cultivating. But what do you do when the pests seem to have the upper hand? You don't want to enforce a "no-fly zone" with pesticides. They're dangerous for you to have and to use, and they harm wildlife and contaminate water. Instead, use safe, organic techniques and products to keep the pests in balance.

Grow healthy plants. The best defenses against insect attack are preventive measures. Pests target weak or unhealthy plants, so choose plants that are suited to the conditions you are putting them in and they'll be less stressed. Don't let plants be too wet, too dry, or too shaded. Use lots of compost, but stay away from high-nitrogen fertilizers that stimulate lush growth that attracts the attention of aphids and mites.

Encourage diversity. Organic gardening relies on increased biodiversity (above- and belowground) to suppress insect damage—very different from fighting one pest at a time with pesticides. Mixing different vegetables, herbs, and flowers together in your beds keeps pests from zeroing in on a whole crop of their target plant. The more diverse and abundant the habitat, the more beneficial insects—and the fewer pest insects. Crop rotations in plots, enhanced vegetation on the borders, flowers throughout the growing season, and biologically active soil all become parts of a dynamic balance of forces that keep pests in check.

Encourage pests' predators. The most effective and natural way to control pests is to rely on the food chain. Plant herbs and flowers among your vegetables to lure predatory insects such as ladybugs and green lacewings, which feed on flowers' nectar while their larvae consume pests. Put out a birdbath to enlist the appetites of songbirds to your cause. Treat toads, lizards, and garter snakes as welcome allies, too.

Build barriers. Row cover is a woven fabric that lets light, air, and water reach plants but keeps pests (including deer) away from them. You'll find it in local garden centers, in seed and garden supply catalogs, and online. A simple cardboard collar around the base of a newly transplanted pepper can protect it from fatal feeding by soil-dwelling cutworms.

PEST ROGUES

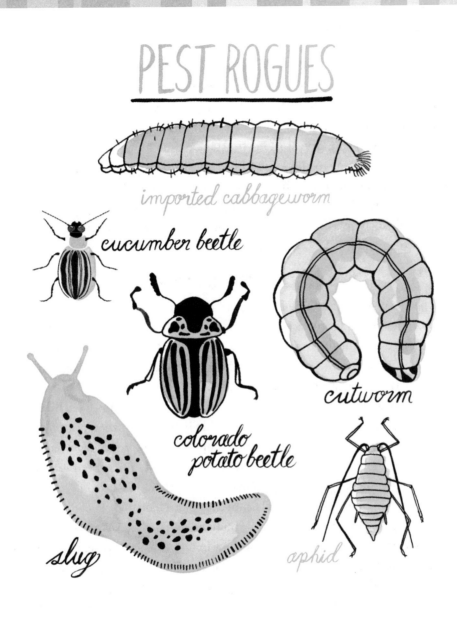

imported cabbageworm

cucumber beetle

colorado potato beetle

cutworm

slug

aphid

Five of the most common vegetable garden insect pests are aphids, imported cabbageworms, Colorado potato beetles, cucumber beetles, and cutworms. Slugs are not insects, but these slimy pests can cause as much damage in a garden as the most determined insect. All of these pests attack more than one kind of crop, and they can be problematic in almost any part of the United States.

Target the treatment. When prevention is no match for infestation, take the time to choose the right organic tool to solve your problem. Start by making sure you have correctly identified the pest and confirmed it is the cause of the symptoms you've found. Consult your local Cooperative Extension office (csrees.usda.gov) if you need help. Then, depending on the pest, you can arm yourself with the treatment most likely to do the trick.

Give in but don't give up. Pests attack plants under stress. Do you have enough healthy plants to allow you to sacrifice the sickly ones? Can you restore sickly plants to robust health so they can resist insect attack? If not, let the pests do their worst, then watch as their predators flock to your garden and protect your healthy plants. Or consider the afflicted plants as a pest trap and remove them and the pests occupying them from your garden.

Bring On the Beneficials

Encouraging so-called beneficials—insects, animals, birds, arachnids, and other organisms that prey on or parasitize pests or pollinate our plants—is an important tool in the organic gardener's collection of ways to protect plants and prevent problems. For ideas on how to get these garden good guys on your side, take a cue from the natural world.

Nature keeps the populations of the insects we call pests in check by providing natural enemies, the ones we think of as beneficial insects. But few of us fully appreciate the vast number of potentially beneficial organisms that inhabit the land around us. It's not only the handful we read about most often, but dozens—probably hundreds—of insects and other creatures.

You'll find many of the beneficials native to your region in meadowlike settings, particularly if the area edges along a woodland and includes running water and perhaps a marshy spot. By comparison, how many of those beneficials are in your garden? If you're growing strictly corn, beans, and tomatoes in the midst of a close-cropped lawn, it will be only a few. If you have flowers, fruiting trees and shrubs, and herbs along with your vegetables, perhaps near a weedy hedgerow, you will have more. The number will increase with the diversity of the planting you create.

The mere presence of pests like aphids isn't enough to lure predators to your garden and keep them there. Beneficial insects need places to breed, and most of them need other sources of food. Take, for example, the huge family of minuscule wasps that parasitize several kinds of pests, from aphids to Mexican bean

(continued on page 266)

GARDEN BENEFICIALS

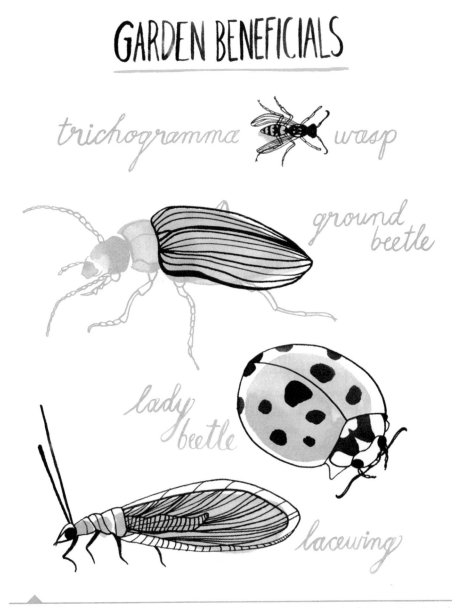

trichogramma wasp

ground beetle

lady beetle

lacewing

From teeny tiny, 1/25-inch (1 mm) *Trichogramma* wasps to almost alarmingly large, 1- to 3-inch ground beetles, beneficial insects do a super-size job of keeping pests from overrunning our gardens. Lady beetles (adults and larvae) and lacewing larvae feed on aphids, scale insects, mealybugs, and other small soft-bodied pests. *Trichogramma* species and other parasitic wasps attack the eggs and caterpillars of many garden pests. And ground beetles prey on cutworms, slugs, fly eggs and maggots, and other soft-bodied larvae and pupae in the soil.

Plant the flowers that pest-controlling insects love most. Insectary plants have flowers that provide the protein (in pollen) and carbohydrates (in nectar) that lady beetles, lacewings, and other beneficials need to thrive and produce more offspring. When the pest insects they feed on are in short supply, some adult beneficials seek out pollen and nectar as a supplemental food source. Others feast on flower power exclusively (and their larvae feed on the pests).

While nearly all flowers have pollen and nectar, scientists are discovering that specific blossoms are more attractive to beneficials than others. Here's what the research has revealed:

The amount of available nectar or pollen and how accessible the food sources are determine what makes one flower more appealing than another. Most beneficial insects are minute, with shorter mouthparts suited to small, shallow flowers equipped with a nice landing platform and exposed nectaries (where nectar is produced). Flowers that meet these specifications include umbel-type plants (flower clusters shaped like flattopped umbrellas) like those found in the carrot family (dill, fennel, parsley, cilantro, etc.) and certain daisylike flowers found in the composite family.

An added attraction in some plants is the presence of extrafloral nectaries, which are nectar sources located outside the flower, usually in the petiole or stem. A few examples include sunflowers and cover crops such fava beans, cowpeas, and vetch. In peonies, these extrafloral nectaries are located on the bud itself.

A 3-year study at Colorado State University monitored 170 species of ornamental plants to find out which ones were most attractive to five beneficial insect groups: lacewings, syrphid flies (aka hoverflies), mini-wasps, lady beetles, and tachinid flies. Thirty varieties of plants stood out as highly attractive, though only one plant—golden marguerite (*Anthemis tinctoria*)—enticed all five beneficial groups. Fennel, dill, cilantro, and fernleaf yarrow (*Achillea filipendulina*) were found to be highly attractive to all but tachinid flies.

While one plant might be more attractive to beneficials than another, the "appeal factor" can vary depending on climate, location, time of year, and the volume of flowers produced. Nectar production can also vary among varieties of the same species. In the Colorado State study, for instance, creeping thyme (*Thymus serpyllum*) was highly attractive to beneficials, while few or no visitations were observed on some of its cultivars.

Keep in mind that flowering periods vary widely from species to species. Growing a diversity of insectary plants that offer a succession of blooms from early spring through fall will keep beneficial bugs in your garden—and eating pests—all season long.

The following nine insectary plants have been proved indispensable in several studies.

ANISE HYSSOP (*Agastache foeniculum* or *A. rugosa*, aka Korean mint) is a showy, summer-blooming perennial that's highly attractive to many beneficials, especially parasitic wasps.

CILANTRO, AKA CORIANDER (*Coriandrum sativum*), is a favored annual among a variety of beneficial insects, including lady beetles, green lacewings, and parasitic wasps. Oregon State University researchers found this plant to be highly attractive to syrphid flies in the early season.

COREOPSIS annuals and perennials bloom from spring through fall. They help feed syrphid flies, lady beetles, lacewings, and parasitic wasps.

COSMOS belong to the daisy family. Annual and perennial varieties bloom spring through fall, attracting syrphid flies, lady beetles, and lacewings.

FENNEL (*Foeniculum vulgare*) flowers have extreme appeal for all nectar-feeding beneficial insects. Bonus: This easy-to-grow perennial plant serves as fodder for caterpillars of the anise swallowtail butterfly.

GOLDEN MARGUERITE (*Anthemis tinctoria*) entices five essential beneficials—lady beetles, lacewings, syrphid flies, tachinid flies, and mini-wasps—with its golden yellow daisy-type flowers that bloom summer and fall.

LAVENDER (*Lavandula angustifolia*) blooms in early summer, attracting small pollinating insects as well as aphid-eating syrphid flies.

SWEET ALYSSUM (*Lobularia maritima*) is a fast-growing annual with fragrant white flowers that are a widely recognized nectar source for beneficial insects, particularly syrphid flies.

YARROW (*Achillea millefolium*; *A. filipendulina*) is a summer-flowering perennial that feeds syrphid flies, lacewings, tachinid flies, lady beetles, and parasitic wasps.

beetles. The adults lay eggs on the body of the pest, and when the larvae hatch out, they consume the host. The egg-laying adults need nectar for food to continue breeding and producing eggs and for seeking out the pests. They need other plants for rest and shelter. These essentials may be provided by trees for one species, flowers for another, herbs or weeds for yet another.

Take the following steps to support beneficials and encourage them to stick around in your garden:

Give them shelter. Groundcovers—like winter cover crops, grasses, and low-growing thyme—and hedgerows with tall plants such as willows provide a place for beneficials to live and reproduce. Protect beneficial ground beetles by leaving cover crop residues in place. Keep in mind also that both pest insects and beneficials dwell in the garden all season. Often the same plants that attract beneficials when they are in bloom harbor a few pest insects for the beneficials to feed on when they're not in bloom.

Offer water. Beneficials need to drink. A shallow birdbath or dish with pebbles to perch on, filled to within a quarter of an inch of the rim, is ideal.

Don't spray. Synthetic pesticides and even "natural" ones such as rotenone kill beneficials. They are "broad-spectrum" weapons that don't discriminate between helpful and harmful insects. Give the beneficials what they need, and you won't need the spray.

Go native. Native insects prefer native plants. Ornamental plants from China and Europe do not supply food for our native insects. Excellent native insectary plants, including mountain mint (*Pycnanthemum*), blue star (*Amsonia*), butterfly weed (*Asclepias tuberosa*), shrub dogwoods, sassafras, and certain viburnums, are often available at nurseries. To find more native choices for your garden, check with a local native plant society, visit a nearby botanical garden or arboretum, or consult plantnative.org to locate a native plant nursery near you.

ORGANIC PEST PREVENTION AND CONTROL TECHNIQUES

It can take a few years for the population of beneficials in your garden to grow to the point of providing adequate protection against pest problems. Once they're well established, beneficials may do most—or all—of the pest control for you. But until the good guys take charge, it's a smart idea to put some preventive measures in place and to be prepared to apply controls if a pest problem threatens your garden.

Prevention and Monitoring Methods

Stopping pests before they reach your garden is far preferable to trying to control them once they've begun munching on your plants. Almost as good is knowing when pests are starting to appear and taking action to keep them from ruining your crops.

FLOATING ROW COVERS

This translucent white porous polyester fabric acts as an insect barrier while letting in up to 80 percent of the available light. You can buy either lightweight or heavyweight types—you'll want to use the lighter one for controlling pests in summer, because it will keep out bugs without cooking your plants. The heavier fabric reportedly traps more warmth and so is better for season extending.

The material is sold by the yard, generally in rolls 4 to 8 feet wide. You cut it to the length you need, then drape it over metal hoops, attach it to wooden supporting frames, wrap it around wire tomato cages, or simply lay it directly on your crops like a blanket. *Important:* You must secure the edges of the row cover with soil, U-shaped pins (either commercial or homemade ones crafted from wire coat hangers), boards, bricks, or rocks.

Use floating row covers as temporary barriers to get plants past critical stages, such as when they are seedlings or while the pest you are deterring is most active. Potatoes, lettuce, and carrots, for example, may spend the whole season under cover, since they don't require insects for pollination. Crops such as tomatoes, squash, and eggplant need to be uncovered when they start blooming so pollinators can visit.

Pests controlled: Row covers are especially useful against mobile pests, including cabbage moths (imported cabbageworms), Colorado potato beetles, most aphids, Mexican bean beetles, flea beetles, squash bugs, and tomato hornworms. Combine row covers with crop rotation if you're dealing with pests that overwinter in the soil.

Another type of barrier that's well worth putting in place is a cutworm collar. Use one around the base of every transplant you put in your garden and you won't have to worry about awaking to find your plants snipped off at soil level by these nocturnal pests. Cut strips of lightweight cardboard to about 8 × 2½ inches, overlap the ends of a strip to form a circle, and fasten with tape or a staple or simply notch the ends and slide them together. When transplanting, slip a collar over each plant and press it into the soil around the stem so about half of the collar is below the soil line. You can also use shallow cans, like the kind tuna comes in, with the tops and bottoms removed, or pretty much any other barrier that can encircle a plant's tender young stem at the soil level.

Pests controlled: Cutworm collars stop the several species of moth larvae that live in the soil and come out at night to feed by curling around plant stems, girdling or completely chewing through young transplants. To reduce the cutworm population, cultivate the top 1 to 2 inches of soil a day or two before setting out transplants in the garden. Hand-pick any cutworms you uncover, and drop them into soapy water or toss them on a paved surface where they'll be easy prey for hungry birds.

Prevention is the key to protecting tender transplants from cutworm damage. Put a simple collar—of cardboard, plastic, or heavy-duty paper— around every seedling when you set it out in the garden, and avoid losing your crop to nocturnal stem-snipping cutworm caterpillars.

PHEROMONE TRAPS

Many insects produce powerful smells called pheromones that they use to lure the opposite sex. Scientists have duplicated several of these scents and used them to bait special traps for luring the target insect. But because these "sex" traps attract mostly male insects, they aren't completely effective at controlling pest damage. They're useful as an early warning that a particular pest is moving into your area. When you find the first pests in your trap, you know it's time to launch your control strategies, such as putting your row covers in position or applying *Bacillus thuringiensis* (page 271).

Pests monitored: Pheromone lures are available for diamondback moths and moths that produce armyworms, cabbage loopers, corn earworms, European corn borers, tomato pinworms, and cutworms.

STICKY TRAPS

These traps—a rigid material of a particular color that's coated with a sticky substance—are used to catch insects that are attracted to that color. To be effective, the traps must be clean and sticky. Also, use at least one trap (hung at plant height and close to the plant) every 3 to 5 feet.

You can buy packaged sticky traps or make them yourself. To make your own, use any rigid material of the right color (for colors, see below) or that you can spray paint. Cut the material to size (4 × 6-inch rectangles are the standard), and if needed, paint it the correct color. Cover the trap with a plastic bag or clingy plastic wrap, then coat it with a sticky substance, such as Tangle-Trap. (The plastic wrap makes cleanup easy—when your trap is covered with bugs, just remove the plastic and rewrap the trap with a new piece of plastic. Then coat it with more sticky stuff.)

For cucumber beetles, use a mobile trap: Wrap clingy plastic food wrap around a white bucket or other large object, then coat the plastic with Tangle-Trap. Carry the bucket along the rows of vines, shaking and brushing the plants as you go. The beetles will fly up and stick to the traps.

Pests monitored/controlled: Yellow traps attract whiteflies, fruit flies, male winged scales, leafhoppers, fungus gnats, midges, male winged mealybugs and leaf miners, thrips, psyllids, and winged aphids. White traps lure whiteflies, plant bugs, cucumber beetles, and flea beetles. Light blue traps attract flower thrips, and red spheres attract the flies whose eggs hatch into apple maggots.

Control Methods

For pests that slip past the barriers, elude the beneficials, and escape early detection to reach damaging levels on your plants, there are organically acceptable ways to defend your garden. Observe commonsense safety rules when applying organic pest control products: Follow label instructions, wear protective clothing, don't eat or drink while spraying, and wash up afterward. While organic controls typically are gentler for the environment, that does not guarantee that they are safe to swallow, breathe, or get in your eyes or on your skin.

Focus control methods on the areas where pests are most likely to be found to limit the amount of pesticide you have to use and to reduce the risks to nontarget beneficials. For example, check the undersides of leaves when applying organic pest control—pests often hide out of sight.

INSECTICIDAL SOAP

Insecticidal soap contains unsaturated long-chain fatty acids (derived from animal fats) that dissolve the cuticle (skin) of insects. Insecticidal soap sprays are commercially formulated products sold specifically for insect control. (Don't confuse these products with herbicidal soaps, which kill vegetation instead of insects, or household soaps, which are detergents.)

To be effective, the insecticidal soap must come in contact with the insects while it's still liquid—it has no effect after it dries on the plants. Spray only on pests and try to avoid hitting beneficial insects with the spray. *Caution:* Insecticidal soap can burn some plant leaves. Test each type of plant before spraying the entire plant. Spray a few leaves, then wait 48 hours. If there's no damage, go ahead and spray the entire plant. Don't spray on hot days, and rinse the soap off your plants after a few hours if the plants are receiving a lot of sunshine. If you have hard water, mix the soap with distilled water to help the soap dissolve.

Pests controlled: Insecticidal soap sprays are highly effective against mites, aphids, whiteflies, and other soft-bodied insects as well as the softer nymph stages of some tough-bodied bugs.

OIL SPRAYS

Oil sprays work by suffocating pests. To be effective, the oil spray must hit the pest directly.

Use "dormant" oils to kill insect pest eggs and disease spores on the bare branches of trees and shrubs during the dormant season. To treat growing plants, use a lighter-weight, more refined horticultural oil (called "summer," "supreme," or "superior" oil). Lighter oils evaporate more quickly than dormant oils and are less likely to damage plants.

To avoid plant damage, don't spray any plants suffering from moisture stress. Also, don't spray on very hot days. Test the spray on just a few leaves before you spray the entire plant. Wait 48 hours to make sure no leaf spotting or discoloration occurs.

To minimize potential harm to beneficial insects, limit your spraying to small areas where you can see pests lurking, and leave a couple of unsprayed "refuges" for any good bugs you can't see. Protect nectar-feeding beneficials and pollinators by not spraying during peak flowering times and by not spraying blossoms. Spray early in the morning, before bees become active. And if you plan to release beneficials, do it after you apply the oil spray.

Pests controlled: Use horticultural oils to combat aphids, mites, beetles, leaf miners, caterpillars, thrips, leafhoppers, and whiteflies.

BACILLUS THURINGIENSIS

Bacillus thuringiensis (Bt) is a naturally occurring bacterium found in the soil. There are many different types, and some can be used to kill a specific insect or class of insects. When a target insect takes a bite of a plant sprayed with the type of Bt the insect is sensitive to, the insect gets infected and stops feeding. Inside the insect, the bacterium releases a protein that causes the pest to die within a few days.

Each type of Bt is effective only on one specific insect (or group) and only on insects that actually eat it. However, that doesn't mean you should spray it indiscriminately. For example, the type that kills cabbage loopers can also kill the caterpillars of the beautiful butterflies you're trying to attract to your garden. Spray it only when you know you have a pest problem, and spray only the pest-infested plants.

Most formulations of this bacterium are sold as a liquid or a wettable powder that you dilute with water and then spray on the plants you want to protect. Some products are sold in the form of dusts or granules that you dust directly on plants.

Because Bt usually is effective only against the nonadult stage of pest insects, you must time applications carefully. As soon as you spot the pest larvae, thoroughly coat the affected plants with the spray or dust. (For corn pests, deposit a little of the granular product into the whorl or on the corn silk.) Avoid spraying during the heat of the day. Bt breaks down a day or two after spraying, so you may need to reapply it if you're up against a severe infestation. As with all sprays or dusts, always wear goggles and a mask to prevent contact with the bacterium when you apply it to your plants (there have been a few reports of allergic reactions in those who have inhaled it).

Pests controlled: The most common strain of the bacterium—Bt var. *kurstaki* (sometimes called Bt var. *berliner*)—kills hundreds of different kinds of caterpillars, including cabbage loopers, tomato hornworms, cabbageworms, corn earworms, European corn borers, and squash vine borers. Bt var. *tenebrionis* (a new name—until recently this one was called Bt var. *san diego*) kills Colorado potato beetles.

PARASITIC NEMATODES

Don't confuse these beneficial nematodes with destructive root-knot nematodes. Once inside a pest, parasitic nematodes release bacteria that kill the insect host within a day or two. Although these good nematodes occur naturally in the soil, there usually aren't enough of them in one place to control pests that have gotten out of hand in your garden. But you can buy them by the billions for use as a living—and organic, safe, and nontoxic—form of pest control.

The dormant nematodes are shipped in a moist medium, which you mix with water when you're ready to apply. When you receive a shipment, put the sealed container in your refrigerator until you are ready to use it (the nematodes will keep there for about 4 months). Try to use them as soon as possible, though; their effectiveness declines the longer you store them. Once the nematodes are mixed with water for application, they are viable for only a very short time. Use all of the mix within a few hours—don't try to save any of it.

Apply nematodes to moist soil that has reached a temperature of at least 60°F, either in the evening or when it's overcast, at a rate of about 23 million nematodes per 1,000 square feet. Thoroughly cover the area with the nematodes, then water them in. Exception: If your pest is in the plant (the squash vine borer or corn earworm), mix up a small batch of nematodes and use a garden syringe or

talk the talk
Pest and Disease Control

BACTERIA: Single-celled microorganisms that reproduce by simple cell division. Beneficial bacteria can help control insect pests, but some bacteria species can cause serious plant diseases, such as bacterial wilt and fire blight.

BACTERIAL PESTICIDE: A pesticide that kills a target pest by infecting it with a living bacterium that inhibits the function of the host and causes it to die. Bt (see opposite) is one example of a bacterial pesticide.

BENEFICIALS: Helpful creatures—such as birds, bats, bees, earthworms, toads, snakes, spiders, and predatory insects—that eat pests, pollinate plants, or otherwise benefit the garden by their presence and activities.

BT (BACILLUS THURINGIENSIS): A spray, powder, or granule derived from naturally occurring bacteria that kills certain insect larvae. One Bt variety, Btk (Bt var. *kurstaki*), controls cabbage loopers, cabbageworms, tomato hornworms, fruit worms, European corn borers, and other caterpillars. Another Bt variety targets mosquito larvae.

FUNGUS: A spore-producing organism that helps the decomposition process. Fungi are important for breaking down materials in a compost pile, but some kinds cause common plant diseases such as powdery mildew and late blight.

FUNGICIDE: A biological organism or chemical compound used to kill or inhibit the action of fungi.

HERBICIDE: A substance used to kill unwanted plants. Some types are selective (they kill only a certain type of plant); others are nonselective and will kill any plants they contact. Systemic herbicide enters a plant's vascular system and kills the entire plant; contact herbicide affects only the parts of the plant it touches.

INSECTICIDAL SOAP: Specially formulated solutions of fatty acids that kill insect pests such as aphids, mites, and whiteflies.

NEMATODE: A microscopic, unsegmented, threadlike worm; some nematodes are beneficial, while others can harm plants.

PESTICIDE: Any substance, synthetic or natural, that is used to kill insects, animals, fungi, or bacteria.

VIRUS: A microscopic organism that must be inside the living cell of a host to reproduce. Viruses can be transmitted by insects, mites, and nematodes as well as through contact with garden tools and plant cuttings.

eyedropper to apply them just inside the tip of the ear of corn or into the squash vine entrance holes.

Pests controlled: Nematodes attack and invade armyworms, corn earworms, squash vine borers, soil-dwelling grubs (including Japanese beetle larvae), weevils, root maggots, and cutworms (in their soil-dwelling stages).

MANAGING ANIMAL PESTS

They may look cute and cuddly, but the furry pests that arrive in your garden on four legs can do a lot of damage, usually at night while you're blissfully unaware of the ravaging being done to your vegetables and flowers. It's possible to curtail late-night snacking by Bambi and friends, but it can be difficult to stop it completely once the local wildlife has identified your garden as their favorite salad bar.

The trickiest part of coping with animal pests can be identifying the pest. Since many animals feed at dawn or dusk, you may need to rely upon such signs as feeding patterns, tracks, tunnels, or excrement to figure out what culprit is invading your garden. For example, damaged strawberries may be the work of birds, mice, or slugs. Controls that work for one pest may do nothing to stop another, so it's important to determine exactly what pest is to blame before you act.

Most animal deterrents fall into one of four categories:

Fences and barriers. These usually work best in vegetable gardens where fencing and netting are unlikely to spoil the view. To be successful, barriers must block an animal's access to your plants without interfering with your ability to tend them.

Repellents. Sprays or scent dispensers that hang in or near affected plants, these products typically must be refreshed after rain to keep them at their peak potency. Repellents that make your plants taste bad require that animal pests take a bite before they learn their lesson. Repellents can be a good choice for protecting ornamentals that you don't want to fence, but keep in mind that when food is scarce, hungry animals may ignore bad flavors and smells to get the food they need to survive.

Scare tactics. Gadgets such as inflatable owls, plastic snakes, hawk-shaped kites, and elaborate scarecrows have limited effectiveness. Moving them frequently from one spot to another can help. Scare devices that move in the wind—kites, balloons, and dangling CDs or pie tins—work better than stationary items, but their ability to scare still fades the longer they dangle in the same place.

Traps. Live trapping animal pests may seem like a humane solution, but it rarely is. Animals trapped and released in another location rarely adapt successfully. Plus, there are regulations governing the transport and release of wild animals. Snap traps (which capture and kill the animal) can be effective for small pests, such as mice and voles.

Protecting your garden from hungry wildlife requires a thoughtful approach that considers an animal's behavior, its place in the local ecosystem, and your garden's place in its environment. A successful strategy may involve a combination of deterrent methods—netting and scare devices over a berry patch, for example. Or you may need to replace a plant that deer find particularly tasty with something less appealing. With patience and perseverance, you can usually find a way to peacefully coexist with your wild neighbors.

Prevent Future Disease Problems

Here are five steps that can make a world of difference if your garden is plagued by disease:

1. **Clean up the garden in fall. Remove fallen fruit, cut back perennials, and rake up leaves—all prime breeding grounds for fungal pathogens.**

2. **Increase spacing for better airflow. Divide perennials when they become too crowded.**

3. **Water at ground level instead of overhead. Fungal spores that cause leaf spot, wilt, and blight thrive on wet plant leaves. Also, water deeply but infrequently. Constantly damp soil encourages pathogens that lead to root rot.**

4. **Rotate your vegetables to different spots in the garden from one season to the next.**

5. **If you've had problems in the past, look for disease-resistant varieties, sometimes indicated by letters following a variety name. For example, "VFNT" after the name of a hybrid tomato means that it is less prone to verticillium, fusarium, root-knot nematodes, and tobacco mosaic virus. Many heirlooms have been preserved for their disease resistance, too.**

DEALING WITH PLANT DISEASES

Dealing with plant diseases can be one of the most challenging aspects of gardening. Unlike garden pests, which are usually easy to spot, most organisms that cause disease are too small to see without a magnifying glass or a microscope. Disease symptoms can be variable and subtle, so they're tricky to diagnose and sometimes easy to miss until a problem is quite severe.

Symptoms and Signs

Scientists who study plant disease separate the visible characteristics of disease into two categories: symptoms and signs. A symptom is a plant's response to a disease-causing organism or condition. Two common disease symptoms are wilting and changes in plant color. Disease symptoms usually result from the death of cells, inhibited cell development, or overstimulated cell development.

A sign of an infectious disease is the disease-causing organism itself or its products (such as spores). Examples of signs produced by fungi include the white powdery spores of mildew, the black film of fungal strands on leaves with sooty mold, and the galls on cedar trees produced by cedar-apple rust. One common sign of bacteria is slimy ooze that often has a foul odor. While it's not critical to know the technical difference between a symptom and a sign, it is helpful to know the terms used to describe common symptoms and signs of disease.

What to Do About Disease

Find the source. Fungal diseases are spread by spores, which travel by air currents or rain splashes from one plant to another. Viruses, such as the dreaded tobacco mosaic virus, spread when sap from an infected plant is transferred to a healthy one via your hands or tools. Bacterial diseases are transmitted by insects like leafhoppers, aphids, and thrips.

If you suspect your plant is diseased, study its symptoms and signs, then seek advice from your local Cooperative Extension office, a Master Gardener, or knowledgeable staff at a local nursery or public garden to try to identify the cause and determine what to do about it. Knowing what caused the problem is a vital piece of information you'll need to decide how to care for that plant—or what to grow instead—next season.

Rx for Ailing Plants

Organic gardeners don't have to accept disease problems as a death sentence for their plants, nor do they have to reach for a nonorganic fungicide to save the day. Good cultural practices, like those described in "Prevent Future Disease Problems," go a long way toward keeping disease pathogens from causing distress. Here are a few other options for resolving disease woes without reaching for a toxic treatment:

Ailment: Black spot on your rosebush

Remedy: Mix 2 tablespoons baking soda, 2 teaspoons liquid hand soap, and 2 quarts water. Put it in a spray bottle and coat the leaves, top and bottom. This solution changes the pH on the leaves' surfaces, making them inhospitable to the black spot spores.

Ailment: Powdery mildew on your zinnias or pumpkins

Remedy: Spray a solution of 1 part milk to 2 parts water on plants with powdery mildew. Mist the problem plants with the solution, making sure you hit the stems and undersides of leaves. Reapply after it rains.

Ailment: Anthracnose on your tomato plants

Remedy: To protect against diseases that splash up from the soil, spread several layers of newspaper around the plants. Moisten the paper, then top with 2 or 3 inches of grass clippings or other organic mulch. This traps disease spores in the soil.

Excessive stress is unhealthy. Plants suffering from over- or underwatering, overfertilization, extreme weather, or other forms of stress are more susceptible to disease than their robust neighbors. For example, if your bee balm plants have suffered leaf drop and tissue damage from powdery mildew year after year, they become extra vulnerable to other diseases and insects. Some stressed plants even produce compounds that make them more attractive to insects.

Beware of family connections. Pests and diseases spread readily from plant to plant in the same family. Some cross family lines. For instance, tomatoes, delphiniums, and marigolds are in separate plant families, but they are among the 150 plants that host tobacco mosaic virus.

Cut your losses. No amount of gardening triage will save plants hit with viruses or phytoplasmas (bacteria-like organisms). These nasties cause stunted growth in healthy plants and can lead to twisted leaves and stems, mosaic leaf patterns, distorted or discolored flowers, and other strange-looking symptoms.

Release the guilt. It's not your fault. A dead or diseased plant isn't necessarily a reflection of your gardening skills. Before giving another chance to a plant you didn't succeed with, review its needs for sunlight, soil conditions, and water so you can be sure to meet them. And hope for better weather—the culprit of last resort.

AWAY WITH WEEDS

Pests, diseases, harsh weather, wild animals: A lot of things are out to get your garden plants—including other plants, in the form of those vigorous, unwanted garden invaders we describe as weeds. Even if you subscribe to the notion that weeds are just plants growing in the wrong place, it's important to keep them under control. That's because weeds steal important nutrients and moisture from the soil at the expense of your garden's chosen fruits, flowers, and vegetables. Weeds also can block air circulation and cast shadows that prevent your plants from soaking up the sun.

Some particularly bad actors, such as bindweed, will even wrap themselves around your preferred plants and clamber right over them, choking them with twining stems and weighing them down with sheer aggressive growth. Finally, weeds with family ties to your garden's crops can harbor diseases and pests that may easily spread to their domesticated kin. All in all, plenty of reasons for keeping weeds out of your garden's picture.

Chapter 6 addressed weeding as a part of regular garden maintenance. Here's a look at weeds as part of the cadre of pests that may disrupt your garden and some tips on how best to get them under control.

Winning the weed battle on the home front starts by learning all you can about your enemy. As with pests and diseases, developing an effective control strategy for weeds is easiest when you know what you're up against. Weeds fit into four general categories:

Annuals spread by seed. The original plant blooms, produces seeds, and dies. Their root systems don't usually get big, deep, or wide, so annuals are the easiest to eradicate. Pigweed, cocklebur, and sow thistle are annuals.

4 WEED TYPES

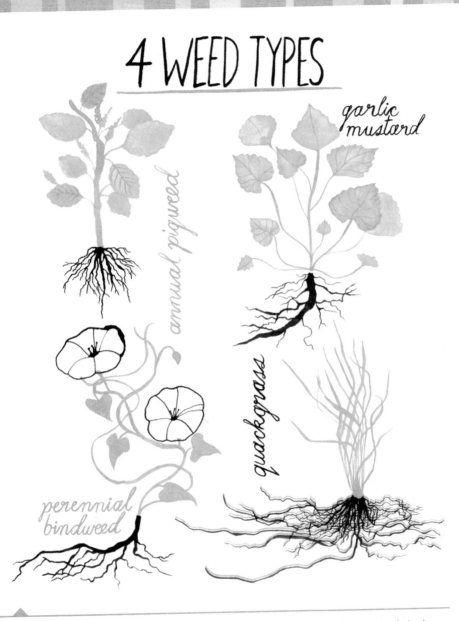

garlic mustard

annual pigweed

quackgrass

perennial bindweed

Let a weed's life cycle guide your efforts to control it. Hoe annuals like pigweed early in the season, before they make seeds. Dig out taproots of first-year biennials like garlic mustard to prevent seed production in year two. Perennials like bindweed have fleshy, rampant roots that can reproduce from even a tiny piece left in the soil; they also spread by seed. Remove every piece of these pests as soon as you spot them and never, ever put them in the compost. Weedy grasses spread by seeds and rambling rhizomes; pull out every bit and keep after them to get control.

Biennials spread by seed in their second year. The first year, they put out leaves and a taproot. Dig up most or all of the taproot to stop its growth. Poison hemlock, garlic mustard, and bull thistle are biennials.

Perennials spread by seed, too, but their roots survive winter to grow the next year. Removing all the roots is key to eliminating them. Dandelion and field bindweed are perennials.

Grasses spread by seed and by rhizomes—stringy stems that send up shoots away from the original plant. As is the case with perennial weeds, if you don't remove the entire root system, the plant grows back. Johnson grass, quack grass, and Bermuda grass are in this category.

Once you identify which weeds you have and the ways they grow, fit the eradication method to the weed:

Tease them out. Tedious but satisfying, hand-weeding is the best solution for dealing with perennial taprooted weeds or grasses with rhizomes.

Cut them off. Cutting down or hoeing weeds before they produce seed is crucial to keeping them under control. It works best on annuals and biennials. Perennial weeds may need to be cut back every 2 to 3 weeks in spring and summer and into fall.

Turn up the heat. A quick pass with a flame weeder (a propane tank with a long wand that lets you stand upright while putting the flame to weeds on the ground) boils, then bursts, the water cells in the leaves, wilting the plant. No need to set it on fire, no matter how enjoyable that may be. Flaming is most efficient for young seedlings, big-leaved weeds, or ones that form ground-hugging rosettes.

Toast them. Organic contact herbicides, such as clove, orange and cinnamon oils, and horticultural (full strength, not supermarket) vinegar burn a weed's foliage (and if you're not careful, any other plant in the vicinity) but don't kill the roots. But spray them every few weeks, and you'll eventually . . .

Starve them. Any method that kills foliage or cuts weeds off at the soil line—leaves, stems, and all—eventually depletes the roots of energy, killing the plants. And remember, just like the desirable plants in your garden, weeds require light, air, nutrients, and water. Withhold one or more of these and, eventually, a weed dies. This takes time, however, so be persistent. Organic weed control isn't a do-it-once-and-be-done proposition.

Keep Them Gone

To keep weeds from coming back:

- Don't leave bare ground. Choose plants vigorous enough to outcompete your most troublesome weeds, and plant them close enough so that once mature, their foliage touches, shading out competition.

- Water only the base of desired plants. That keeps the rest of the soil dry, depriving surrounding weed seeds of water.

- Disturb the soil as little as possible when planting, because weed seeds exposed to even dim light can germinate. How dim? Moonlight is enough for some.

- Mulch, mulch, mulch. Newspaper covered by bark mulch, grass clippings, or seed-free straw makes a good barrier to keep light from triggering weed seed germination.

Wage your weed war, but realize that complete and utter annihilation isn't achievable or desirable. Learn to live with some weeds. Console yourself with the knowledge that although you despise them, your garden's weeds feed and shelter beneficial insects, pollinators, birds, and other wildlife.

Weeds by the Numbers

Why worry about weeds? A few examples of their statistical advantage over your garden plants:

72,000: **Average number of seeds produced by a single plant of lamb's-quarters**

16 feet: **Depth to which Canada thistle roots can grow**

50 years: **Period of time field bindweed seeds remain viable in the soil**

ORGANIC GARDENING THROUGH THE SEASONS

Gardens are where people and the land come together in
the most inspiring way. In almost every garden, the land is made better
and so is the gardener. Each is being kind to the other.

—ROBERT RODALE, *ORGANIC GARDENING,* **1988**

Some gardeners feel relief when cold temperatures—or extreme heat—arrive to enforce a break in gardening activities. Others take adverse conditions as a challenge and use every available tactic to keep their gardens growing no matter what the calendar says.

Season extension can be as simple as tossing a cover over the tomatoes to protect them from an early frost or as elaborate as a greenhouse equipped with heat and lights to allow year-round growing. Whether you welcome a respite when your local climate turns inhospitable for outdoor planting or are determined to do everything you can to keep the harvest coming, there are a few simple techniques every gardener should know to stretch the growing season.

STRETCHING THE OUTDOOR GROWING SEASON

One simple way to extend the growing season outdoors is to start seedlings indoors ahead of the traditional schedule and then plant the seedlings outdoors with individual cloches (see below) for protection. On a larger scale, you can use heavyweight row covers supported by wire hoops, switching to lightweight covers as the weather warms up. You can also reverse this process in fall, planting crops in late summer and covering them once the weather turns cool.

Keep in mind that season extenders such as cloches and row covers are most effective if you prewarm the garden soil before planting. Seeds will not germinate and transplants will establish poorly in cold soil, even if the air temperature is warm enough. To warm the soil, put the season extender in place 1 to 2 weeks prior to planting, or cover the soil with clear or black plastic several weeks before planting.

Cloches. Once made of glass, most cloches are now made of paper or plastic, and you can easily make your own out of any translucent material. Short ultraviolet rays from the sun pass through the cloche and warm the soil and air inside. The soil collects and stores the heat, then releases it slowly, creating a greenhouselike atmosphere and protecting plants from frost. The warmer conditions under a cloche also encourage growth. Commercial cloches include the popular Wall O'Water and similar plastic structures that are filled with water and set around plants. To make a simple cloche, cut off the bottom section of a gallon plastic jug and set the jug over an individual plant. You can mimic the effects of water-filled commercial cloches by circling a plant with a ring of clear plastic soda bottles fastened together and filled with water. Or you can wrap clear plastic around a tomato cage to create a miniature greenhouse.

Cold frames. Homemade cold frames usually are made of wood with a transparent glass or plastic top; garden suppliers sell cold frames made of various types of plastic or polycarbonate with aluminum or plastic frames and bases. Use cold frames to trap the sun's energy and keep transplants and seedlings warm at night. You can add passive heating to a cold frame by tucking dark-colored plastic jugs filled with water in the corners of the frame. During the day

SEASON EXTENDERS

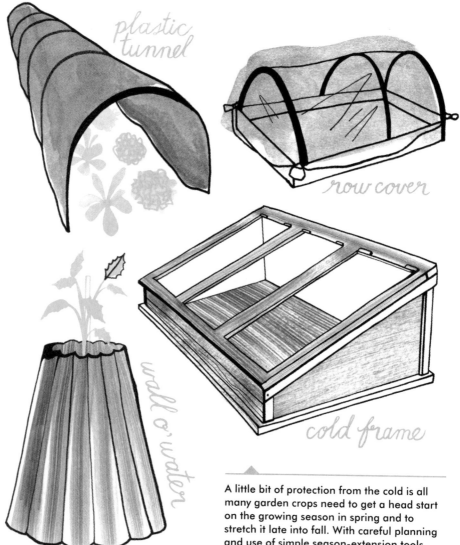

plastic tunnel

row cover

wall o' water

cold frame

A little bit of protection from the cold is all many garden crops need to get a head start on the growing season in spring and to stretch it late into fall. With careful planning and use of simple season-extension tools, you can have the earliest tomatoes in your neighborhood and enjoy fresh-picked salad with Thanksgiving dinner.

they'll absorb sunlight; at night the stored warmth will help keep plants from freezing. A hotbed is essentially a cold frame to which a heat source has been added.

Row covers. A row cover is a versatile season extender that you can use to protect rows, small garden areas, or the whole garden from frost or cold temperatures. Row covers are sheets of transparent or translucent plastic or fabric. They're available in different weights and sizes and may be used to warm the soil, to provide a few degrees of frost protection, or to protect plants from pests. By using row covers, you can extend the season by a month or more.

Doubling up. If extending your growing season captures your imagination, you may want to build your own garden-scale plastic tunnel and raise crops under it throughout winter. This requires covering the beds under the tunnel with cold frames or heavyweight row covers to provide enough insulation from freezing temperatures.

Hotbeds

Hotbeds and cold frames share similar construction—rectangular, boxlike structures covered by glass tops—but a hotbed includes a heat source. Traditionally, rotting manure put the heat in a hotbed, but most gardeners now rely on electric heating cables to supply the warmth. Because hotbeds have a steady source of heat, they can be used earlier in the season than most cold frames, and they create ideal conditions for starting most types of seeds.

Add a heating cable to any frame built on a dug foundation to turn it into a hotbed. You can also make a hotbed from a portable frame, but you'll need a pit at least a foot deep to hold the heating cable. For best control over temperatures within the frame, choose a heating cable with a thermostat.

To make a hotbed, spread a 2-inch layer of vermiculite on top of a gravel layer at the bottom of your pit or foundation. Spread the cable on top of the vermiculite, using long loops to distribute the heat evenly. Don't let the cable wires cross; keep loops at least 8 inches apart and 3 inches away from the frame edges. Cover the cable with 1 inch of sand, followed by a layer of screen or hardware cloth to protect it from being damaged by sharp objects. Cover the screen with 4 to 6 inches of coarse builder's sand in which to sink pots.

talk the talk
Season Extension

CLOCHE: Light-permeable plant covers made out of a variety of materials that are primarily used to protect plants from frost. They work much like miniature greenhouses.

COLD FRAME: A small outside structure meant to give plants some protection from environmental factors such as extreme cold, drying winds, and pounding rain.

ROW COVERS: Sheets of lightweight, permeable material, usually polypropylene or polyester, that can be laid loosely on top of plants to act as a barrier against insect pests or that can give a few degrees of frost protection at the beginning or end of the growing season.

SEASON EXTENSION: Using warming devices and techniques to make the growing season longer by allowing an earlier start for plants in spring and a longer harvest in fall. Cold frames, cloches, row covers, and prewarming the soil are all ways to extend the growing season.

Extending the Season in Hot or Dry Sites

If you garden where soaring summer temperatures or extended periods of drought are the norm, your season-extending efforts may be focused on keeping your crops cool rather than warming them up. Choosing varieties with good heat tolerance is important, as is timing your gardening to take advantage of mild winter temperatures and moderate to warm spring and fall conditions. Instead of row covers to keep off the frost, your favorite season extender might be shade cloth, which is open-weave plastic sheeting that you can support over the top of your garden beds to give your plants some protection from the hottest rays of the sun. Sheets of lattice or lengths of snow fencing may also be positioned to cast partial shade over garden beds.

Where dry spells are a concern, take advantage of every moisture-conservation method you can. Drip irrigation, mulching to conserve soil moisture, and capturing rainwater all can contribute to keeping your garden going without wasting a precious drop. Instead of gardening in raised beds, gardeners in dry regions may choose to garden in sunken beds; likewise, making compost in pits rather than piles helps keep things moist enough for ongoing decomposition.

For many gardeners, record keeping—if it happens at all—is barely an after-thought. At the end of a day of digging and weeding, planting and picking, most of us just want to clean up and sit down. We feel like we're going above and beyond if we manage to clean our tools and put them back in their proper spots. But taking a few more minutes to jot down even the scant facts of the day can create a valuable tool that will serve you nearly as well as the fanciest hoe money can buy.

Call it a journal, a garden diary, a record book, or a log. Keep it in a notebook or a desk calendar or on your preferred electronic device. But definitely keep it, add to it, and refer to it in future gardening seasons as a reminder of what you planted (you think you'll remember, but you probably won't), as a reminder of when things bloomed, as a reminder of when the first tomato ripened or when the last spinach was harvested. Enhance it with sketches or photos of favorite flower combinations or that insect you want to look up later. Staple seed packets to the pages or tuck garden center receipts into pockets. All this information will add up to a practical history of your garden that can guide future decisions about what seeds to order, when to plant, when to be on the lookout for pest or disease problems, and so much more. And all you have to do is get started.

Why Keep a Garden Journal?

To document the history of your garden. This gives you a clear picture of what, where, and when to cultivate while adding to the value of your home.

To plan maintenance tasks. By monitoring frost warnings, you'll know when to move tender potted plants to the warmest part of the garden and cover new plants with floating row covers. By noting the spring arrival of songbirds, you'll know when to stock up on seed for next year's migration.

To track the progress of your garden and your gardening skill. Note milestones: your first attempt at grafting fruit trees or the year you dug your koi pond, planted a tree, started the asparagus bed, or helped your children plant their first gardens. Also record seasonal information, such as the date you harvest your first crop of tomatoes or asparagus, and report the growth of plants to learn which thrive in certain microclimates.

To anticipate challenges such as pests and diseases. Problems often appear at particular times of year or under specific conditions.

Tools for Easy Record Keeping

Start simple. As your garden grows, your desire for details will lead you to try some of these creative ideas:

- Spiral notebooks are portable and lie flat for easy note-taking. Index cards are handy to use, carry, organize, and store.

- Color-code your notes to distinguish among perennials, annuals, shrubs, trees, and bulbs. Keep a few index cards with you and take notes in pencil—it doesn't smudge when wet. Preprinted garden journals offer useful tips on what to note.

- A small spiral-bound watercolor pad and a traveling watercolor set may help you illustrate what you see. Or try a sketchpad and a set of drawing pencils. Not artistic? Carry a small digital camera. Keep a visual record of your own garden or other gardens you visit for ideas by shooting a close-up of each plant with its label. Assemble the snapshots into a photo album.

- Staple seed packets and plant labels onto sheets of paper or organize them into photo sleeves to establish a record of everything you've tried in your garden.

- Keep a separate wall or desk calendar for each year, and review the previous few years' calendars to see what you did and when you did it.

- Draw a map or design of the overall garden, as well as detailed drawings of garden beds, to remind yourself where bulbs are planted and to plan the rotation of your vegetable beds. Gather the materials listed above into a three-ring binder, an empty drawer, or a storage box so the information about your garden is all in one location.

Technology for Gardeners

Garden weblogs (try digindirt.com) are perfect for sharing information. Research favorite topics or chat with other gardeners at OrganicGardening .com. Microsoft Excel and other spreadsheet programs let you create a filing system using databases such as FileMaker Pro and Microsoft Access. Set up data fields (plant name, height, flower color, and so on), then assign each plant its own record, which can be searched, sorted, and categorized. Online calendars work just like paper ones but are easier to search—and perpetual. Digital

What to Write Down

Recording plant information is good for planning. Go over notes in the off-season and sketch ideas to try in spring. Some suggestions for what to record:

Annuals (flowers and vegetables)	Perennials, trees, shrubs
Plant name	Plant name
Source of seed	Source of plant
Date started/method	Planting date
Germination	Location in the garden
Transplant date	Fruiting or flowering period
First fruit or bloom time	Pests and diseases
Date of death	Season(s) of interest
Pests and diseases	Bird/wildlife appeal
Comments	Comments

photo libraries, such as iPhoto and MediaDex, allow you to organize your images into "albums" as well as assign names and keywords to each image. Of course, you could just rely on your memory, but after a few seasons all the years seem to blend into one.

SEASONAL GARDEN-CARE CALENDAR

Where you garden will be the chief determiner in *when* you garden. Obviously, plants in Texas grow on different schedules than those in North Dakota, and gardeners in Denver are sowing seeds at different times than gardeners in Atlanta. This seasonal care calendar is based on gardening roughly in the "middle" of the USDA Hardiness Zone Map's range of 13 temperature zones, eight of which (Zones 3–10) are represented in the lower 48 states. As such, this calendar offers only a loose guide to timing for any particular garden, especially those at the northern or southern ends of the hardiness zone spectrum.

JANUARY

- Garden resolution time? Resolve to go easier on yourself when you make mistakes. Resolve to keep better/any records of your garden. Resolve to enjoy your garden more and worry less.

- Look through seed catalogs to get an idea of what you want to plant. If you plan to start some of your plants from seed, order the seed now. Catalogs often have a wider seed selection than your garden center, with more heirlooms, more organic choices, and varieties with resistance to the most common disease problems.

- Inventory your garden supplies and make sure you have the essentials (such as row covers and plant cages); shop for items or materials that are in short supply.

- Make a 3-year rotation plan for your vegetable garden. By changing the positions of plants in different plant families from year to year, you interrupt disease and pest cycles. Plan to alternate deep-rooted plants with shallow-rooted plants and heavy feeders with light feeders to avoid exhausting soil nutrients.

- Give your houseplants some love: Clean leaves and freshen up containers; scratch some worm castings into the surface of the soil or water with a mild solution of liquid fertilizer. If you can't slide a knife between the soil and a houseplant's pot, repot in a larger container. When indoor plants get stressed from too much heat, inadequate light, and excessive dryness, they become more susceptible to opportunistic pests like mealybugs, spider mites, and whiteflies. Keep a watchful eye: Mealybug clusters resemble cotton balls, spider mite webs can be spotted in leaf axils, and tiny whiteflies hide under leaves. Stick plants under the shower to help control these pests.

- Feed the birds but watch out for the deer. Be on the lookout for signs that hungry deer have taken a liking to plants in your landscape. If deer are common in your area, proactively protect young landscape plants and fruit trees with cages or netting to exclude browsing Bambis. If you rely on repellents to deter the deer, be prepared to reapply them often to maintain their effectiveness.

- Start seeds of pansies, snapdragons, begonias, and hardy perennials indoors under lights.

FEBRUARY

- Map your garden and decide when and where you'll plant each vegetable crop you plan to grow. Estimate the number of annual and perennial flowers you'll need, based on their mature sizes, to fill your flowerbeds.

- Keep adding kitchen scraps to your compost pile, even though you may have to trudge through the snow to do it. If wintry conditions keep you from delivering materials to your outdoor compost site, set up a temporary holding container in a more accessible location like an unheated garage or shed or outside your back door. Put a lidded plastic garbage can where you can get to it as needed and use it to hold kitchen scraps until you can get them to your main compost bin or pile. Cover kitchen scraps with dried leaves or shredded paper to keep the interim bin from becoming too soggy.

- Near the end of the month, prepare for indoor seed starting, beginning with any cool-season crops, such as broccoli, cabbage, and bok choy, that will go into the garden extra-early in a cold frame or other protective covering.

- Order seeds for your soil-building cover crops. Save money by buying a big bag of seed and splitting the cost—and the seed—with your gardening friends or neighbors.

- Prune apple and pear trees in late winter, when they're still dormant. Now is also the time to prune grapevines, brambles, and shrubs that bloom in late summer. Sharpen your shears to deliver the kindest cuts.

- Bring in spring: Cut branches with plump buds of forsythia, cherry, serviceberry, quince, or maple and put them in a vase with water. Change the water every 4 days, and in 2 to 3 weeks, you'll have an early taste of spring in your house.

MARCH

- Explore local sources for compost. Many counties and municipalities compost leaves and yard wastes for residents' use. Find out what materials are accepted at your municipal compost facility and how they are processed. Get samples to check for quality and—if it meets your standards—look into the cost and timing of having a load delivered to your garden.

- Start preparing beds by working compost into the soil as soon as the ground has thawed and dried sufficiently. Pull away organic mulch from beds where early spring crops will grow; use black or clear plastic to warm the soil before sowing seeds.

- Start pepper seedlings 8 weeks before your last frost date; start tomato and eggplant seedlings 6 weeks before your last frost date.

- Plant pea seeds directly in the garden near the middle of the month if the weather cooperates. Inoculate them prior to planting for better germination.

- Prepare for outdoor planting by making seed tapes out of 1-inch-wide strips of newspaper. Space seeds along the paper at the recommended distance and "glue" them to the paper with a mix of water and flour. At sowing time, the thin paper dissolves under moist soil, leaving you with perfectly spaced seedlings.

- Low soil temperatures mean slow seed germination and plant growth in spring. Early planting in cold soil won't save you time, and it may actually stunt the growth of your plants.

- If the weather's mild, plant roses, trees, and shrubs.

- Cut back ornamental grasses to a few inches above ground level.

APRIL

- Heavy spring rains may reveal erosion and drainage problems, especially on bare or newly planted beds. Watch for places where water runs off the soil surface and consider mulching or changing the surface grading to stop runoff and prevent erosion.

- Fight the temptation to work the soil too early when it's still cold and wet.

- Begin soil-building activities. If spring cover crops are in your rotation plan, plant them now. If you planted a cover crop last fall, incorporate it as soon as you can work the soil. Dig it into your vegetable and flower beds.

- Plant spring vegetables and—to give summer crops such as peppers, melons, and tomatoes an earlier start—lay black plastic over the planting bed for a couple of weeks to warm the soil.

- Plant seed potatoes and lettuce, spinach, and mesclun seed directly in prepared garden soil.

- Plant radish, carrot, and beet seeds as well as onion sets and shallots.

- Near the end of the month, plant those broccoli and cabbage seedlings that you started last month out in the garden.

- Make sure to mulch your beds or you'll spend the next 5 months or so weeding.

- Reduce weed potential in garden beds by lightly cultivating bare soil and leaving it uncovered for a few days to let weed seeds freshly brought to the surface germinate. Once you see sprouts, grab a hoe and lay them low. Do this a couple of times before you plant. Use mulch between seedling rows and around transplants to keep light from reaching any weed seeds that remain.

- Rake mulch away from your strawberry beds and rosebushes, but keep the materials nearby in case of a late frost. Give your soil the spring squeeze test. If a handful crumbles in your fist and doesn't form a dense ball, it's dry enough to work in.

- Break out the bulbs: Time to plant summer-flowering bulbs and tubers, such as gladiolas, lilies, begonias, and cannas. Mix organic bulb fertilizer, compost, or leaf mold into the planting hole to get them off to a strong start.

- Dig, divide, and replant perennials such as asters, bee balm, chrysanthemums, hostas, and phlox.

MAY

- If you don't have a compost bin, build one (or just make a loose pile of compostable materials), then begin to fill it.

- Take corrective action based on your lawn and garden soil test results, using lime or sulfur to adjust pH and organic fertilizers to improve nutrient levels.

- Use straw or grass clippings to mulch around your vegetables.

- Gradually expose tender transplants to increasing time outdoors to harden them off in preparation for planting them in the garden once the danger of frost has passed.

- After the soil has warmed to 60°F, transplant out tomatoes, peppers, eggplants, melons, cucumbers, and sweet potatoes. Supports and trellises are easier to install at planting time when there is less risk of accidentally harming your plants' roots. Small, 3-foot-tall "tomato" cages work well for supporting peppers and eggplants; for tomatoes, use sturdier, 6-foot-tall rings made from 4-inch-square wire fencing.

- Protect cucumbers, melons, and squash from pests by using row covers. (Be sure to remove them when the plants blossom to let pollinators do their job.)

- Squeeze some last plantings of cool-season crops into the garden; try some mâche (corn salad), a tasty cool-weather green. For late-spring crops of lettuce and other greens, choose varieties noted for their heat resistance.

- If you haven't started your own tomato and pepper seedlings, buy transplants and plant them in the garden after the soil has warmed up and night temperatures are remaining consistently above 50°F. Place collars around the transplants' stems at planting time for protection against cutworms.

- Sharpen your mower blade before cutting the lawn for the first time. The blade should cut—not tear—the grass as you mow. Remove only a third of the grasses' top-growth each time you mow to keep the turf healthy and vigorous. In general, the higher you cut your grass, the deeper its roots will grow, increasing its tolerance of heat and drought.

- Plant seeds of snap beans, corn, squash, melons, and cucumbers in your prepared garden beds.

- When you plant your cucumbers, be sure to sow dill seeds, too—beneficial insects flock to dill's flowers, and you'll want the seeds and flowers to flavor your pickles. Plant radishes between your cucumbers (and melons, too) to deter cucumber beetles, which can transmit bacterial wilt to vine crops.

- Plant dahlias when your soil is warmer than 60°F.

- Liven up homegrown salads by adding basil, mint, rosemary, or nasturtiums to your usual mix of leafy greens.

- Potato leafhoppers begin feeding in May in some regions. Find out when pests become active, then time your control tactics for maximum effect.

- Keep an eye on developing pea pods. Start harvesting snow peas as soon as pods are present and before the peas inside begin to swell. Pick sugar snap types when the fleshy pods and the peas within are full-size. Harvest garden peas when the fresh, green pods are filled out by their contents. Sample a few pods/peas for quality control while you pick but fight the urge to eat them all before you make it out of the garden.

- Grow a garden for the birds by planting sunflowers, purple coneflowers, and black-eyed Susans—all favorites of finches and other seed-eating birds.

- Prune lilacs, azaleas, spirea, and other spring-flowering shrubs after they bloom.

- Transplant evergreen shrubs and trees, and pop annual flowers into beds. Sow sunflowers, zinnias, marigolds, nasturtiums, portulaca, and cosmos wherever you need an extra splash of color.

- Mulch roses with a 1-inch layer of compost.

JUNE

- Harvest salad greens such as lettuce, spinach, and mesclun mixes before the weather gets too warm and they begin blooming and producing seeds (aka bolting).

- Preserve the flavor: Dried herbs taste four times stronger than fresh. Harvest your herbs just before flowering, when the leaves contain maximum oils. Gather herbs in the morning after the dew dries. Tie the stems into small bundles and hang them upside down in a warm, dry, airy place out of the sun. Keep bundles loose to allow air circulation.

- Pull out weeds that crop up through your mulch or in your rows.

- Give your beds plenty of water so they stay moist for good seed germination and growth and good root establishment by transplants.

- Mulch your landscaped areas. There are good reasons to wait until your soil warms, despite the fact that your neighbors applied mulch 2 months ago. Your plants will get a healthier start and you'll be giving desirable self-sowing annual flowers a chance to get going.

- As early vegetable crops go to seed, you can follow them with a summer cover crop (e.g., buckwheat, cowpeas, oats). Don't let these summer cover crops go to seed!

- Plant scarlet or pink flowers such as zinnias, sage, bee balm, and begonias to attract hummingbirds and butterflies. Tubular blossoms of any color also invite hummingbirds to visit. Treat pollinators to catmint, black-eyed Susan, oregano, or trumpet vine flowers.

- Deadhead spent annual flowers often to ensure a steady supply of fresh blooms. Prune the tips of Cuban oregano and coleus to promote bushiness.

- Stay out late on the summer solstice, the longest day of the year, and enjoy the sounds and scents of your garden at dusk. Watch for emerging fireflies—in addition to the pleasure of watching them blink in the summer darkness, you'll appreciate knowing that their larvae prey on slugs.

- Protect your skin from sun damage by applying sunscreen with an SPF rating of 15 or higher and by wearing a wide-brimmed hat and tightly woven clothing.

- Eliminate standing water in your garden and landscape to keep mosquitoes from breeding around your home. Even the water in the saucer under a potted plant is enough for the bloodsuckers to lay eggs and for the resulting larvae to mature into biting pests. Refresh the water in birdbaths regularly and screen rain barrels. Use mosquito "dunks" with Btk (*Bacillus thuringiensis* var. *kurstaki*) in water gardens or rain barrels to kill mosquito larvae. Avoid becoming a feast for mosquitoes by using a repellent that contains DEET—which also repels ticks—or natural oil of lemon eucalyptus. Follow label instructions for using repellents safely.

- Use a layer of straw mulch under potatoes and tomatoes to thwart voracious Colorado potato beetles. The young beetles hatch in soil and can't fly for a week, so the mulch halts or at least slows their progress.

- Take advantage of summer sales to stock up on seeds for season-stretching fall crops like broccoli and spinach.

- Plant moonflower (*Ipomoea alba*), caladium, coleus, zinnia, and other heat-tolerant ornamentals. Continue planting daisies, asters, coreopsis, marigolds, and sunflowers—they nourish beneficial insects, which will help keep pests in check.

- Plant pole, lima, and bush beans, summer and winter squash, luffa gourds, okra, tomatoes, eggplant, peppers, sweet potatoes, southern peas, and other heat-loving vegetables.

- Mulch peas and cole (broccoli, cauliflower, cabbage, Brussels sprouts) crops to keep the soil cool; water them regularly.

- Thin peaches, plums, pears, and apples to about 6 inches apart.

- Check your drip-irrigation system—you'll be depending on it soon. Use drip irrigation or soaker hoses to provide a steady supply of moisture to beds; also mulch with organic materials, such as dried grass clippings, pine needles, or leaves.

JULY

- Continue watering during dry spells. Avoid letting plants wilt to show you they need water—pay attention to soil moisture and rainfall (or lack thereof) to know when it's time to give your gardens a drink.

- Water in the morning to give plants a chance to take up moisture before sun and wind evaporate it. Minimize water loss to evaporation by watering the soil at the base of your plants rather than wetting plants' leaves and stems. Wet foliage encourages disease problems, since many common disease organisms spread readily in a film of water.

- Pay close attention to container plants' water needs. Hanging baskets and window boxes can dry out quickly on hot, sunny days, and peat-based potting mixes can be difficult to re-wet once they get completely dry. Crowded containers look lush and lovely, but they may need to be watered twice a day in hot, dry weather.

- Harvest onions, green (snap) beans, summer squash, cucumbers, carrots, beets, and the first tomatoes. Pick cucumbers, zucchini, and other squashes when they are small so the vine continues producing fruit. When you let a zucchini (or cucumber) approach baseball-bat size, the plant's energy goes to maturing the seeds within that fruit rather than toward making more blossoms and new zukes.

- Plant more snap beans every 2 to 3 weeks to keep a steady supply of beans coming from your garden through summer. Likewise, make successive plantings of basil and cilantro to replace earlier plants that have reached the end of their productivity and to ensure you'll have these herbs' signature flavors available for tomato sauces and salsas, respectively.

- Pull out spring crops that are finished producing for the season, such as peas, lettuce, and broccoli. Add the spent plants to your compost pile.

- Mulch tomatoes, peppers, eggplant, and rows of corn and beans to keep the soil moist and cool and to prevent weeds from competing for water and nutrients. Hoeing too close to shallow-rooted vegetable crops risks injuring the roots and reducing the harvest.

- Let the decomposers do their thing this month—toasty summer temperatures support rapid decomposition, as long as the contents of your compost bin are adequately moist and well aerated. Lend the microorganisms a helping hand by dampening and turning the compost occasionally.

- Start seeds for fall greens, broccoli, cabbage, and cauliflower in a cool, shady spot (or indoors) so they'll be ready to transplant to your garden when summer vegetables are finished. Because of waning daylight, leafy crops planted in late summer and early fall will take at least 2 weeks longer to reach maturity than those sown in spring.

- Place netting over summer fruits like raspberries and blueberries to keep the birds from eating the entire crop. Support the netting so it is at least a few inches above the plants—if it rests on fruiting branches, the birds will dine through the mesh. Fasten down protective netting at ground level to keep robins and other fruit lovers from going under the net to feast.

- Prune out old, woody raspberry and blackberry canes. Cut back canes that have finished fruiting.

- Mulch the soil around melons and winter squash to prevent weeds from coming up amid the spreading vines. A layer of mulch helps keep developing fruits clean, too, and reduces the risk of rots and pest problems that can damage young melons and squashes that are resting directly on the soil.

- Presprout and sow snap, shelling, or snow peas for fall crops.

- Harvest potatoes when the plants begin to die back.

- Start seeds of biennials, such as foxglove, hollyhock, evening primrose, and lunaria for next year's blooms.

- Sow a couple of containers with seeds of basil so you'll have pots of this useful herb already up and growing when cold weather arrives. It's far easier to get seeds of heat-loving basil started in midsummer than in the shorter days and chilly nights of early fall.

- Put a pot of cherry tomatoes or a couple container-grown blueberry plants on your deck or patio where you can "graze" on sweet morsels while you relax outdoors.

AUGUST

- Visit your garden early in the morning, before the heat is unbearable. Patrol for pests and hand-pick them while they're moving slowly in the cool, moist air. Pull any weeds that are peeking through the mulch or between plants in rows or beds.

- Can tomatoes and continue harvesting corn, peppers, beans, and other vegetable crops.

- As your vegetable crops mature and garden beds empty, clean up the debris and plant a fall cover crop (for example, oats or crimson clover). Cut down your summer cover crops and turn them under the soil.

- Sit in the shade and relax with a cold glass of lemonade or iced tea with a sprig of homegrown mint.

- Turn and moisten compost as needed. Boost a slow, dry pile by adding fresh grass clippings from your mower bag.

- Direct-seed carrots, kohlrabi, and radishes early this month for a fall vegetable garden.

- Sow leafy greens like lettuce, Chinese cabbage, Swiss chard, and mustard for fall salads. Set out transplants of broccoli, Brussels sprouts, cauliflower, and collards.

- When the days become noticeably shorter, 'Autumn Joy' sedum opens clusters of tiny deep red flowers. Soon those flowers will be thronged by butterflies feasting on the nectar before cool weather sets in.

SEPTEMBER

- Can more tomatoes and make salsa or spaghetti sauce.

- Be ready to cover tomatoes, peppers, and other tender crops that are still productive if an early frost threatens. Often many warm growing days remain in the wake of a late-summer cold snap, if plants can be protected for just a night or two.

- Harvest pumpkins, carrots, and beets as they mature.

- Continue harvesting summer crops as long as they keep producing and are unclaimed by frost.

- As more crops reach the end of their productivity, remove them from the garden and add them to the compost bin. Plant cover crops in the empty spaces they leave behind. You can still plant fall cover crops (for example, annual rye, vetch, winter wheat, crimson clover).

- Start a new compost project using the mixed grass clippings and chopped dry leaves captured from late-season lawn mowing along with spent garden plants.

- Dig up tender dahlias, cannas, caladiums, and gladiolis before frost hits; store tubers and bulbs in slightly moistened sphagnum moss or vermiculite in a cool spot.

- Sow spinach for spring harvest.

- Dig, divide, and replant overgrown perennials.

- Pot up a few herbs—parsley and basil are good candidates—to prepare them for moving indoors for ongoing harvest into winter.

- Clean up houseplants that have spent summer outdoors and prepare them to go back inside before frost gives them a chill.

OCTOBER

- Plant garlic cloves for next year's crop. Mulch with a layer of straw to keep them cozy for the winter months and to prevent weeds from competing next spring.

- Plant spring-flowering bulbs such as tulips, daffodils, hyacinths, and crocuses.

- Harvest any remaining tomatoes and peppers before frost arrives.

- Continue cleaning out spent plants and replacing them with cover crops.

- Collect stakes, cages, temporary trellises, and row covers used for insect barriers, and scrape or brush off clinging soil before storing for winter.

- Carve a pumpkin or two for Halloween.

- Fertilize cool-season grasses and top-dress your lawn with a thin layer of compost.

- If indicated by a soil test, add lime or sulfur to adjust the pH of your soil.

- Top off your empty vegetable beds with raked-up grass clippings and fall leaves. Leaving soil bare exposes it to erosion and nutrient leaching.

- Order some worms and start an indoor worm composting bin for your kitchen scraps.

- Don't haul all the leaves to your compost pile. Simply mow over them to chop them up, then spread them around your perennials.

- You can preserve herbs that don't dry well, such as basil, chives, parsley, and chervil. Right after harvesting them, wash and dry the leaves, then mix the herbs (chopped or whole) with water or olive oil. Pour the mixture into an ice tray to freeze and pop out the cubes whenever you want to add a taste of homegrown herbal flavor to sauces or soups.

- Before hard frost, cover fall crops of salad greens with heavyweight row covers or double layers of clear plastic supported on hoops to keep them growing into fall.

NOVEMBER

- Run over your fallen leaves with the lawn mower and either allow them to remain on your lawn or, if the leaf layer is too thick, drag them to your compost pile. You could also bag them to use as mulch next year. Stockpile some dry leaves to mix with kitchen scraps in temporary compost containers during winter months.

- Cut back perennials (except for spring bloomers, roses, mums, and ornamental grasses) to a few inches above soil level.

- Harvest frost-sweetened Brussels sprouts, carrots, parsnips, cabbages, and kale. Mulch over any crops you want to overwinter in the garden with a thick layer of straw.

- Sharpen, clean, and repair hand tools before storing them; wipe metal blades with an oily cloth to prevent rusting.

- Clean, repair, and fill bird feeders. Watch the birds that come and go in your yard and note the changing species as some travel south to spend winter in warmer climates and new arrivals fly in from the north.

- Impress Thanksgiving guests with a salad of greens harvested from your garden—assuming you got those row covers on in time!

- Pot up a clump of mint, let it freeze one time, then bring it indoors for snipping throughout winter.

- Last chance to plant spring-flowering bulbs in most parts of the country.

DECEMBER

- Cut back asparagus fronds.

- Refill bird feeders as needed. Provide fresh water for birds, too, if natural sources are all frozen.

- As weather permits, keep harvesting leeks and kale and any other sturdy survivors. Add a second layer of row cover over leafy crops at night.

- Recycle your Christmas greens by laying them over your perennials. Pine needles, straw, or shredded leaves also make good materials for winter mulch, which helps to insulate the soil and protect your plants from alternate freezing and thawing that can heave their roots out of the soil.

- Give strawberries extra insulation with a mulch layer of straw or shredded leaves when temperatures drop to 20°F.

- To keep houseplants from drying out, place them on a tray of water filled with pebbles to raise humidity.

- Force some paper-white narcissus bulbs: Put them in a bowl with pebbles and water, set the bowl in a bright, cool window, then enjoy their flowers and fragrance. Discard the bulbs after they bloom.

- Make as point of getting outdoors for a bit of daylight and fresh air on the winter solstice, the year's shortest day.

- Protect upright evergreens like juniper and arborvitae from snow damage by wrapping the stem and branches with wire, twine, or nylon fishing line. Start from the bottom and wind upward. This will prevent snow from collecting in the center of the tree, which can cause bending and splitting.

ACKNOWLEDGMENTS

Our gardens connect us to the past and commit us to the future, while anchoring us firmly in the present. Among the remaining examples of humankind's earliest written materials are agricultural records: accounts of crops planted and harvested, notes of successes and failures, descriptions of tools and inventions, almanacs, and timetables. Even when it seems to grow tenuous, our connection with the soil and its productivity runs deep.

The writers and editors of this book humbly and gratefully acknowledge the rich legacy of garden-tested advice that fills its pages and especially want to thank the thousands of contributors to *Organic Gardening* and Rodale Garden Books for knowledge beyond words. This collection of practical guidance represents decades of work by gardeners who were willing to try new things (and old ones), who were willing to endure ridicule and skepticism, and—most of all—who were willing to share their successes and failures with others.

The roots of this book rest in the enduring history of gardening and farming in the United States, a pursuit as revered and respected by the nation's founding fathers as the raising of a new country. Its techniques span centuries of land stewardship, from early colonists learning to tend strange crops in unfamiliar conditions to J. I. Rodale's awakening to the connections between soil health and human health to modern-day recognition that organic methods produce wholesome food without damaging and depleting the environment.

To all the planters and growers, the weeders and waterers, to all the nibblers and tasters, to the risk takers and explorers, to the diggers and the gatherers, we offer our thanks and share our hopes for a future of successful, healthy, organic growing.

ORGANIC GARDENER'S RESOURCE GUIDE

When you discover the joys of gardening, you inevitably begin searching for additional information to enrich your experience. This resource guide features an extensive list of organizations, companies, and publications to help you gain skills and knowledge to feed your newfound passion.

GETTING FAMILIAR WITH ORGANIC GARDENING

The Basic Book of Organic Gardening, by Robert Rodale, Rodale, 1971

The Garden Primer, by Barbara Damrosch, Workman, 2008

Grow the Good Life: Why a Vegetable Garden Will Make You Happy, Healthy, Wealthy, and Wise, by Michele Owens, Rodale, 2011

Maria Rodale's Organic Gardening Secrets Spring, eBook, by Maria Rodale, Rodale, March 2012

Maria Rodale's Organic Gardening Secrets Summer, eBook, by Maria Rodale, Rodale, June 2012

Maria Rodale's Organic Gardening Secrets Fall, eBook, by Maria Rodale, Rodale, September 2012

Maria Rodale's Organic Gardening Secrets Winter, eBook, by Maria Rodale, Rodale, December 2012

Organic Manifesto, by Maria Rodale, Rodale, March 2010

Our Roots Grow Deep: The Story of Rodale, 2009: http://ourrootsgrowdeep.com/uof/ourrootsgrowdeep/

Pay Dirt, by J. I. Rodale, Rodale, 1945

Rodale's Ultimate Encyclopedia of Organic Gardening, by Fern Marshall Bradley, Barbara W. Ellis, and Ellen Phillips, 2010

You Grow Girl: The Groundbreaking Guide *to Gardening,* by Gayla Trail, Simon & Schuster, 2005

Mother Earth News magazine: www.motherearthnews.com/organic-gardening.aspx#axzz2hoeiQHM3

Not your grandmother's guide to gardening by a young urban gardener: http://yougrowgirl.com/about/

Organic Gardening magazine: www.organicgardening.com/learn-and-grow/beginners-guide-organic-gardening

The Rodale Institute
http://rodaleinstitute.org/
A nonprofit dedicated to pioneering organic farming through research and outreach

National Gardening Association
www.garden.org
Plant-based education for kids and communities

Timber Press, Chelsea Green, and Storey Publishing all have books on gardening and agriculture:
www.timberpress.com/
www.chelseagreen.com/
www.storey.com

The Brooklyn Botanic Garden produces a nice series of handbooks:
www.bbg.org/gardening/handbooks

FINDING GREAT GARDEN TOOLS, SUPPLIES, AND CLOTHING

A.M. Leonard
www.gardenersedge.com/default.aspx
Horticultural tool and supply business with emphasis on doing business the "old fashioned way"

Bogs
www.bogsfootwear.com/shop/index.html
Gardening footwear

Corona
coronatoolsusa.com
Pruning and gardening tools

DripWorks
dripworks.com
Drip irrigation systems; watering tools and supplies

Felco
http://www.felco.com/felco/home.page?
Professional pruning shears and cable cutters

Fiskars
http://www2.fiskars.com/
Supplier of branded consumer products for the home, garden and outdoors

Garden Girl
http://www.gardengirlusa.com/
Practical yet stylish gardening clothes for women

Gardener's Supply Co.
gardeners.com
Tools, supplies, and accessories

Garden Tool Co.
gardentoolcompany.com
Tools and equipment

Garrett Wade
www.garrettwade.com/
De Wit garden tools, among others

Green Heron Tools
greenherontools.com
Gardening and farming tools for women

Kinsman Company
www.kinsmangarden.com/
Specialty garden supplies, especially containers

Lee Valley Tools
leevalley.com
Gardening and woodworking tools, supplies, and accessories

Lehman's
www.lehmans.com/default.aspx
A general store with old-fashioned, nonelectric merchandise, including homesteading supplies and tools

Peaceful Valley Farm & Garden Supply
www.groworganic.com/
State-of-the-art organic growing supplies and the information and tools needed to apply them

Plow & Hearth
www.plowhearth.com/
Gardening tools and supplies, mostly decorative, including composting, watering, and raised beds

ShovelandHoe.com
www.shovelandhoe.com/
Garden hand tools, including Burgon & Ball

Sneeboer
www.sneeboerusa.com/
Fine hand-forged Dutch garden tools

Womanswork
womanswork.com/
Garden and work gloves for women

LEARNING ABOUT GARDEN DESIGN

Ann Lovejoy's Organic Garden Design School, by Ann Lovejoy, Rodale, 2001

Homescaping, by Anne Halpin, Rodale, 2005

Tomorrow's Garden: Design and Inspiration for a New Age of Sustainable Gardening, by Stephen Orr, Rodale, 2011

EXPLORING CONTAINER GARDENING, INCLUDING RAISED BEDS AND LASAGNA GARDENING

The Container Gardener's Bible, by Joanna K. Harrison and Miranda Smith, Rodale, 2009

The Edible Balcony, by Alex Mitchell, Rodale, 2011

Edible Spots & Pots: Small-Space Gardens for Growing Vegetables and Herbs in Containers, Raised Beds, and More, by Stacey Hirvela, Rodale, 2014

Lasagna Gardening, by Patricia Lanza, Rodale, 1998.

Vertical Gardening, by Derek Fell, Rodale, 2011

Trellises

The Cedar Store
www.CedarStore.com
Vertical gardening structures including arches, arbors, and trellises

Kinsman Company
www.kinsmangarden.com
Vertical gardening units and containers

DIGGING DEEPER INTO SOIL

The Soil Will Save Us: How Scientists, Farmers, and Ranchers Are Tending the Soil to Reverse Global Warming, Kristin Ohlson, Rodale, 2014

Teaming with Microbes: The Organic Gardener's Guide to the Soil Food Web, by Jeff Lowenfels and Wayne Lewis, Timber Press, 2010

Soil Testing

In addition to the suggestions below, soil test kits and meters are available from many garden supply retailers.

Cooperative Extension Service
The Cooperative Extension service provides valuable information through its local offices on subjects like lawn care, home canning, financial management, frost dates, soil testing, and weeds to consumers. Check out this site to find your local branch: www.csrees.usda.gov/Extension/index.html

Logan Labs, LLC
www.loganlabs.com
Agricultural, commercial, and residential soil and water testing

Soil and Plant Laboratory, Inc.
www.soilandplantlaboratory.com/index.html
Soil, compost, water, plant tissue testing for agricultural, commercial, residential customers

Wallace Labs
us.wlabs.com
Soil testing, water testing and plant tissue testing for farmers, professional landscaping companies and home owners

Compost

The Complete Compost Gardening Guide, by Barbara Pleasant and Deborah L. Martin, Storey Publishing, 2008

The Rodale Book of Composting: Easy Methods for Every Gardener, by Grace Gershuny and Deborah L. Martin, Rodale, 1992

Worms Eat My Garbage, by Mary Appelhof, Flower Press, 1997

Earthworms and Other Soil Organisms

OrganicGardening.com: Understanding Earthworms: Earthworms, worm casting, and vermicomposting. www.organicgardening.com/learn-and-grow/understanding-earthworms

UNCO Industries
www.vermiculture.com/

Vermicomposting
www.bae.ncsu.edu/topic/vermicomposting/vermiculture/directory-by-state.html
Earthworms, supplies, and information plus a state-by-state listing of organizations involved in the vermiculture or vermicomposting industry

www.workingworms.com/
Raise red worms and African nightcrawlwers

LOCATING ORGANIC SEED/ PLANT COMPANIES

Annie's Annuals & Perennials
http://anniesannuals.com/
*Specializing in rare and unusual annual and
    perennial plants, including cottage
    garden heirlooms and hard-to-find
    California native wildflowers*

Arrowhead Alpines
www.arrowheadalpines.com/shop/
*Rare, unusual, beautiful and sometimes just
    odd plants*

Bluestone Perennials
bluestoneperennials.com
Perennials, bulbs, shrubs

Brent & Becky's Bulbs
brentandbeckysbulbs.com
Bulbs; tools and supplies

Burpee Seeds
burpee.com
*Vegetable, herb, flower seeds and plants;
    tools and supplies*

Chamblee's Rose Nursery
http://chambleeroses.com/
Environmentally friendly roses

The Cook's Garden
cooksgarden.com
*Vegetable, herb, flower seeds and plants;
    tools and supplies*

EcoTulips
www.ecotulips.com/
Organic flower bulbs

Fedco Seeds
www.fedcoseeds.com/
*Cold-hardy untreated vegetable, herb, and
    flower seeds*

Gilbert H. Wild & Son
gilberthwild.com
Peonies, irises, daylilies, hostas

Gurney's Seed & Nursery Co.
gurneys.com
*Vegetable, herb, flower, fruit seeds and
    plants; tools and supplies*

Harris Seeds
harrisseeds.com
*Vegetable, herb, flower, fruit seeds and
    plants; tools and supplies*

Henry Field's Seed & Nursery Co.
henryfields.com
*Vegetable, herb, flower, fruit seeds and
    plants; perennials; tools and supplies*

High Mowing Organic Seeds
highmowingseeds.com
Vegetable, herb, flower seeds

Hoffman Nursery
http://hoffmannursery.com/
Ornamental and native grasses

Italian Seed & Tool Company
www.italianseedandtool.com/
*North American distributor for Bavicchi of
    Italy flower, herb, and vegetable seeds and
    garden supplies*

Kitazawa Seed Co.
www.kitazawaseed.com/
Asian vegetable seeds

Johnny's Selected Seeds
johnnyseeds.com
*Vegetable, herb, flower, fruit seeds and
    plants; perennials; tools and supplies*

John Scheepers Kitchen Garden Seeds
www.kitchengardenseeds.com/index.html
Vegetable, herb, and flower seeds

Klehm's Song Sparrow Nursery
songsparrow.com
Perennials, trees, shrubs; tools and supplies

Nichols Garden Nursery
nicholsgardennursery.com
*Herb seeds and plants; vegetable, flower
    seeds; supplies*

Park Seeds
parkseed.com
*Flower, herb, vegetable seeds; fruits and
    perennials; tools and supplies*

Peaceful Valley Farm Supply
www.groworganic.com
*Organic seeds, fertilizers, weed and pest
    control, garden tools, irrigation, growing
    supplies, books, and homesteading
    supplies*

Pinetree Garden Seeds
superseeds.com
*Vegetable, herb, flower seeds; tools and
    supplies*

Plant Delights Nursery
plantdelights.com
Perennials, shrubs, trees

Plant Information Online
http://plantinfo.umn.edu/
Search tool to find published information about a particular plant and nurseries that sell it

Rainbow Iris Farm
www.rainbowfarms.net/index.cfm?
Irises

Seeds from Italy
www.growitalian.com/
Distributor for Franchi Seeds of Italy, plus garden gifts and supplies

Select Seeds
www.selectseeds.com/
Flower seeds and plants, specializing in old-fashioned fragrant varieties, flowering vines, and rare cottage garden annuals

Simply Succulents
www.simplysucculents.com/
Specializing in hardy succulents

Southern Exposure Seed Exchange
www.southernexposure.com/
Vegetable, herb, flower, cover crop seeds; books, DVDs, tools, and supplies

Sow True Seed
sowtrueseed.com/
Vegetable, herb, flower, cover crop seeds; books, DVDs, tools, and supplies

Stargazer Perennials
www.stargazerperennials.com/
Roses, perennials, seed potatoes and garden plants

Stokes Seeds
stokeseeds.com
Vegetable, herb, flower, cover crop seeds; books, DVDs, tools, and supplies

Sustainable Seed Company
http://sustainableseedco.com/
Vegetable, herb, flower seeds; tools and supplies

Territorial Seed Company
territorialseed.com
Vegetable, herb, flower, fruit seeds and plants; tools and supplies

Thompson & Morgan
tmseeds.com
Flower, herb, vegetable, tree and shrub seeds; supplies

Tierra Madre Farm
www.tierramadrefarm.com/Default.aspx
Rare fruit trees

Tomato Growers Supply Co.
tomatogrowers.com
Tomato, pepper, eggplant, tomatillo seeds; supplies

Veseys
www.veseys.com/us/en/
Vegetable, herb, and flower seeds, bulbs, tools and supplies, light gardens, greenhouses

Victory Seeds
www.victoryseeds.com/
Rare, open-pollinated, and heirloom garden seeds plus composting redworms, books, garden kits

Well-Sweep Herb Farm
wellsweep.com
Herb plants and perennials

White Flower Farm
whiteflowerfarm.com
Perennials, bulbs, shrubs; tools and supplies

Western Native Seed
www.westernnativeseed.com/
Native plant seed for the Rocky Mountains and western Great Plains

Heirloom Seeds and Books

Baker Creek Heirloom Seeds
rareseeds.com
Heirloom vegetable, herb, flower seeds; tools and supplies

D. Landreth Seed Company
http://landrethseeds.com/
Heirloom seeds, bulbs, tubers, and garden accessories

Heritage Grain Conservancy
http://growseed.org/
Heritage grains from around the world

Native American Seed
www.seedsource.com/
Native wildflower and grass seeds

Native Seeds/SEARCH
www.nativeseeds.org/
Nonprofit seed conservation organization

Old House Gardens
www.oldhousegardens.com/
Heirloom bulbs

Renee's Garden
www.reneesgarden.com/
Heirloom and gourmet vegetable, flower, and herb seeds

Seed Savers Exchange
seedsavers.org
Nonprofit seed exchange; vegetable, herb, flower seeds

Seeds of Change
seedsofchange.com
Vegetable, herb, flower seeds; tools and supplies

Terroir Seeds
www.underwoodgardens.com/
Heirloom vegetable, herb, flower seeds; tools and supplies

Thomas Jefferson Center for Historic Plants at Monticello
www.monticelloshop.org/farm-garden.html

Tomatofest
http://tomatofest.com/
Heirloom tomato seeds

Seed to Seed: Seed Saving and Growing Techniques for Vegetable Gardeners, by Suzanne Ashworth, Seed Savers Exchange, 2002

Vegetable Gardening the Colonial Williamsburg Way: 18th-Century Methods for Today's Organic Gardeners, by Wesley Green, Rodale, 2012

DISCOVERING MORE PLANTS

Annuals for Every Purpose, by Larry Hodgson, Rodale, 2002

Derek Fell's Grow This! by Derek Fell, Rodale, 2013

Grow It, Heal It, by Christopher Hobbs and Leslie Gardner, Rodale, 2013

Perennials for Every Purpose, by Larry Hodgson, Rodale, 2000

The Pruner's Bible: A Step-by-Step Guide to Pruning Every Plant in Your Garden, by Steve Bradley, Rodale, 2005

Rodale's Illustrated Encyclopedia of Perennials, by Ellen Phillips and C. Colston Burrell, Rodale, May 2004

Rodale's 21st-Century Herbal, by Michael Balick, Rodale, 2014.

Rodale's Ultimate Encyclopedia of Organic Gardening, by Fern Marshall Bradley, Barbara W. Ellis, and Ellen Phillips, Rodale, 2010

STARTING SEEDS

The Plant Propagator's Bible, by Miranda Smith, Rodale, 2007

HELPING WITH THE HARVEST AND BEYOND

Cooking from the Garden

The Four Season Farm Gardener's Cookbook, by Barbara Damrosch and Eliot Coleman, Workman, 2013

Grow Cook Eat: A Food Lover's Guide to Vegetable Gardening, Including 50 Recipes, Plus Harvesting and Storage Tips, by Willi Galloway, Sasquatch, 2012

Grow Great Grub: Organic Food from Small Spaces, by Gayla Trail, Clarkson Potter, 2010

Homegrown: A Growing Guide for Creating a Cook's Garden, by Marta Teegan, Rodale, 2010

Preserving Food from the Garden

The Complete Root Cellar Book: Building Plans, Uses and 100 Recipes, by Steve Maxwell and Jennifer MacKenzie, Robert Rose, 2010

Preserving Summer's Bounty: A Quick and Easy Guide to Freezing, Canning, and Preserving, and Drying What You Grow, by Susan McClure, Rodale, 1998

Saving the Season: A Cook's Guide to Home Canning, Pickling, and Preserving, by Kevin West, Knopf, 2013

Tart and Sweet, by Kelly Geary and Jessie Knadler, Rodale, 2011

GAINING GROUND ON GARDEN PESTS, DISEASES, AND WEEDS

Attracting Beneficial Bugs to Your Garden: A Natural Approach to Pest Control, by Jessica Walliser, Timber Press, 2014

Deer-Resistant Landscaping: Proven Advice and Strategies for Outwitting Deer and 20 Other Pesky Mammals, by Neil Soderstrom, Rodale, 2009

Garden Insects of North America: The Ultimate Guide to Backyard Bugs, by Whitney Cranshaw, Princeton University Press, 2004

Good Bug Bad Bug: Who's Who, What They Do, and How to Manage Them Organically, by Jessica Walliser, St. Lynn's Press, 2011

Insect, Disease & Weed I.D. Guide, Jill Jesiolowski Cebenko and Deborah L. Martin, eds., Rodale, 2001

The Organic Gardener's Handbook of Natural Pest and Disease Control, Fern Marshall Bradley, Barbara W. Ellis, and Deborah L. Martin, eds., Rodale, 2010

Rodale's Vegetable Garden Problem Solver, by Fern Marshall Bradley, Rodale, 2007

What's Wrong with My Plant? (And How Do I Fix It?): A Visual Guide to Easy Diagnosis and Organic Remedies, by David Deardorff and Kathryn Wadsworth, Timber Press, 2009

Arbico Organics
http://www.arbico-organics.com/
Beneficial insects and organisms, fertilizers and soil amendments, weed and disease controls, composting supplies, insecticides, critter controls, horse care, traps, lures, pheromones, botanicals and more

Gardens Alive!
www.gardensalive.com
Natural solutions for pest control and fertilization

Peaceful Valley Farm Supply
www.groworganic.com
Organic seeds, fertilizers, weed and pest control, garden tools, irrigation, growing supplies, books, and homesteading supplies

EXTENDING THE SEASON

Four-Season Harvest: Organic Vegetables from Your Home Garden All Year Long, 2nd Edition, by Eliot Coleman, Chelsea Green, 1999

The Year-Round Vegetable Gardener: How to Grow Your Own Food 365 Days a Year, No Matter Where You Live, by Niki Jabbour, Storey, 2011

KEEPING RECORDS— SAMPLING OF GARDEN JOURNALS

Organic Gardening 2014 Desk Calendar, Rodale, 2013

Five-Year Garden Journal, Gardener's Supply Co.: www.gardeners.com/5-Year-Garden-Journal

Garden Journal from ARBICO Organics: www.arbico-organics.com/category/garden-journal/13

Garden Scribe Plant Organizer: www.gardenscribe.com

Monticello Garden Journal, www.monticelloshop.org

WELCOMING WILDLIFE

Attracting Native Pollinators: Protecting North America's Bees and Butterflies, by The Xerces Society and Dr. Marla Spivak, Storey, 2011

Backyard Bird Secrets for Every Season: Attract a Variety of Nesting, Feeding, and Singing Birds Year-Round, by Sally Roth, Rodale, 2009

Bird-by-Bird Gardening: The Ultimate Guide to Bringing in Your Favorite Birds—Year after Year, by Sally Roth, Rodale, 2009

My Pet Chicken Handbook, by Lissa Lucas and Traci Torres, Rodale, 2014

Projects for the Birder's Garden: Over 100 Easy Things That You Can Make to Turn Your Yard and Garden into a Bird-Friendly Haven, by Fern Marshall Bradley, Rodale, 2004

RSPB Gardening for Wildlife: A Complete Guide to Nature-Friendly Gardening, by Adrian Thomas, Bloomsbury, 2010

Secrets of Backyard Bird Feeding Success, by Deborah L. Martin, Rodale, 2011

TECHNOLOGY FOR GARDENERS

Eden Garden Designer

http://www.edengardendesigner.com/
Design your gardens on your iPhone or iPod Touch

Garden Pilot

http://download.cnet.com/GardenPilot/3000-317131/44-75029179.html
Guide to vegetables, annuals, perennials, roses, trees, shrubs and more, including useful tips from gardening professionals

The Southern Exposure Seed Exchange Garden Planner

http://gardenplanner.southernexposure.com/
Online garden planner

AWaytoGarden.com

An online blog and radio show about gardening

You Bet Your Garden

http://whyy.org/cms/youbetyourgarden/
Radio show on gardening hosted by Mike McGrath

BEYOND THE BASICS

Organic Certification

Organic Materials Review Institute (OMRI)

www.omri.org/
A national nonprofit organization that determines which input products are allowed for use in organic production and processing

USDA's National Organic Program

www.usda.gov/wps/portal/usda/usdahome?navid=ORGANIC1/4CERTIFICATIO
Regulates the standards for any farm, wild crop harvesting, or handling operation that wants to sell an agricultural product as organically produced

Eating Locally

Community Supported Agriculture (CSAs)

www.localharvest.org/csa/
Read about how they work and find CSAs in your area

SustainableTable.org

Search for local, sustainable, and/or organic food at eatwellguide.org

GMOs

The Non-GMO Project

www.nongmoproject.org/learn-more/what-is-gmo
www.nongmoshoppingguide.com
The Non-GMO Project offers North America's only third-party verification for products produced according to rigorous best practices for GMO avoidance

The Organic Consumers Association

www.organicconsumers.org
This is an online and grassroots non-profit public interest organization, campaigning for health, justice, and sustainability, including issues of food safety, industrial agriculture, and genetic engineering.

Books and Web Sites with More Ideas to Pursue

Easy Garden Projects to Make, Build, and Grow: 200 Do-It-Yourself Ideas to Help You Grow Your Best Garden Ever, by Barbara Pleasant, Rodale, 2006

Gardening with Native Wildflowers, by Samuel B. Jones, Jr., and Leonard E. Foote, Timber Press, 2010

Grow Fruit Naturally: A Hands-On Guide to Luscious, Homegrown Fruit, by Lee Reich, Taunton, 2012

Hope's Edge: The Next Diet for a Small Planet, by Frances Moore Lappé and Anna Lappé, Tarcher, 2003

The Omnivore's Dilemma, by Michael Pollan, Penguin, 2007

100 Easy-to-Grow Native Plants for American Gardens in Temperate Zones, by Lorraine Johnson, Firefly Books, 2009

Plant Breeding for the Home Gardener: How to Create Unique Vegetables and Flowers, by Joseph Tychonievich, Timber Press, 2013

Teaming with Nutrients: The Organic Gardener's Guide to Optimizing Plant Nutrition, by Jeff Lowenfels, Timber Press, 2013

Lady Bird Johnson Wildflower Center
www.wildflower.org/
Information about native plants and how to incorporate them into your landscape, plus a directory of suppliers that sell native plants or seeds

Plant Native
www.plantnative.com/index.htm
Information about native plants and a search tool to find sources for native plants in your state

The Pollinator Partnership
www.pollinator.org/
Downloadable regional guides listing plants for pollinators, and other educational material about pollinators

USDA Natural Resources Conservation Service PLANTS Database
http://plants.usda.gov/java/
Fact sheets and planting guides, plus lists of plants that are invasive or noxious, threatened or endangered, culturally significant, and more

The Xerces Society
www.xerces.org/
Focused on conservation of invertebrates, including bees, butterflies, and worms

INDEX

Boldface page numbers indicate photographs or illustrations. Underscored references indicate boxed text, charts, and graphs.

P

Paeonia (peony) (*Paeonia* cultivars), 222–23
  supporting, 253
Pansy (*Viola xwittrockiana*), 48, 192, 290
Papaver orientale (Oriental poppy), 229
Parasitic nematodes, 272, 274
Parsley, 173, 301, 302
Parsnips, 25, 303
Patio Produce Garden, 34
Peaches, thinning, 297
Pears, 291, 297
Peas (*Pisum*)
  harvesting, 295
  mulching, 297
  presprouting for fall crop, 299
  saving seeds of, 120
  sugar snap, 128, 153–54
  sweet (garden), 153–54
  trellising, 253
  viability of old seeds, 121
  when to plant, 25, 26, 292
Peas (*Vigna*)
  cowpea (black-eyed pea, crowder pea,
      southern pea) (*V. sinensis*), 94–95, 143,
      296, 297
Pelargonium x hortorum (bedding geranium),
      44, 184–85
Penstemon (beardtongue), 229
Peony (*Paeonia* cultivars), 222–23, 253
Peppers, 155–56
  mulching, 298
  protecting from early frosts, 301
  supporting, 252, 294
  viability of old seeds, 121
  when to plant, 25, 26, 292, 294, 297
Perennials, 167, 203, 203–4
  for containers, 69
  deadheading, 251, **251**
  dividing, 251, 301
  fall tasks, 301, 303
  garden plans for
      Garden for a Shady Spot, 46, **47**
      Multiseason Perennial Border, 50, **51**
  long-lasting, 203
  pinching, 251
  popular, 204–27
  spring tasks, 293
  thinning, 251
  winterizing, 256
  winter tasks, 304
Periwinkle, Madagascar (catharanthus)
      (*Catharanthus roseus*), 181
Perlite, 105

Pesticides, 8, 273
  beneficial insects and, 266
Pests. *See* Animal pests; Insect pests
Petunia (*Petunia xhybrida*), 48, 193–94
pH, 74, 75, 78, 81
Pheromone traps, 269
Phlox (garden phlox) (*Phlox paniculata*), 223–24
Phosphorus, 75, 81
Physostegia virginiana (obedient plant), 229
Pigweed, annual, 279, **279**
Pinching, 251, **251**
Pine needles, as mulch, 239
Pinks, garden (*Dianthus* spp.), 228
Plantain lily (hosta) (*Hosta* spp. and cultivars),
      216–17
Plant families, 178
Plant propagation, language of, 104–5
Plants
  cold-sensitive crops, 25
  cool-season crops, 25
  parts of, **126**, 127
  processes of, 127
  selecting
      cold hardiness and, 22
      for containers, 68–69
      disease resistance and, 275
      heat tolerance and, 22
  shopping for, 102, 107
  warm-season crops, 25
  watering, 233–34
Plant supports, 252–53, **252**, **253**, 294
Plant types, 167
Plastic tunnels, **284**
Plums, thinning, 297
Pocketknife, **30**, 31
Pollination, 105, 115–17
Poppy, Oriental (*Papaver orientale*), 229
Portulaca (moss rose) (*Portulaca grandiflora*),
      48, 195, 295
Potassium, 75, 81
Potatoes, 156–57. *See also* Sweet potatoes
  harvesting, 255, 299
  mulching, 297
  when to plant, 25, 293
Potato leafhoppers, 295
Powdery mildew, remedy for, 277
Propagation, language of, 104–5
Pruners, **30**, 31
Pruning
  brambles, 299
  February tasks, 291
  spring-blooming shrubs, 295
Pumpkins, powdery mildew and, 277

Shrubs
  mulches and, 242
  pruning spring-flowering, <u>295</u>
  pruning summer-flowering, <u>291</u>
  selecting for containers, 69
  spring tasks, <u>295</u>
  transplanting evergreen, <u>295</u>
  when to plant, <u>292</u>
  winter tasks, <u>291</u>
Side-dress, <u>247</u>
Site selection, 18, 20–22, <u>21</u>
Slug, **261**
Snapdragon (*Antirrhinum majus*), 198–99, <u>290</u>
Sneezeweed (*Helenium autumnale*), <u>228</u>
Snowdrop (*Galanthus* spp.), <u>230</u>
Soaker hose, <u>236</u>
Soil
  acid, <u>74</u>, 81
  aeration of, <u>74</u>
  alkaline, <u>74</u>, 81
  amendments, 81, <u>83</u>
  clayey, 72, **72**
  constituents of, 71–78, **72**, <u>74–75</u>, <u>76</u>, **76**, <u>77</u>,
      77
    air, 72–73
    living organisms, 74–75, 74–77, <u>76</u>, **76**, <u>77</u>,
        77
    minerals, 71–72
    organic matter, 73–74
    particle types, 72, **72**
    water, 72–73, 233–34, <u>234</u>
  for containers, 67–68, 96
  cover crops and (*See* Cover crops)
  digging, 56–57, 82–84, <u>85</u>, 257 (*See also*
      Beds)
    alternative patterns of, 83–84
    avoiding with lasagna gardening, 64
    double, 83
    single, 83, 84
    tilling, 56, <u>85</u>, 257, <u>293</u>
  drainage of, <u>74</u>, 78–79
  earthworms and, <u>76</u>, **76**, 79
  erosion prevention, <u>293</u>
  fall care of, 256–57, <u>302</u>
  fertilizers for (*See* Fertilizer)
  humus in, <u>74</u>
  loamy, 72, **72**
  micronutrients in, <u>74</u>, 82
  minerals in, 71–72, **72**, <u>81</u>
  moisture in, 233–34, <u>234</u>
  mycorrhiza in, <u>74</u>
  neutral, <u>74</u>

nitrogen in, <u>74</u>, 81
organic matter in, 73–74, <u>75</u>
pH of, <u>74</u>, <u>75</u>, 78, 81
phosphorus in, <u>75</u>, 81
potassium in, <u>75</u>, 81
potting, 67–68, 96
preparing garden beds (*See* Beds)
properties of, <u>74–75</u>
for raised beds, 63
ribbons, <u>79</u>
sandy, 72, **72**
silt in, 72
spring tasks, <u>292</u>, <u>293</u>, <u>294</u>
structure of, <u>75</u>
summer tasks, <u>300</u>
symbiotic relationships and, <u>75</u>
tests of, 78–82, <u>79</u>, <u>80</u>, **80**
  for drainage, 78–79
  earthworms and, 79
  getting accurate readings, 81
  laboratory, 81–82
  nutrient content, 81–82
  ribbons, <u>79</u>
  taking samples for, 82
  for texture, 79, <u>79</u>, <u>80</u>, **80**
texture of, <u>75</u>
warming in spring, <u>292</u>, <u>293</u>
Soil amendments, 81, <u>83</u>, <u>247</u>
Soybean (edamame), 159–60, **159**
Spading fork, **28**, <u>29</u>
Species, <u>178</u>
Speedwell (*Veronica spicata* cultivars), <u>229</u>
Spider mites, houseplants and, <u>290</u>
Spinach, <u>128</u>, 160–61
  harvesting, <u>296</u>
  viability of old seeds, <u>121</u>
  when to plant, <u>25</u>, <u>26</u>, <u>293</u>, <u>301</u>
Spiraea, false (astilbe) (perennial) (*Astilbe*
    spp.), 206–7
Spring tasks, <u>292</u>, <u>293</u>, <u>294–95</u>
Squash, 65, 161–62
  mulching, <u>299</u>
  protecting from pests, <u>294</u>
  saving seeds of, 117, 120
  viability of old seeds, <u>121</u>
  when to harvest, <u>255</u>, <u>298</u>
  when to plant, <u>25</u>, <u>26</u>, <u>295</u>, <u>297</u>
Stakes, 252, **252**
Sticky traps, 269
Stonecrop (sedum) (*Sedum* cultivars), <u>203</u>,
    226–27
Straw, as mulch, 239